# International Financial Institutions and Their Challenges

# INTERNATIONAL FINANCIAL INSTITUTIONS AND THEIR CHALLENGES
## A GLOBAL GUIDE FOR FUTURE METHODS

*Felix I. Lessambo*

palgrave
macmillan

IFC does not guarantee the accuracy, reliability or completeness of the content included in these works, and accepts no responsibility or liability for any omissions or errors (including, without limitation, typographical errors and technical errors) in the content whatsoever or for reliance thereon.

First published in 2015 by
PALGRAVE MACMILLAN®
in the United States—a division of St. Martin's Press LLC,
175 Fifth Avenue, New York, NY 10010.

Where this book is distributed in the UK, Europe and the rest of the world, this is by Palgrave Macmillan, a division of Macmillan Publishers Limited, registered in England, company number 785998, of Houndmills, Basingstoke, Hampshire RG21 6XS.

Palgrave Macmillan is the global academic imprint of the above companies and has companies and representatives throughout the world.

Palgrave® and Macmillan® are registered trademarks in the United States, the United Kingdom, Europe and other countries.

ISBN: 978–1–137–52269–6

Library of Congress Cataloging-in-Publication Data

Lessambo, Felix I.
    International financial institutions and their challenges : a global guide for future methods / Felix I. Lessambo.
        pages cm
    Includes bibliographical references and index.
    ISBN 978–1–137–52269–6 (hardback : alk. paper)
    1. Financial institutions. 2. Banks and banking. 3. Globalization—Economic aspects. I. Title.

HG173.L47 2015
332.1'5—dc23                                                    2015006193

A catalogue record of the book is available from the British Library.

Design by Newgen Knowledge Works (P) Ltd., Chennai, India.

First edition: August 2015

10 9 8 7 6 5 4 3 2 1

Printed in the United States of America.

# CONTENTS

# ILLUSTRATIONS

## FIGURES

## TABLES

# ACKNOWLEDGMENTS

Writing a book is always a challenge. But writing a book on "International Financial Institutions" is a more daring intellectual exercise, especially when the objectives are evolving so fast. The information for this book is based mostly on publicly available materials on the websites of the international financial institutions discussed here: the IMF, the World Bank Group, the regional development banks, and the regional investment banks.

I would like to express my gratitude to those who motivated me through the project, knowing my dedication to the subject and believing me more than able to complete this project: Dr. Gordon Marsha, Fouad Sayegh, Esq., and Brice Thionnet, Esq.

Several goods friends provided me with needed guidance and materials to complete this book, while others took from their busiest time to review and comb the manuscripts: Pastor Roland Dalo, Aline Kabongo.

# ABBREVIATIONS

| | |
|---|---|
| ADB | Asian Development Bank |
| AfDB | African Development Bank |
| AMC | Asset Management Company |
| AS | Advisory Services |
| BED | Board of Executive Directors |
| BMC | Borrowing Member Country |
| BIS | Bank for International Settlements |
| BIT | Bilateral Investment Ttreaty |
| BoP | Balance of Payment |
| CAF | Corporación Andina de Fomento |
| CAO | Office of the Compliance Advisor Ombudsman |
| CAS | Country Assistance Strategy |
| CCL | Contingent Credit Lines |
| CDB | Caribbean Development Bank |
| CEB | Council of Europe Development Bank |
| CFF | Compensatory Financing Facility |
| CLEERE | Climate Change, and Energy Efficiency and Renewable Energy Facility |
| CODE | Committee on Operations and Development Effectiveness |
| CPIA | Country Policy and Institutional Assessment |
| CPR | Country Performance Rating |
| CSF | Countercyclical Support Facility |
| DEM | Deutsche Mark |
| DMCs | Developing Member Countries |
| DRC | Democratic Republic of Congo |
| EA | Emergency Assistance |
| EBRD | European Bank for Reconstruction and Development |
| EC | European Commission |
| ECF | Extended Credit Facility |
| ED | Executive Directors |
| EIB | European Investment Bank |
| ESAP | Enhanced Structural Adjustment Facility |
| EP | European Parliament |
| ETF | Extended Fund Facility |
| EU | European Union |
| EVP | Executive Vice President |

| | |
|---|---|
| FCL | Flexible Credit Line |
| FDI | foreign direct investment |
| FSI | Financial Soundness Indicators |
| FSO | Fund for Special Operations |
| GAB | General Arrangements to Borrow |
| GBS | Global Broadband Solution Inc |
| GNI | Gross Net Income |
| GPG | Global Public Goods |
| GRA | General Resource Account |
| HIPC | Heavily Indebted Poor Countries |
| IADB | Inter-American Development Bank |
| IBRD | International Bank of Reconstruction and Development |
| ICD | Islamic Cooperation for the Development |
| ICSID | International Center for the Settlement of Investment Disputes |
| ICIEC | Islamic Corporation for the Insurance of Investment and Export Credit |
| ID | Islamic Dinars |
| IDA | International Development Association |
| IDB | Inter-American Development Bank |
| IEO | Independent Evaluation Office |
| IFC | International Finance Corporation |
| IFIs | International Financial Institutions |
| IMF | International Monetary Fund |
| IMFC | International Monetary and Financial Committee |
| IPRSP | Interim Poverty Reduction Strategy Paper |
| IRTI | Islamic Research and Training Institute |
| IsDB | Islamic Development Bank |
| ITFC | International Islamic Trade Finance Corporation |
| JASPERS | Joint Assistance to Support Projects in European Regions |
| LADB | Latin America Development Bank |
| LICs | Low-income countries |
| MCE | Microfinance Centre of Expertise |
| MCI | Mid-Cap Initiative |
| MD | Managing Director |
| MDB | Multilateral Development Bank |
| MDG | Millennium Development Goal |
| MDRI | Multilateral Debt Relief Initiative |
| MED | Monetary and Economic Department |
| MENA | Middle-East and North Africa |
| MIC | Middle-Income Countries |
| MIL | Environmental Investment Loans |
| MIFs | Microfinance Institutions |
| MIGA | Multilateral Investment Guarantee Agency |
| MSMEs | Micro-, Small-, and Middle-Size Enterprises |
| NAB | New Arrangements to Borrow |

| | |
|---|---|
| NDB | New Development Bank |
| NEPAD | New Partnership for Africa's Development |
| NIB | Nordic Investment Bank |
| NTF | Nigeria Trust Fund |
| ODA | Official development Assistance |
| OECD | Organization for Economic Cooperation and Development |
| OED | Operation Evaluation Department |
| OIC | Organization of Islamic Cooperation |
| OIE | Office of Independent Evaluation |
| OPCS | Operations Policy and Country Services |
| OPEV | Operations Evaluation Department |
| OPIC | Overseas Private Investment Corporation |
| PC | Performance Criteria |
| PCDR | Post-Catastrophe Debt Relief |
| PCG | Partial Credit Guaranty |
| PCL | Precautionary Credit Line |
| PLL | Precautionary and Liquidity Line |
| PIL | Project Investment Loans |
| PPPs | Public-Private Partnerships |
| PRAP | Poverty Reduction Action Plan |
| PRGF | Poverty Reduction and Growth Facility |
| PRI | Political Risk Insurance |
| PRSP | Poverty Reduction Strategy Paper |
| PSES | Policy on Social and Environmental Sustainability |
| PSI | Policy Support Instrument |
| PSP | Private Sector Participation |
| RCF | Rapid Credit Facility |
| RFI | Rapid Financing Instrument |
| ROSC | Report on the Observance of Standards and Codes |
| RSFF | Risk-Sharing Finance Facility |
| SAPRI | Structural Adjustment Participatory Review Initiative |
| SBA | Stand-By Arrangement |
| SCF | Standby Credit Facility |
| SDD | Sustainable Development Department |
| SDR | Special Drawing Rights |
| SMEs | Small and Medium-Sized Enterprises |
| SOEs | Sstate owned enterprises |
| SRF | Supplemental Reserve Facility |
| TCP | Technical Cooperation Program |
| UNCITRAL | United Nations Commission on International Trade Law |
| UNDP | United Nations Development Program |
| WB | World Bank |

# DISCLAIMER

While the author has made every effort to ensure that the information in this book is correct at the time of publication, he does not assume and hereby disclaims any liability to any Party for any loss, damage, or disruption caused by errors or omissions, whether such errors or omissions result from negligence, accident, or any other cause.

This publication is designed to provide accurate and authoritative information in regards to the subject matter covered. It is sold on the understanding that the publisher is not engaged in rendering professional services. If professional advice or other expert assistance is needed, the services of a competent professional should be sought.

# PART I

---◆◆◆---

# THE BRETTON WOODS AND
# AFFILIATES INSTITUTIONS

The International Financial Institutions' framework has become inefficient. The equilibrium reached in the aftermath of World War II—the Bretton Woods Institutions—is outdated and can no longer face the challenges of the twenty-first century. While many have argued for a major governance reform of the Bretton Woods institutions whose representation structures are dominated by the West and fail to accurately reflect the distribution of power in the global economy, such reform alone would not or is far not responding to our world's stringent challenges. More is needed. The modus operandi needs to be revisited to attract the best policy thinkers imbued with a sense of mission and understanding of the multiple-faceted challenges. No institution standing alone has the answers to all the problems, and thus, cooperation becomes the mantra.

# CHAPTER 1

———◆━◆◆━◆———

# INTERNATIONAL FINANCIAL INSTITUTIONS: ARCHITECTURE, FLAWS, AND LEGITIMACY

## GENERAL

International financial institutions need to be adjusted to the needs and challenges of the twenty-first century. Today's economy differs significantly from the world status of economy of the 1940s, which led to the creation of the Bretton Woods System and most of the existing international financial institutions. The globalization of financial markets, the debt crisis, cross-border flows of capital, and the rise of new economic powers have weakened the current system.

As Solimano stated, "The dividing lines between the balance of payments financing (the realm of the IMF) and development lending (the scope of multilateral development banks) have become less clear."[1] In the same vein, the *Report of the High-Level Commission on Modernization of World Bank Group Governance* pointed out:

> Regional institutions have become increasingly important in the economic and political life of the Bretton-Woods institutions, serving as catalysts for regional integration, cooperation, and development assistance.[2]

Thus, time has caused the reevaluation of an adequate balance of power between the Bretton Woods institutions, the regional development banks, and even the international investment banks, as many countries seem to prefer their regional development banks to the distant global Bretton Woods institutions. As Jose Antonio Ocampo has said:

> The current system will only be workable if it is based on stronger regionalism. A stronger regionalism is the only way to balance the huge asymmetries in power that we have in the system that is centre-periphery.

It is good to have competition between regional and sub-regional development banks and among the bilateral donor community. Similarly, it is good to
have various regional monetary funds.[3]

Indeed, the governance within these development banks is more
inclusive—relative to the corporate structure still in existence within the
Bretton Woods institutions dominated by the West. There is a greater degree
of representation for developing countries in the most important decision-
making bodies.

## THE BRETTON WOODS ARCHITECTURE

The Bretton Woods Conference, officially known as the United Nations
Monetary and Financial Conference, was a gathering of delegates from
44 nations who met from July 1 to 22, 1944, in Bretton Woods, New
Hampshire, to devise a new financial architecture for the post–War World II
economy. The two major accomplishments of the conference were the creation of the International Monetary Fund (IMF) and the International Bank
for Reconstruction and Development (IBRD).[4]

Participants in the conference believed, to some extent, that free trade pro-
moted not only international prosperity, but also international peace. The conference discussion was dominated by two rival plans developed, respectively, by
Harry Dexter White, Special Assistant to the Secretary of the US Treasury, and
John Maynard Keynes, an adviser to the Treasury of Great Britain.

The Keynes plan involved the creation of an International Clearing
Union, which would act as an international central bank and issue its own
currency (the bancor), the value of which would be determined at a relative
fixed price to gold. Each member country would establish a fixed but adjust-
able exchange rate in relation to the bancor. International payments balances
would be settled by using the bancor as a unit of account. The bancor would
have very limited convertibility; countries could purchase bancors but would
not be able to convert them into gold. In other words, bancor reserves would
remain within the system to avoid the possibility of a drain on reserves. Each
country would also be allocated a quota of bancor based upon their levels of
imports and exports.

Dexter White, the "assistant secretary," pushed for the exchange rates of
member-country currencies to be fixed to the dollar; and foreign governments and central banks could exchange dollars for gold at $35 per ounce.
Dexter convinced other participants that the newly designed architecture
would help reduce trade barriers and allow capital to flow freely between
member countries.

### The Broader Compromise: 1945–1971

The compromise that ultimately emerged was much closer to Dexter White's
plan than to that of Keynes, reflecting the overwhelming power of the

United States as World War II drew to a close.[5] Under the new architecture, trade would be progressively liberalized, but restrictions on capital movements would remain.[6]

White and Keynes independently drafted plans for organizations that would provide financial assistance to countries experiencing short-term deficits in their balance of payments. This assistance would help ensure that such countries would not adopt protectionist or predatory trade and monetary policies to improve their balance of payment positions. Both plans envisioned a world of fixed exchange rates: the US$ was to be pegged to gold at $35 per ounce, while other countries of the world were to be pegged to the US$ or directly to gold. Thus, the US$ became the currency of international financial institutions—a role it still plays today. The fixed exchange rate regime established at Bretton Woods endured for the better part of three decades. However, in the late 1940s, the United States found it difficult to cope with the growing balance of payment deficits coupled with the pressure facing the US$ in global currency exchanges. After some failed monetary policies in the 1960s, the US Treasury took various palliative measures to fix the system. In January 1961, for instance, the Kennedy administration pledged to maintain the $35 per ounce convertibility. The United States and its European allies set up a gold pool in which their central banks would buy and sell gold to support the $35 price on the London market. The effort was not successful, until 1968, when the rush out of dollars began—capital flight. Investors and multinational companies began to flow out of dollar assets and into German mark assets.[7]

Advocates of the gold-exchange system argue that the system economizes on gold because countries can use not only gold but also foreign exchange as an international means of payment. However, the gold-exchange system, as devised, contained its own germ of failure.

Professor Robert Triffin,[8] on the other hand, predicted that the system was programmed to collapse in the long run. He pointed out that (i) to satisfy the growing need for reserves, the United States needed to run continuous balance-of-payment deficits and (ii) continuous balance-of payment deficits would impair the public confidence in the US$. Robert Triffin's prediction, known as the "Triffin Paradox," came to pass in the early 1970s.

## The Floating-Rate Dollar Standard: 1973–1984

After the dollar exchange crises of August 1971 (when President Richard Nixon suspended the dollar's convertibility into gold), it was only in February/March 1973 that floating exchange rates became the norm for the currencies of the major industrialized nations. To understand the situation, it is worth bearing in mind that the United States entered a recession in 1970. The markets believed that, in order to counter the recession, the United States should devalue its dollar currency. In 1971, President Nixon announced that the United States would no longer automatically sell gold to foreign banks in exchange for the US$, and the Nixon administration imposed a 10 percent tax on all imports to the United States. Put differently, in August 1971, the United States announced that it is abandoning the convertibility of the dollar because of the worldwide lessening of confidence in the US$, and was seeking to convert of the dollars into gold from other nations. This was achieved through the Smithsonian Agreement entered into by ten countries in 1971. Among other things, the Smithsonian Agreement allowed each one of the ten countries gathered to (i) reevaluate its currency against the US$ by up to 10 percent and (ii) the range within which the exchange rates were allowed was raised from 1 percent to 2.25 percent in either direction.

The US$ was devaluated against foreign currencies by about eight percent. The markets reacted again on February 1973, attacking the US$ and forcing the FOREX market to close. On February 12, 1973, the US administration announced another 10 percent depreciation of the US$. The US treasury also announced a second devaluation of the dollar against gold to $42.

## The Plaza and Louvre Accords: 1985–1999

The Plaza Accord was a growth transfer policy for Europe and Japan that was wholly detrimental to the United States. It was a pro-growth agreement signed by the "former G-5[9] nations" constraining the United States to devalue its currency due to a current account deficit approaching an estimated 3 percent of GDP. The Plaza Accord allowed the dollar to slide 20 percent against the Japanese yen, 15 percent against the French franc, and 15 percent against the German deutsche mark. Some considered the Plaza Accord as being broadly detrimental to the United States. However, US manufacturers would again become profitable due to favorable exchange rates abroad—an export regimen that became quite profitable. A high US$ means American producers cannot compete at home with cheap imports coming from Japan and European nations, because those imports are much cheaper than what American manufacturers can sell according to their profitability arrangements.

The United States pushed for a multilateral intervention, designed to allow for a controlled decline of the dollar and the appreciation of the main anti-dollar currencies. Each country agreed to make changes in its economic policies and to intervene in currency markets as necessary to bring down the value of the dollar. The United States agreed to cut the federal deficit and to lower interest rates. Japan promised a looser monetary policy and financial-sector reforms, and Germany agreed to institute tax cuts. France, the United Kingdom, Germany, and Japan agreed to raise interest rates. The impact of the intervention was immediate, and within two years, the dollar had fallen 46 percent to the deutsche mark (DEM) and 50 percent to the Yen (JPY). By the end of 1987, the dollar had fallen by 54 percent against both the deutsche mark and the yen, from its peak in February 1985. The US economy became more geared toward exports, while Germany and Japan increased their imports. This helped resolve the current account deficits and helped to minimize protectionist policies.

Despite these efforts, the US$ continued to decline vis-à-vis the deutsche and other concurrent currencies. The United States was sustaining huge twin deficits in its domestic and current account budgets. In 1986, the trade deficit arose to approximately $166 billion, with exports at about $370 billion and imports at about $520 billion. The trade deficit alone approached approximately 3.5 percent of the GDP, while the Japanese had a surplus of 4.5 percent and the Germans were at 4 percent of the GDP.

To halt the decline, the G-6 entered into a new arrangement—"the Louvre Accord"—aimed at stabilizing the US$, cooperating to achieve exchange rate stability, and closely monitoring macroeconomic policies. The United States pledged to tighten its fiscal policy while Japan agreed to loosen its monetary policy. The participants agreed to intervene if major currencies moved outside a set of predetermined ranges. The dollar rose shortly after the accord was signed.

## THE POST–BRETTON WOODS ERA: NEW MANDATES

The post–Bretton Woods era that started in 1973 has altered the mandates of the two key institutions from Bretton Woods: the IMF and the World Bank. The IMF was assigned new roles in the international monetary system, and the World Bank champions the fight against poverty in order to uplift its member countries in the path of sustainable economic growth. Further new global challenges, mainly (i) the prevention and emergence of the spread of infectious diseases, (ii) climate change, (iii) international financial stability, (iv) international trading imbalances, (v) the threat of terrorism, and (vi) wars and other insecurities compel several experts in these fields to rethink our own world. As far as the international financial institutions are concerned, the enhancement of international financial stability has become an emergency: the quality and the management of the international financial institutions need to be rethought, and their governance revisited, in order to face the new challenges. They need to set up or upgrade monitoring and evaluation systems to properly assess their performances.

## INTERNATIONAL FINANCIAL STABILITY

While the causes of global financial instability are well documented—unsustainable macroeconomic policies, fragile financial systems, institutional weaknesses and structural flaws in international capital markets—the debate focuses more on the appropriate remedies, given the lack of an international body to oversee all the markets. Though the primary responsibility for preventing financial crises lies upon each and every sovereign country, the Bretton Woods Institutions as well as the regional development banks shall work together for a better effort in coordinating their surveillance programs. This encompasses the management of the member countries' debt and assistance in their social, economic, and environmental policies. Many expect the IMF to provide a better and more well-articulated framework.

## THE LEGITIMACY OF INTERNATIONAL FINANCIAL INSTITUTIONS

The legitimacy of actual international financial institutions is more challenged than at any time in the past. The concern is more than legitimate. According to Cotteralli, the ability of an international organization to achieve its goals ultimately rests on its legitimacy. An institution that is not regarded as legitimate will face key obstacles in achieving its goals and will likely be ineffective.[10] The under representation of the developing countries within the decisional instances of the both the IMF and the World Bank Group is well documented. According to Daniel D. Bradlow, only 16 directors represent the remaining 176 member states of both institutions. This means that each of these directors represents on average of slightly less than 11 states.

This unrepresentativeness has largely blown the Bretton Woods Institutions' credibility. Often it has led to a profound sense of hard feeling toward the IMF. The unfairness of their institutional processes has led the IMF and World Bank to lose a part of their moral influence, reduced the value of their recommendations, and thus caused states to be reluctant to implement their advice.

It is clear that the unfairness of the decision-making process inside the Bretton Wood Institutions, and the under representation of the developing world inside their executive board, has largely blown their credibility and legitimacy.

# CHAPTER 2

---◆◆◆◆---

# THE INTERNATIONAL MONETARY FUND

## GENERAL

The IMF is an international cooperative institution, whose main mission consists of promoting and assisting in global monetary stability. The IMF was set up in 1944, at Bretton Woods, with the aim of preventing the competitive exchange rate adjustments that characterized the interwar period. At the beginning, 44 nations gathered at the resort community of Bretton Woods, led by two key figures: the British economist, Sir John Maynard Keynes and the American deputy secretary of state, Harry Dexter. The 44 representatives agreed, primarily, to create the IMF as the second international institution to aid member states in need of foreign exchange conduct international trade and, secondarily, to facilitate the removal of the exchange controls for trade benefits.

Under the IMF original plan, only the US$ was pegged to gold at a rate of $35 per ounce. The other member states' currencies were pegged directly to the US$. From 1944 to 1971, the fixed exchange system created under the Bretton Woods Agreement and overseen by the IMF worked quite perfectly, with some breaches and problems. The overall system collapsed in 1973, paving the way to a greater-flexibility exchange rate among the major currencies. The Smithsonian Agreement with the floating foreign exchange rate system was seen by many as the end of the IMF. However, in 1978, the IMF altered its constitution, with new roles to conform to the new realities. It became an international cooperative bank with the aim of extending loans to developing member states.

Under Article 1 of the IMF's Articles of Agreement, the purposes of the International Monetary Fund are:

- To promote international monetary cooperation.
- To facilitate the expansion and balanced growth of international trade, and to contribute thereby to the promotion and maintenance of high levels of

employment and real income, and to the development of the productive resources of all members as primary objectives of economic policy.

- To promote exchange stability, to maintain orderly exchange arrangements among members, and to avoid competitive exchange depreciation.
- To assist in the establishment of a multilateral system of payments in respect of current transactions between members, and in the elimination of foreign exchange restrictions that hamper the growth of world trade.
- To give confidence to members by making the general resources of the IMF temporarily available to them under adequate safeguards, thus providing them with opportunity to correct maladjustments in their balance of payments without resorting to measures destructive to national or international prosperity.
- In accordance with the above, to shorten the duration and lessen the degree of disequilibrium in the international balances of payments of members.

After1973, the IMF was given two new mandates, which became the foundation for its role in the post–Bretton Woods international monetary system: to oversee the international monetary system to insure its effective operation, and to oversee the compliance by member states with their new obligations.[1]

After almost seven decades from its inception, IMF membership has increased from 44 countries to 187 countries in 2013. IMF member states have a dual role as both shareholders and borrowers. Though some incremental changes have been made in these seven decades, its corporate governance remains obscure, raising concerns as to the transparency of its decision-making process.

In the midst of the 2008 financial crisis, the so-called G-20 called for the reform of the IMF's corporate governance in order to refurbish the tarnished legitimacy of the institution; but six years later, little progress has been made.

While the IMF's representatives are going around the world preaching corporate governance principles (transparency, meritocracy, accountability) to their members, the institution lives far below the standards it imposes on its members. Its corporate governance deviates from "corporate best practice." The replacement of its disgraced managing director, Dominique Strauss-Khan, by the current managing director Christine Lagarde through an obscure process did little to honor the institution.

Though I argued that the IMF, at best, must be consolidated with the Bank for International Settlements,[2] here I am arguing for a remake of the institution's corporate governance—if it is to be relevant and before the merger with the Bank for International Settlements.

## THE ORGANIZATIONAL STRUCTURE OF THE IMF

Under Article XII of the IMF's Articles of Agreement, the organizational structure of the IMF is composed of (i) the board of governors, (ii) the Interim

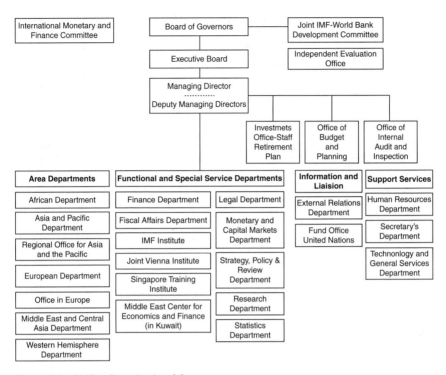

**Figure 2.1** IMF—Organizational Structure.
*Source*: IMF.

Committee, (iii) the International Monetary and Financial Committee, and (iv) the executive board (figure 2.1).

## The Executive Board

The executive board is the main decision-making body within the IMF. It is composed of 24 executive directors (ED), five appointed by the countries with the largest quotas and the other 19 elected by their constituencies—three of them being single-country constituencies. EDs are both the representatives of their respective countries and guardians of the IMF Articles of Agreement. EDs appointed by their countries are at the mercy of their countries, which can at all times and even for no reason, replace them. However, EDs elected by constituencies have a two-year tenure. In December 2010, the IMF agreed to amend its Articles of Agreement so that the executive board will comprise only elected directors. The executive board meets three times a week and is responsible for conducting the IMF's business. Beside its administrative duties, the executive board has specific powers: it selects the managing director, conducts the surveillance of the international monetary system and provides consultations under Article IV of the IMF agreement, approves the use of the IMF resources, sets strategies, and monitors their implementation.

## The Board of Governors

The IMF board of governors is overseen by finance ministers and central bank governors from 187 member states. As such, the board is not directly and indirectly accountable to people in countries it operates. It is the highest decision making body within the IMF. The Board of Governors has overall responsibility for the IMF's direction and performance.

The board of governors meets once a year. It oversees the executive board, appoints the EDs, approves the new entrants, disapproves, or disqualifies a member, increases the IMF quotas, and arbitrates issues related to the management of the international monetary and financial system. The board of governors also elects the twenty-four members executive board on a quota voting system. The voting right is determined based on the principle of "one dollar, one vote." Although the world wealth has shifted eastward, the IMF still functions as if it were the 1940s. The supermajority may require 70 percent or 85 percent of the vote, depending on the issue. For instance, a supermajority of 85 percent will be required for issues such as the change in the quotas or any amendment to the IMF's Article of Agreement.

## The Management

The IMF's management is composed of the Managing Director (MD) and the First Deputy Managing Director. The office of the MD comprises eight senior staff, with a budget of about $7 million. The MD is accountable to the Board for his job performance, decisions, and personal behavior, but in reality, the Board plays only a pro forma role in selecting the MD or renewing its tenure. The MD is selected through an opaque process among the European countries. While in the private sector, companies separate the office of the chairman of the board with the office of the chief executive officer, the managing director of the IMF is both the chairman of the board and the chief executive officer.

Since the creation of the IMF, the managing director has always been a European, and the first deputy managing director has been a US Citizen, despite the merits. In July 2011, the new MD, Christine Lagarde appointed Mr. Zhu Min, a Chinese national as a deputy managing director.

## The International Monetary and Financial Committee

The International Monetary and Financial Committee replaced the Interim Committee since 1999. It is composed of 24 members, all governors of the IMF. It advises and reports to the board of governors on issues related to the management of the international monetary and financial system. It is often considered to be the duplicate of the board of governors.

## The Joint IMF-World Bank Development Committee

The Joint Committee was established in 1974 as a forum that regroups the boards of governors of the IMF and the World Bank (WB). The Joint

Committee is made of 24 members representing all the shareholders that elect an executive director to the boards of the two institutions. The chairperson of the Joint Committee is usually from a developing member country. It reports on all aspects related to transfer of resources to developing countries.

### The Independent Evaluation Office

To respond to criticisms pursuant to its lack of transparency, the IMF has created an internal Independent Evaluation Office (IEO), which reports to the executive board on the efficiency of the IMF's mandates. The IEO is headed by a director, an official of the IMF, appointed and terminated at the pleasure of the executive board, for a renewal term of six years.

Besides its director, the IEO is composed of twelve members in charge of the conducting of investigations and reporting to the executive board. However, the IMF executive board has, under extraordinary circumstances, the right to keep secret the IEO investigations, findings, or recommendations. While such an office lacks independence toward the executive board, the IMF has praised its IEO as an example of "horizontal accountability" due to the fact that the IEO itself is evaluated regularly by an external agency hired by the IMF. What could be seen as an open conflict of Interest is seen as an appropriate response by the IMF resisting any outside checking or auditing of its unpopular policies.

## REFORMING THE IMF CORPORATE GOVERNANCE

For decades, the IMF has resisted any effort to reform its corporate governance. It has established its own Independent Evaluation Office to deal with recurrent countries. In 2008, the G-20 Summit in London agreed to reform the corporate governance of The IMF, effective March 3, 2011. The 2008 reform focused on strengthening the representation of emerging countries and the quota system, a key component of the IMF's financial resources. In 2009, the Committee on IMF governance reform, headed by Trevor Manuel, the South African Minister in the Presidency recommended, among other things, the following changes.

### A Review of the Quotas at the IMF

Quota subscriptions are key components of the IMF's financial resources. A member state's quota delineates basic aspects of its organizational relationship with the IMF, inter alia, (i) subscription, (ii) voting power, and (iii) access to financing. Voting power at the IMF is highly concentrated. Ten countries control over 50 percent of all the voting shares (figure 2.2).

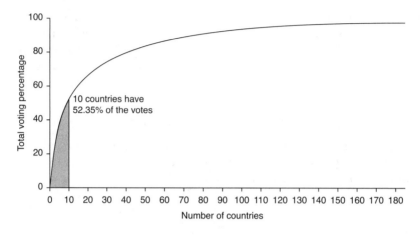

**Figure 2.2**    IMF—Total Voting Percentage.
*Source*: International Monetary Fund.

## Subscription

A member state's quota subscription determines the maximum amount of financial resource it must provide to the IMF. Usually, the quota subscription is paid in full any time a member-country joins the IMF. The IMF has some country-specific modalities concerning the subscription payment: a quarter of the sum should be paid in Special Drawing Rights (the IMF unit), and the remaining 75% is paid in the member state's local currency, or any other currencies accepted by the IMF.

## Voting Power

A member state's voting power is determined based upon a quota system which is based on its financial strength vis-à-vis the IMF. However, a member state's quota does automatically change whether that member state's economy flows or shrinks. A change in the quota must be approved by a majority of 81 percent of the voting members. Needless to say, the quota system is inadequate, or outdated, at best.

The five countries with the largest voting rights are the United States, Japan, Germany, France, and the United Kingdom.

## Access to Financing

The amount in loans that a member state can obtain from the IMF is also dependent upon its quota contribution. It should be noted that the initial quota granted to a new member state is determined through a comparison with an existing member state of comparable economic size and characteristics. The quota formula, per se, is a weighted average of GDP (50%), its openness (30%), its economic variability (15%), and its international reserves (5%). The quota is reviewed every five years by the board of governors.

To reach an important decision within the IMF, a majority of 85 percent was required. Such a threshold has reduced the big group of developing countries to a pro forma role, where they cannot have a say on IMF policies. Such a monopoly of the IMF policies was criticized, and the 2008 reform calls for an expansion of the double majority system, which would include, if not all, some developing countries.

Table 2.1 details both the quotas and the votes.

**Table 2.1**    IMF Members/Quotas and Votes

| Members | Quotas | | Votes | |
| --- | --- | --- | --- | --- |
| | Millions of SDRs | Percent of Total | Number | Percent of Total |
| Afghanistan | 161.9 | 0.07 | 2.360 | 0.09 |
| Albania | 60.0 | 0.03 | 1.341 | 0.05 |
| Algeria | 1,254.7 | 0.53 | 13,288 | 0.53 |
| Angola | 286.3 | 0.12 | 3,604 | 0.14 |
| Antigua & Barbuda | 13.5 | 0.01 | 876 | 0.03 |
| Argentina | 2,117.1 | 0.89 | 21,912 | 0.87 |
| Armenia | 92.0 | 0.04 | 1,661 | 0.07 |
| Australia | 3,236.4 | 1.36 | 33,105 | 1.31 |
| Austria | 2,113.9 | 0.89 | 21,880 | 0.87 |
| Azerbaijan | 160.9 | 0.07 | 2,350 | 0.09 |
| Bahamas | 130.3 | 0.05 | 2,044 | 0.08 |
| Bahrain | 135.0 | 0.06 | 2,091 | 0.08 |
| Bangladesh | 533,3 | 0.22 | 6,074 | 0.24 |
| Barbados | 67.5 | 0.03 | 1,416 | 0.06 |
| Belarus | 386.4 | 0.16 | 4,605 | 0.18 |
| Belgium | 4,605.2 | 1.94 | 46,793 | 1.86 |
| Belize | 18.8 | 0.01 | 929 | 0.04 |
| Benin | 61.9 | 0.03 | 1,360 | 0.05 |
| Bhutan | 6.3 | 0.003 | 804 | 0.03 |
| Bolivia | 171.5 | 0.07 | 2,456 | 0.10 |
| Bosnia and Herzegovina | 169.1 | 0.07 | 2,432 | 0.10 |
| Botswana | 87.8 | 0.04 | 1,619 | 0.06 |
| Brazil | 4,250.5 | 1.79 | 43,246 | 1.72 |
| Brunei Darussalam | 215.2 | 0.09 | 2,893 | 0.11 |
| Bulgaria | 640.2 | 0.27 | 7,143 | 0.28 |
| Burkina Faso | 60.2 | 0.03 | 1,343 | 0.05 |
| Burundi | 77.0 | 0.03 | 1,511 | 0.06 |

continued

**Table 2.1**   Continued

| Members | Quotas | | Votes | |
| --- | --- | --- | --- | --- |
| | Millions of SDRs | Percent of Total | Number | Percent of Total |
| Cambodia | 87.5 | 0.04 | 1,616 | 0.06 |
| Cameroon | 185.7 | 0.08 | 2,598 | 0.10 |
| Canada | 6,369.2 | 2.68 | 64,433 | 2.56 |
| Cape Verde | 9.6 | 0.004 | 837 | 0.03 |
| Central African Republic | 55.7 | 0.02 | 1,298 | 0.05 |
| Chad | 66.6 | 0.03 | 1,407 | 0.06 |
| Chile | 856.1 | 0.36 | 9,302 | 0.37 |
| China | 9,525.9 | 4.00 | 96,000 | 3.81 |
| Colombia | 774.0 | 0.33 | 8,481 | 0.34 |
| Comoros | 8.9 | 0.004 | 830 | 0.03 |
| Congo, Democratic Republic | 533.0 | 0.22 | 6,071 | 0.24 |
| Congo, Republic of | 84.6 | 0.04 | 1,587 | 0.06 |
| Costa Rica | 164.1 | 0.07 | 2,382 | 0.09 |
| Cote D'Ivoire | 325.2 | 0.14 | 3,993 | 0.16 |
| Croatia | 365.1 | 0.15 | 4,392 | 0.17 |
| Cyprus | 158.2 | 0.07 | 2,323 | 0.09 |
| Czech Republic | 1,002.2 | 0.42 | 10,763 | 0.43 |
| Djibouti | 15.9 | 0.01 | 900 | 0.04 |
| Dominica | 8.2 | 0.0003 | 823 | 0.03 |
| Dominican Republic | 218.9 | 0.09 | 2,930 | 0.12 |
| Ecuador | 347.8 | 0.15 | 4,219 | 0.17 |
| Egypt | 943.7 | 0.40 | 10,178 | 0.40 |
| El Salvador | 171.3 | 0.07 | 2,454 | 0.10 |
| Equatorial Guinea | 52.3 | 0.02 | 1,264 | 0.05 |
| Eritrea | 15.9 | 0.01 | 900 | 0.04 |
| Estonia | 93.9 | 0.04 | 1,680 | 0.07 |
| Ethiopia | 133.7 | 0.06 | 2,078 | 0.08 |
| Fiji, Republic of | 70.3 | 0.03 | 1,444 | 0.06 |
| Finland | 1,263.8 | 0.53 | 13,379 | 0.53 |
| France | 10,738.5 | 4.51 | 108,126 | 4.29 |
| Gabon | 154.3 | 0.06 | 2,284 | 0.09 |
| Gambia, The | 31.1 | 0.01 | 1,052 | 0.04 |
| Georgia | 150.3 | 0.06 | 2,244 | 0.09 |
| Germany | 14,565.5 | 6.12 | 146,396 | 5.81 |
| Ghana | 369.0 | 0.16 | 4,431 | 0.18 |
| Greece | 1,101.8 | 0.46 | 11,759 | 0.47 |

continued

**Table 2.1** Continued

| Members | Quotas | | Votes | |
|---|---|---|---|---|
| | Millions of SDRs | Percent of Total | Number | Percent of Total |
| Grenada | 11.7 | 0.005 | 858 | 0.03 |
| Guatemala | 210.2 | 0.09 | 2,843 | 0.11 |
| Guinea | 107.1 | 0.05 | 1,812 | 0.07 |
| Guinea-Bissau | 14.2 | 0.01 | 883 | 0.04 |
| Guyana | 90.9 | 0.04 | 1,650 | 0.07 |
| Haiti | 81.9 | 0.03 | 1,560 | 0.06 |
| Honduras | 129.5 | 0.05 | 2,036 | 0.08 |
| Hungary | 1,038.4 | 0.44 | 11,125 | 0.44 |
| Iceland | 117.6 | 0.05 | 1,917 | 0.08 |
| India | 5,821.5 | 2.45 | 58,956 | 2.34 |
| Indonesia | 2,079.3 | 0.87 | 21,534 | 0.86 |
| Iran, Islamic Republic of | 1,497.2 | 0.63 | 15,713 | 0.62 |
| Iraq | 1,188.4 | 0.50 | 12,625 | 0.50 |
| Ireland | 1,257.6 | 0.53 | 13,317 | 0.53 |
| Israel | 1,061.1 | 0.45 | 11,352 | 0.45 |
| Italy | 7,882.3 | 3.31 | 79,564 | 3.16 |
| Jamaica | 273.5 | 0.11 | 3,476 | 0.14 |
| Japan | 15,628.5 | 6.57 | 157,026 | 6.23 |
| Jordan | 170.5 | 0.07 | 2,446 | 0.10 |
| Kazakhstan | 365.7 | 0.15 | 4,398 | 0.17 |
| Kenya | 271.4 | 0.11 | 3,455 | 0.14 |
| Kiribati | 5.6 | 0.002 | 797 | 0.03 |
| Korea | 3,366.4 | 1.41 | 34,405 | 1.37 |
| Kosovo | 59.0 | 0.02 | 1,331 | 0.05 |
| Kuwait | 1,381.1 | 0.58 | 14,552 | 0.58 |
| Kyrgyz Republic | 88.8 | 0.04 | 1,629 | 0.06 |
| Lao People's Republic | 52.9 | 0.02 | 1,270 | 0.05 |
| Latvia | 142.1 | 0.06 | 2,162 | 0.09 |
| Lebanon | 266.4 | 0.11 | 3,405 | 0.14 |
| Lesotho | 34.9 | 0.01 | 1,090 | 0.04 |
| Liberia | 129.2 | 0.05 | 2,033 | 0.08 |
| Libya | 1,123.7 | 0.47 | 11,978 | 0.48 |
| Lithuania | 183.9 | 0.08 | 2,580 | 0.10 |
| Luxembourg | 418.7 | 0.18 | 4,928 | 0.20 |
| Macedonia | 68.9 | 0.03 | 1,430 | 0.06 |
| Madagascar | 122.2 | 0.05 | 1,963 | 0.08 |
| Malawi | 69.4 | 0.03 | 1,435 | 0.06 |

continued

**Table 2.1**  Continued

| Members | Quotas | | Votes | |
|---|---|---|---|---|
| | Millions of SDRs | Percent of Total | Number | Percent of Total |
| Malaysia | 1,773.9 | 0.75 | 18,480 | 0.73 |
| Maldives | 10.0 | 0.004 | 841 | 0.03 |
| Mali | 93.3 | 0.04 | 1,674 | 0.07 |
| Malta | 102.0 | 0.04 | 1,761 | 0.07 |
| Marshall Islands | 3.5 | 0.001 | 776 | 0.03 |
| Mauritania | 64.4 | 0.03 | 1,385 | 0.05 |
| Mauritius | 101.6 | 0.04 | 1,757 | 0.07 |
| Mexico | 3,625.7 | 1.52 | 36,998 | 1.47 |
| Federated States of Micronesia | 5.1 | 0.002 | 792 | 0.03 |
| Moldova | 123.2 | 0.05 | 1,973 | 0.08 |
| Mongolia | 51.1 | 0.02 | 1,252 | 0.05 |
| Montenegro | 27.5 | 0.01 | 1,016 | 0.04 |
| Morocco | 588.2 | 0.25 | 6,623 | 0.26 |
| Mozambique | 113.6 | 0.05 | 1,877 | 0.07 |
| Myanmar | 258.4 | 0.11 | 3,325 | 0.13 |
| Namibia | 136.5 | 0.06 | 2,106 | 0.08 |
| Nepal | 71.3 | 0.03 | 1,454 | 0.06 |
| Netherlands | 5,162.4 | 2.17 | 52,365 | 2.08 |
| New Zealand | 894.6 | 0.38 | 9,687 | 0.38 |
| Nicaragua | 130.0 | 0.05 | 2,041 | 0.08 |
| Niger | 65.8 | 0.03 | 1,399 | 0.06 |
| Nigeria | 1,753.2 | 0.74 | 18,273 | 0.73 |
| Norway | 1,883.7 | 0.79 | 19,578 | 0.78 |
| Oman | 237.0 | 0.10 | 3,111 | 0.12 |
| Pakistan | 1,033.7 | 0.43 | 11,078 | 0.44 |
| Palau | 3.1 | 0.001 | 772 | 0.03 |
| Panama | 206.6 | 0.09 | 2,807 | 0.11 |
| Papua New Guinea | 131.6 | 0.06 | 2,057 | 0.08 |
| Paraguay | 99.9 | 0.04 | 1,740 | 0.07 |
| Peru | 638.4 | 0.27 | 7,125 | 0.28 |
| Philippines | 1,019.3 | 0.43 | 10,934 | 0.43 |
| Poland | 1,688.4 | 0.71 | 17,625 | 0.70 |
| Portugal | 1,688.4 | 0.43 | 11,038 | 0.44 |
| Qatar | 302.6 | 0.13 | 3,767 | 0.15 |
| Romania | 1,030.2 | 0.43 | 11,043 | 0.44 |
| Russian Federation | 5,945.4 | 2.50 | 60,195 | 2.39 |

continued

**Table 2.1** Continued

| Members | Quotas | | Votes | |
|---|---|---|---|---|
| | Millions of SDRs | Percent of Total | Number | Percent of Total |
| Rwanda | 80.1 | 0.03 | 1,542 | 0.06 |
| Samoa | 11.6 | 0.005 | 857 | 0.03 |
| San Marino | 22.4 | 0.01 | 965 | 0.04 |
| Sao Tome and Principe | 7.4 | 0.003 | 815 | 0.03 |
| Saudi Arabia | 6,985.5 | 2.94 | 70,596 | 2.80 |
| Senegal | 161.8 | 0.07 | 2,359 | 0.09 |
| Serbia | 467.7 | 0.20 | 5,418 | 0.22 |
| Seychelles | 10.9 | 0.005 | 850 | 0.03 |
| Sierra Leone | 103.7 | 0.04 | 1,778 | 0.07 |
| Singapore | 1,408.0 | 0.59 | 14,821 | 0.59 |
| Slovak Republic | 427.5 | 0.18 | 5,016 | 0.20 |
| Slovenia | 275.0 | 0.12 | 3,491 | 0.14 |
| Solomon Islands | 10.4 | 0.004 | 845 | 0.03 |
| Somalia | 44.2 | 0.02 | 1,183 | 0.05 |
| South Africa | 1,868.5 | 0.79 | 19,426 | 0.77 |
| Spain | 4,023.4 | 1.69 | 40,975 | 1.63 |
| Sri Lanka | 413.4 | 0.17 | 4,875 | 0.19 |
| St. Kitts and Nevis | 8.9 | 0.004 | 830 | 0.03 |
| St. Lucia | 15.3 | 0.01 | 894 | 0.04 |
| St Vincent and the Grenadines | 8.3 | 0.003 | 824 | 0.03 |
| Sudan | 169.7 | 0.07 | 2,438 | 0.10 |
| Suriname | 92.1 | 0.04 | 1,662 | 0.07 |
| Swaziland | 50.7 | 0.02 | 1,248 | 0.05 |
| Sweden | 2,395.5 | 1.01 | 24,696 | 0.98 |
| Switzerland | 3,458.5 | 1.45 | 35,326 | 1.40 |
| Syrian Arab Republic | 293.6 | 0.12 | 3,677 | 0.15 |
| Tajikistan | 87.0 | 0.04 | 1,611 | 0.06 |
| Tanzania | 198.9 | 0.08 | 2,730 | 0.11 |
| Thailand | 1,440.5 | 0.61 | 15,146 | 0.60 |
| Timor-Leste | 8.2 | 0.003 | 823 | 0.03 |
| Togo | 73.4 | 0.03 | 1,475 | 0.06 |
| Tonga | 6.9 | 0.003 | 810 | 0.03 |
| Trinidad and Tobago | 335.6 | 0.14 | 4,097 | 0.16 |
| Tunisia | 286.5 | 0.12 | 3,606 | 0.14 |
| Turkey | 1,455.8 | 0.61 | 15,299 | 0.61 |
| Turkmenistan | 75.2 | 0.03 | 1,493 | 0.06 |

continued

Table 2.1    Continued

| Members | Quotas | | Votes | |
|---|---|---|---|---|
| | Millions of SDRs | Percent of Total | Number | Percent of Total |
| Tuvalu | 1.8 | 0.001 | 759 | 0.03 |
| Uganda | 180.5 | 0.08 | 2,546 | 0.10 |
| Ukraine | 1,372.0 | 0.58 | 14,461 | 0.57 |
| United Arab Emirates | 752.5 | 0.32 | 8,266 | 0.33 |
| United Kingdom | 10,738.5 | 4.51 | 108,126 | 4.49 |
| United States | 42,122.4 | 17.70 | 421.965 | 16.75 |
| Uruguay | 306.5 | 0.13 | 3,806 | 0.15 |
| Uzbekistan | 275.6 | 0.12 | 3,497 | 0.14 |
| Vanuatu | 17.0 | 0/01 | 911 | 0.04 |
| Venezuela | 2,659.1 | 1.12 | 27,332 | 1.09 |
| Vietnam | 460.7 | 0.19 | 5,348 | 0.21 |
| Yemen, Republic of | 243.5 | 0.10 | 3,176 | 0.13 |
| Zambia | 489.1 | 0.21 | 5,632 | 0.22 |
| Zimbabwe | 353.4 | 0.15 | 4,275 | 0.17 |
| Totals: General Department and Special Drawing Rights Department | | | | |
| | 237,993.4 | 100.0 | 2,518,501 | 100.0 |

*Source*: IMF, http://www.imf.org/external/np/sec/memdir/members.aspx

## THE KEY FUNCTIONS OF THE IMF

Due to subsequent changes in its Articles of the Agreement, the IMF nowadays performs three essential functions: (i) surveillance, (ii) financing, and (iii) technical assistance

### Surveillance

Under the Article IV of the agreement, the IMF is mandated to oversee the exchange rate policies of its member countries to ensure the effective operation of the international monetary system. IMF staff would therefore assess a member country's economic policy to ensure that it is consistent with the achievement of sustainable growth and macroeconomic stability. The surveillance function is conducted through continuous and open discussions between the IMF representatives and the member country's officials in charge of the financial and macroeconomic stability. The IMF conducts both bilateral and multilateral surveillances. However, the IMF surveillance recommendations are not binding or enforceable per se. Member countries comply merely based upon peer pressure and the publicity surrounding these general recommendations.

By and large, the IMF surveillance conducted under Article V focuses mainly on:

- exchange rate, monetary and fiscal policies;
- balance of payments and external debt developments;
- capital-account, financial and banking-sector issues;
- the impact of the member country's policies on its external accounts
- the international and regional implications of its policies;
- the identification of potential vulnerabilities.

In recent years, the IMF surveillance mandate has also evolved in scope to include simultaneous consultations among several member countries, and the IMF staff are inquiring more into member country exchange rate policy to deter any unfair competitive advantage.

## Financing

The IMF finances its operations primarily by collecting quota subscriptions from its members, sale of gold, multilateral borrowing arrangements, general borrowing arrangements, and new arrangements to borrow.

- Members' Quotas

The total member countries' quota subscription is approximately of US$376 billion. When a country joins the IMF, it pays up to one-quarter of its quota, the so-called "reserve tranche" in the form of reserve assets in an accepted foreign currency. The remaining three-quarters are paid in the country's own currency.

- Sale of Held Gold

The IMF holds around 90.5 million ounces (2,814.1 metric tons) of gold at designated depositories. On the basis of historical cost, the IMF's total gold holdings are valued at Special Drawing Rate (SDR) 3.2 billion (about US$4.8 billion), but at current market prices, their value is closer to SDR 73.8 billion (about US$113.2 billion).

- Multilateral Borrowing Arrangements

Currently, the IMF has two standing multilateral borrowing arrangements. The Multilateral Debt Relief Initiative (MDRI) provides for 100 percent relief on eligible debt from three multilateral institutions to a group of low-income countries. The initiative is intended to help low-income countries advance toward the United Nations' Millennium Development Goals (MDGs), which are focused on halving poverty by 2015.

- General Arrangements to Borrow (GAB)

The GAB was established in 1962 and expanded in 1983 to SDR 17 billion, from about SDR 6 billion. It has been activated ten times, the last time in 1998. The GAB and the associated credit arrangement with Saudi Arabia have been renewed, without modifications, for a period of five years from December 26, 2013. The GAB involved the central banks of eleven countries contributing to and maintaining a US$6 billion pool to maintain the stability of the Bretton Woods system. The GAB and the New Arrangement to Borrow (NAB) are currently funded to US$750 billion.

• New Arrangement to Borrow

The NAB is a set of credit arrangements between the IMF and 38 member countries and institutions, including a number of emerging market countries. In January 1997, the IMF's executive board adopted a decision establishing the NAB, which became effective in November 1998. The NAB is used in circumstances in which the IMF needs to supplement its quota resources for lending purposes. Once activated, it can provide supplementary resources of up to SDR 370.0 billion (about $575 billion) to the IMF. As part of efforts to overcome the global financial crisis, in April 2009, the group of twenty industrialized and emerging market economies (G-20) agreed to increase the resources available to the IMF by up to $500 billion (which would triple the total pre-crisis lending resources of about $250 billion) to support growth in emerging markets and developing countries. This broad goal was endorsed by the International Monetary and Financial Committee (IMFC) in its April 25, 2009 communiqué. The increase was made in two steps:

• First, through bilateral financing from IMF member countries;
• Second, by incorporating this financing into an expanded and more flexible NAB. On September 25, 2009, the G-20 announced it had delivered on its promise to contribute over $500 billion to a renewed and expanded NAB.

The amended NAB, which became effective on March 11, 2011, increased the maximum amount of resources available to the IMF under the NAB to SDR 370 billion (about $575 billion), from the SDR 34 billion under the original NAB. As of 2009, the total resources available to the IMF were increased to US$750 billion.

The multilateral borrowing arrangements, the New Arrangements to Borrow (NAB),[3] and the General Arrangements to Borrow (GAB) are intended to temporarily supply funds to the IMF. With these funds, it extends credits and loans to member country seeking its financial assistance. Member Countries borrowings are prorated to their shares within the IMF. These credits and loans come with string attached, known as conditionality. These conditionalities have become a contentious point between the IMF and the borrowing member countries. The similarities of these conditionalities have led some to question their relevance. As Antonio Ocampo stated: IMF member countries have had stable macroeconomic regimes under different structural conditions: high very interventionist states with very good macro balances and very neo-liberal states with a lot of macro imbalances.[4]

Applying the same conditionalities to regional countries despite their differences is counterproductive. Further, the IMF needs to work with the borrowing countries and draft "conditionalities" acceptable to and implementable by the borrowing countries. In so doing, borrowing countries would "own" the program and the string attached as part of the overall package with a commitment to achieve the economic goals.

## Technical Assistance

The IMF has often used its technical assistance mission as a tool to achieve a stabilization policy. Technical assistance accounts for approximately 20 percent of the IMF's annual operating budget.[5] The IMF technical assistance mission covers several areas, among others:

- training of officials;
- institution building;
- design and implementation of monetary and fiscal policy;
- collection and refinement of statistical data;
- management and accounting of transactions with the IMF.

# CATEGORIES OF IMF LENDING

In 1944, when the IMF was founded, it was expected to extend loans to the 44 member countries in need of short-term loans to overcome their temporary balance of payment (BoP) issues. With the transformation of its mission in the 1970s, the types of needs for IMF financing also need to change. While some member countries still need a temporary assistance to fix their BoP imbalances, other member countries become different in nature, scope, and even length in timing.

The IMF lends to a member country by providing it with reserve assets obtained from other member countries. The IMF makes two types of loans (i) concessional loans, and (ii) non-concessional loans.

IMF lending takes place through a complex process involving three stages:

- Reserve tranche: 25 percent of quota
- Credit tranche
- Special or extended facilities

The reserve tranche is considered to be part of a member's foreign reserves, and is granted automatically and free of policy conditions. However, the credit tranche and special or extended facilities are not automatic and do involve policy conditions.

Each credit tranche is evaluated in terms of 25 percent of a member's quota. The first 25 percent of quota above the reserve tranche is referred to as the "lower credit" tranche, and all subsequent 25 percent allotments above the reserve tranche, referred to as upper credit tranches are obtained through Standby Arrangements (SBAs), under the conditions set out in the letter of intent. IMF lending above the reserve tranche is deemed as a purchase-repurchase (REPO) arrangement in that when the IMF lends to a member, that member purchases foreign reserves using its own domestic currency. Nevertheless, later on when the borrower repays to the IMF, it repurchases its domestic currency reserve with foreign reserves.

## Concessional Loans

Concessional loans are loans provided to poorest member countries with lower interest rates and longer repayment periods than typical or standard market or multilateral loans. They are also known as soft loans and bear less pressure in terms of cutting spending and other abrupt economic-enhancing growth reforms. The most common types of concessional loans given to member states are the Extended Credit Facility (ECF), the Standby Credit Facility (SCF), the Rapid Credit Facility (RCF), the Post-Catastrophe Debt Relief (PCDR), and the Policy Support Instrument (PSI).

- The ECF provides flexible medium-term support to low-income member countries with a protracted balance of payment issues.
- The SCF addresses short-term and precautionary BoP needs.
- The RCF provides rapid access to the IMF funds with limited conditionalities in order to assist low-income member states meet their urgent imbalance of payment.
- The PCDR provides debt relief to low-income member states hit by catastrophic natural disasters, such as earthquake, storms, and other acts of God.
- The PSI is less than a loan. Rather, it is the IMF "seal of approval" for low-income countries seeking not a loan from the IMF, but an informal approval by the IMF as to the soundness of their macroeconomic stance.

## Non-Concessional Loans

Non-concessional loans come under different forms: (i) SBA; (ii) Extended Fund Facility (EFF), (iii) Supplemental Reserve Facility (SRF), (iv) Contingent Credit Lines (CCL), (v) Compensatory Financing Facility (CFF), (vi) Emergency Assistance (EA), (vii) Poverty Reduction and Growth Facility (PRGF).

(a) The Standby Arrangement

An SBA is a 12–18 month temporary assistance aimed at assisting a member country fix its temporary BoP imbalance. It comes in two different subforms: whether as a signed arrangement entered into by a member county and the IMF, or as an insurance facility for the borrower to enter later on into such an arrangement. An SBA must be repaid within three and one-quarter to five years. The payment schedule can be reduced to two and one-quarter to four years, anytime a member country wants to get rid of the IMF surveillance. Since 2005, the IMF has experienced a decline, as many borrowers are either getting loans from China, or building up huge foreign exchange reserves to counteract any BoP imbalance.

(b) The Extended Fund Facility

An EFF is a three-year financial assistance program to country members that might be facing structural serious BoP imbalances or a weak economic growth affecting their BoP imbalances. An EFFmust be repaid within four and one-half to ten years. As with the SBA, a member country with improved BoP can repay earlier if its EFF within four and one-half to seven years.

(c) The Supplemental Reserve Facility

An SRF is merely a supplement resource made available to a member country borrower under the SBA and the EFF, with higher interest payment rates. An SRF must be repaid within one and one-half years, but can be extended to two and one-half years under the IMF assessment of the country compliance with the program.

(d) The Contingent Credit Lines

The system of CCLs was established in 1999 and abolished in 2003. The facility of CCL was praised by borrowing member countries, as it comes with lesser conditionalities. However, the IMF member countries providing funds to the program criticized the program as being ineffective.

(e) The Compensatory Financing Facility

A CCF is a financing facility provided to a member country facing temporary export shortfall, or excesses in cereal import costs. A CCF must be repaid within three and one-quarter to five years.

(f) Emergency Assistance

An EA is a financial facility granted to a member country facing a BoP imbalance due to a natural disaster or a post-conflict situation. An EA is, in many cases, a prelude to an SBA between the IMF and the Member country.

(g) Poverty Reduction and Growth Facility

To make financial support more flexible and tailored to the needs of the low-income borrowers, the IMF, through the PRGF, has been providing

Extended Credit Facilities (ECF), Rapid Credit Facilities (RCF), and Stand-by-Credit Facilities (SCF) since January 2010.

ECF provides sustained engagement over the medium-to-long term to low-income borrowers facing medium-term BoP needs. It is more flexible than the financing tools described above.

SCF provides flexible support to low-income borrowers experiencing a short-term BoP imbalance due to external shocks.

RCF provides rapid financial support in the form of a single up-front pay-out to low-income borrowers facing urgent financing needs.

## THE IMF ECONOMIC STABILIZATION PROGRAMS

To promote economic and financial stability, the IMF engages in economic stabilization programs or policies. These policies encompass the following: (i) structural adjustment, (ii) privatization, (iii) civil servant layouts, and (iv) massive budgetary cuts in social and environmental programs to the most vulnerable.

### Structural Adjustments

Introduced in the 1980 under pressure from the United States[6] and the United Kingdom, structural adjustments are the most unfair conditionalities that the IMF attached to its financing model. Structural adjustment policies applied in developing countries have been counterproductive. Structural adjustment policies are often drafted "in the dark" by IMF staff who have no actual knowledge of the realities in the borrowing countries, and without interaction with experts from the developing countries. Group thinking has also contributed to the failure of the structural adjustment policies, as most economists within the IMF come from the same schools without a culture of open debates. Structural adjustment policies, wherever applied (i.e., Asia, Africa) have left many more vulnerable than they were before the IMF's involvement in the name of financial stability. Several measurements have been used to assess the effectiveness of these structural adjustments to several countries. One group of researchers uses the "ex ante benchmarks," while others used a counterfactual methodology. Ex ante benchmark researchers consider the benchmarks imposed by the policy-making institutions (IMF/WB) themselves against the created expectations to assess whether a given structural adjustment policy has worked or failed. The counterfactual researchers, on the other hand, looked at how the intervention changed the outcome, compared to what would have been the economic, social, and environmental result in the absence of the structural adjustment loans. The result of their finding is quite heartbreaking—the structural adjustment loans have failed the recipients.[7]

> The IMF and World Bank declaring a country eligible for debt relief is an admission that past loans, including adjustment loans, did not bring enough current account adjustments and export and GDP growth into that country to keep debt ratios within reasonable bounds.

## Privatization

A component of structural adjustment loans, in many countries, was the dire privatization of state-owned enterprises. Here again, the results were not satisfactory. Developing nations have long viewed the IMF with suspicion, for promoting disastrous, unfettered privatizations that complicated the transition from state-owned enterprises to market oriented models. The Bretton Woods Institutions' failure in Russia has been, is, and will remain a hot topic of the century. The actors of the crisis—the Russian government, the IMF, the World Bank, the Clinton Administration, the advisors—are still blaming one another, and no one is willing to learn from that experience, or even take some responsibility. From the IMF, the policies applied were the best under the circumstances, while other witnesses such as Joseph Stiglitz and Jeffrey Sachs deliver different accounts. For clarity's sake, let us first spell out the policies used in Russia before considering their shortfalls.

The IMF chose to emphasize monetary targets, budget deficits, and the unfettered privatization of Russian state-owned enterprises, despite the lack of legal and economic infrastructures to back up the process. Under pressure from the US government, the World Bank /IMF privatization of Russian state-owned enterprises—the tight monetary, fiscal, and foreign currency policies—turned to be catastrophic. Assets were spoiled by a new group of oligarchs who deposited the money in Swiss bank accounts,[8] inflation remained high, and we saw an increase in poverty and inequality.

*IMF Policies*
The IMF advice was directed primarily toward avoiding hyperinflation and bringing inflation down quickly to low levels, so as to create the conditions for the resumption of growth. In these years, IMF emphasized the necessity for tight monetary and fiscal policies to contain inflation.[9] The IMF's main concern was that the new leadership of the government and the Central Bank of Russia should not move toward more inflationary policies, thereby losing the degree of macroeconomic stability that had been achieved with difficulty over the previous few years.[10] John Odling-Smee, the IMF director of the European department, at that time, still argues that, despite the disappointing overall outcome, many of the specific measures taken to enable Russia to continue to qualify for disbursements were good reform measures with long-term benefits[11]—that the IMF advice and technical assistance contributed to many improvements in budget procedures, tax policy, and tax administration that made it easier to design and execute the budget as planned.

Though Mr. Odling-Smee has the right to his own opinion, a careful analysis of the justifications he laid down in his paper appear to be a list of failures. Below are some of his justifications or excuses:

- The IMF was aware, at the time, of their adverse consequences, although it perhaps did not envisage the full scale of the problems of pending non-payments that were partly caused by government arrears,[12]

- At that time, the IMF generally believed that the chances of implementing the fiscal policy envisaged in the program were greater if postponements were not too frequent or prolonged,
- given the importance of Russia in the region and to the world, it was thought to be worth the risk to the IMF's reputation and finances to persist with the engagement,
- although there was a willingness in principle to introduce private financing and charging, the necessary structural reforms for this and for the overall reduction in the size of the sector were never undertaken in a comprehensive way,[13]
- the implementation of the program was made difficult by the unexpected capital inflows, which, in the absence of adequate sterilization instruments, caused excessive monetary growth in the middle of the year, and inflation remained above the target path,[14]
- despite some doubts about the fiscal situation and the ultimate exit strategy, the IMF was officially supportive of the authorities' proposal, and the next mission worked closely with them on designing the monetary policy framework that was compatible with the new exchange rate policy,[15]
- there was probably a window from November 1997 to March 1998 when people might have been persuaded of the need for an exit, and an orderly exit might have been possible. With hindsight, it is regrettable that the IMF did not spot this opportunity at the time,[16]
- the IMF's influence was not always positive. It was, for example, a mistake to push for early abolition of the oil export duty and liberalization of the Treasury bill market.[17]

### The Criticisms of the IMF Policies

The IMF policies in Russia were flawed from the start, according to several witnesses. For instance, Jeffrey Sachs who advised the Russian government for some period relates that:

> In December 1991 I had continuing discussions with the IMF about Western assistance for Russia. The IMF's point man, Mr. John Odling-Smee, who lasted for a decade as the head of the IMF's efforts, was busy telling the G-7 that Russia needed no aid, that the "balance of payments gap" as calculated by the IMF was essentially zero. The IMF was simply parroting the political decisions already decided by the United States, rather than making an independent assessment. This is just a conjecture, but I make it because of the very low quality of IMF analysis and deliberations. They seemed to be driving towards conclusions irrespective of the evidence. The IMF's approach was in any event just what the rich countries wanted to hear. The technical methodology was primitive beyond belief.[18]

> The IMF advisory process was dangerously narrow and misconceived, and the IMF played a disastrous role by pressing Russia to maintain a common currency among the successor states of the former Soviet Union.[19]

> The IMF contributed to more than a one-year delay in the introduction of national currencies, and thereby to a significant delay in achieving

stabilization. Also, the IMF staffing was incredibly thin in 1992, not a single resident adviser.[20]

Throughout 1992 I warned everybody that I could that the reform process was dangerously blocked, that the IMF was making one mistake after another.[21]

As Jeffrey Sachs goes on to explain, the Clinton Administration, or at least its economic team failed to properly asses the Russian crisis.

There was absolutely no interest in a significant assistance plan for Russia, nor did key officials on Russian policy have any knowledge of economics. At that point the Treasury Secretary was Lloyd Bentsen, and neither he nor his deputy Roger Altman had any interest or knowledge of this issue. Larry Summers, who might have, was just getting started as an Undersecretary of Treasury. Key foreign policy campaign adviser Michael Mandelbaum refused to join the Administration in part because he realized that Clinton indeed would not support a major Western assistance effort to Russia.[22]

In the same vein, Joseph Stiglitz, the Chief Economist at the World Bank at the time of the Russian saga openly denounced the monetary, fiscal, privatization, and foreign currency policies pursued by the IMF, and the lack of social measures to protect the middle class that was impacted by these policies. However, as general objection to Joseph Stiglitz's virulent criticisms of the IMF, M. John Odling-Smee points out that Mr. Stiglitz, as Chief Economist at the World Bank in 1997–2000, knew that the World Bank rather than the IMF was in the lead role for advising on these issues of market and structural institutions, and that the IMF had little influence.[23]

After this clarification, let us consider the policies advocated and implemented by the IMF and their shortfalls under the analysis of both Jeffrey Sachs and Joseph Stiglitz:

(i) IMF Monetary Policy Flaws

The IMF's advice was directed primarily toward avoiding hyperinflation and bringing inflation down quickly to low levels, to create conditions for the resumption of growth. To that end, the IMF emphasized the necessity for tight monetary and fiscal policies to contain inflation, despite its underlying causes.[24]

The IMF poured in US$ to avoid devaluation, with the expectation of boosting confidence in the market. However, even when confidence had still not been restored and Russia started borrowing on high interest rates, the IMF did not adjust its policy or reverse course.

(ii) IMF Fiscal Policy Flaws

The underlying assessment of the Russian fiscal policy was also flawed. The IMF overestimated the capabilities of the Russian government to collect taxes, despite the fact that big companies in Russia negotiated their tax burdens and often ended paying no taxes. The IMF's lack of sufficient personnel on the ground led to a tax policy detached from the realities of the Russian tax system. Thus, the stabilization of the macroeconomic situation revealed an illusion. As Mr. Odling-Smee recognized:

> Although the actual fiscal deficit in 1995 was in line with the target, revenues and expenditures were not as high as originally intended. As in most years in the 1990s, revenues were below the projected level, mainly because well-connected enterprises had been able to reduce their tax liabilities, either by obtaining formal tax exemptions or by informal arrangements.

(iii)  IMF's Foreign Currency Flaws

The IMF's foreign currency policy was misleading. Providing money to maintain exchange rate was a bad economic policy. The fall of the Russian ruble occurred because government intervention in the market to stabilize the value of the currency was futile. According to Jeffrey Sachs, the IMF played a disastrous role by pressing Russia to maintain a common currency among the successor states of the former Soviet Union. He expresses the criticism as follow:

> As long as the 15 new countries, each with its own central bank, continued to use the Soviet ruble as currency, each central bank had the incentive to issue ruble credits, thereby enjoying seignorage gains (the benefits of money issue) while imposing inflation on all the others.[25]

## Budget Cuts

Several of the IMF structural adjustment programs led to drastic budget cuts affecting the most sensitive areas of people's lives. For instance, in Senegal, the IMF stabilization program (1980s) and the StructuralAdjustment Programs in 1986 led to falling health care standards, with maternal mortality increased by 60 percent, from 750 per 100,000 births in 1988 to 1,200 per 100,000.[26] In Hungary, the IMF/WB SAP resulted in a contraction of the budget by 14 percent between 1989 and 1996; industry fell by 34 percent over the same period.[27] In addition, the SAP entered into by Mexico in 1982 increased the level of inequality, and the government was not able to perform its basic governmental functions: education, heath, security.[28]

## Layout

Unfettered privatization of state-owned enterprises (SOEs) led to massive unemployment in developing countries where the SAPs were implemented. In these member states with almost no social nets, the IMF-concocted privatization programs were counterproductive. Professor Stiglitz criticizes the IMF's privatization as a pure confusion of means and goals. Rather than being a well thought-out process of bringing additional revenue to the budget, it was used as a goal.[29]

## ACCOUNTABILITY, TRANSPARENCY AT THE IMF

The IMF is often criticized for its lack of accountability and transparency in its policies toward the creditor member states.

### Accountability

Given the dual role of the member states as both shareholders and creditors, the issue of accountability needs to be considered in both aspects.

Toward its shareholders—The IMF is quite accountable as it grants voting rights based upon member states' subscription to the capital of the IMF. However, the IMF lacks basic mechanisms to protect its minority shareholders (the developing countries) against abuse of domination by the majority block, which has led to a situation where the majority or dominant block imposes its wills, policies, and interests to the detriment of the minority. Today, the majority of IMF votes are in the hands of the G7, with the United States holding a veto power.

Toward it Creditors—The IMF lacks accountability toward its creditors as the policies applied to borrowers are drafted by the majority block based upon the voting system. Within the IMF, the General Resource Account (GRA), which is responsible for all operations and transactions, relies upon the subscription quota explained above. Borrowers have little say.

### Transparency

The IMF's lack of transparency is well documented. From its policy making programs to their implementation on the ground, the IMF's Board of Governors, dominated by the G-7, dictate economic policies that suit their own interests, while the borrower member countries are left with no choice but to get on board. Few or less open debates occur as to the efficiency and effectiveness of the policies put forward, except that there are, from the IMF's viewpoint, good and sound economic policies. The reality is even more dire for borrower member countries as the IMF is the one in charge of the assessment of the conditionalities attached to the loans. These conditionalities apply to four main areas: (i) Performance Criteria (PC), (ii) Program Reviews (PRs), (iii) Prior Actions (PAs), and (iv) Structural Adjustments.

(i) The Performance Criteria

PC set out to evaluate whether the performance being measured is a quantitative performance or a structural performance. PCs are conditions agreed upon by the IMF and the borrower member country from the assets. PCs allow the IMF to assess the borrower member country's commitment or seriousness, as subsequent disbursements are contingent to the success of the precedent conditions. Any breach by a borrower member country can cause the program to be suspended, unless the IMF executive board grants a waiver. Unfortunately for borrowers, the PCs are derived from financial programing models developed by the IMF, and the borrower has no say as to the accuracy or efficiency of the used quantitative assessment of the various measures in the financial program. For transparency's sake, it would make more sense if both the IMF and the borrower elaborate a common model, allowing the borrower the dignity of being part of the system in a transparent way.

#### (ii) Program Reviews

PRs are ex-post, set interval assessments of the facility granted to a borrower member country, often when both the IMF and the borrower are uncertain as to the economic or financial crisis affecting a country. PRs are preferred over PCs because they allow the parties (IMF and Borrower) to adjust the assessment of the facility and objectives.

#### (iii) Prior Actions

PAs refer to prior actions that a borrowing member country needs to take before gaining access to IMF financing. These actions are negotiated and agreed upon between the IMF and the borrower.

#### (iv) Structural Adjustments

Structural adjustment policies applied in developing countries have been counterproductive. It is also well documented that the implementation of structural adjustments in Asia and Africa has led to massive unemployment, increase in poverty, and the suspension of vital government programs— whether to fight AIDs, or educate its own people. Further, the implementation of structural adjustment by the IMF was dictated by the investment banking business model in violation of the spirit of the IMF Charter. Structural adjustment policies are drafted, in the dark, by IMF staff without any knowledge of the realities in the borrowing countries, and without interaction with experts from the developing countries

## IMF's CHALLENGES

One of the biggest challenges facing the IMF is its current governance. Though the IMF remains "fully committed" to pursuing the implementation of the G-20 recommendations in the midst of the 2008 crisis, no substantial reform is as yet done. But for these reforms to go through, the United States must be willing to accept the modernization process. Recently, the IMF general director expressed her frustrations as follows:

There was not much I could do to push reform and give emerging economies a bigger say without the support of the United States. The US Congress must sign off on the IMF funding to complete 2010 reforms that would make China the IMF's third-largest member and revamp the IMF board to reduce the dominance of Western Europe.[30]

A month or so after that, Ms. Lagarde added:

The International Monetary Fund has become a "collateral" victim of US politics, preventing it from completing a sweeping funding increase and reform plan.[31]

Without sound structural and governance reforms, the future of the IMF is gloomy. More and more developing countries are turning to China, Saudi Arabia, and other oil-rich countries for financial facilities, rather than to the IMF. For instance, Egypt declined the IMF's US$ three billion loan (at almost 0%) to turn to Saudi Arabia for the same amount. In 2013, Nigeria negotiated a $3 billion loan—to enhance its infrastructure—with China rather than the IMF. In some parts of the world, mainly in Asia, the IMF is close to becoming history, as these countries are piling on enormous reserves to face any imbalances without calling upon the IMF. With the increase of Sovereign Wealth Funds and the New Development Bank,[32] more countries will turn to those institutions for long-term loans under better conditions than the current IMF lending policies can provide. Further, the IMF should let the World Bank Group deal with the Millennium Development Goals and focus more on technical assistance, not only to developing countries, but also to its ten biggest shareholders. The recent financial meltdown has taught us that financial crises and macroeconomic mismanagements are not the province of developing countries. The IMF would need to reconsider its oversight of the biggest financial markets such as the United States, the Eurozone, and others.

As Mr. Xia Bin, an adviser to the People's Bank of China (PBoC) said:

Unless the United States reduces its dominant voting share in the International Monetary Fund, and re-negotiates the EU monopoly, any serious reform would head toward giving emerging economies more of a say in deciding who should take the helm of the IMF.

China's Foreign Minister went on to add:

The international Monetary Fund leadership should be based on "merit, transparency, and fairness."

The relevance of the IMF is dependent upon its ability to adjust its missions and governance to the needs and desires of all its members, and not just the very few. Otherwise, the IMF will become history.

# CHAPTER 3

---—ЖЕЖ—---

# THE WORLD BANK

## GENERAL

Established in 1944, under the Bretton Woods Agreement, the International Bank for Reconstruction and Development (IBRD) was created to help rebuild Europe after World War II. However, the mission of the World Bank (WB) has evolved with the passage of time. Today, the WB's primary mission is to reduce poverty, by offering developmental assistance to middle and low-income state members. One way to achieve the mission statement is to promote economic and policy prescriptions, which in turn promote economic growth. Good corporate governance is one of the prescriptions. Prior to 1998, the WB was not really preoccupied with good corporate governance and its accompanying politics. However, following the immensity of the Asian financial crisis of the 1990s—increased privatization, financial market liberalization, and high-profile corporate failures—the WB and the leaders of the so-called "G-7" came to the conclusion that corporate governance was much needed globally in order to prevent financial crises such as the Asian crisis from occurring again. In assessing member states, the WB relies upon the principles of corporate governance—as adopted by the Organization for Economic Cooperation and Development (OECD).

The WB group is like an international cooperative composed of 187 member states. To become a member, a state must first join the IMF. At the time of its adhesion to the WB, a member state must pay a subscription fee, which is equivalent to 88.29 percent of the quota allowed to that country by the IMF. The adherent country must also buy 195 shares in the WB. The WB's policies are heavily criticized by borrowing states as unjust, inadequate, obsolete, and designed to protect the interests of the five super-shareholders and the capital markets.

## ORGANIZATIONAL STRUCTURE OF THE WB

The organizational structure of the WB group is to a large extent, similar to the structure of the IMF.

## The Board of Governors

The board of governors consists of one governor and 187 alternate governors per member state. Governors are ministers; about three-quarters are ministers of finance and one quarter from other government ministries, including international development, planning, and foreign affairs. Alternate governors are usually finance ministers, central bank governors, or any senior official of similar rank, appointed by its home country. Under the WB Agreement, the board of governors is vested with the all power to conduct its business, inter alia:

- Admission and suspension of member states;
- Increase and/or decrease of the authorized capital stock;
- Determination of the distribution of the net income of the bank;
- Approval of any amendment to the Articles of Agreement;
- Interpretation of the Articles of Agreement;
- Permanent suspension of the operations of the WB;
- Increase in the number of elected executive directors;
- Arrangement to cooperate with other international organizations.

However, except otherwise stated in the Articles of Agreement, the board of governors delegates most of its powers to the board of directors.

## The Board of Directors

The board of directors is composed of executive directors, who exercise a contradictory dual function as executives of the WB and the representatives of the countries that appoint them. Executive directors are responsible vis-a-vis the board of governors, and have been vested with the power to nominate and revoke the president of the WB. Five executive directors are appointed by the shareholders having the largest shares (the United States, the United Kingdom, France, Germany, and Japan) and 19 are elected by the rest of the members, organized in constituencies. Three countries (China, Russia, and Saudi Arabia) elect their own executive directors, while the 16 other executive directors represent multi-country constituencies. Appointed directors serve at the discretion of their governments, while elected directors serve renewable two-year terms. Powers of the executive directors are listed as executive power or oversight power. Executive power consists of representing the board of governors at the annual meetings, carrying out audits of accounts and administrative budgets, and the preparation of the WB's annual report. The oversight power includes the supervision of the Independent Evaluation Group, the inspection panel, the external audit, and the Conflict Resolution System.

## The President

The President of the WB is the central figure. He conducts the ordinary business of the WB under the direction of the executive directors. The President of the WB serves as the head of the group's five arms[1] and is the chairperson of all its boards of directors.

## THE PURPOSES OF THE WB

The mission statement of the IBRD states that it "aims to reduce poverty in middle-income and creditworthy poorer countries by promoting sustainable development, through loans, guarantees, and non-lending, including analytical and advisory-services." The WB aims at issues such as building infrastructure (roads, dams, and power plants), natural disaster relief, humanitarian emergencies, poverty reduction, infant mortality, gender equality, education, and long-term development issues. Furthermore, the WB tries to foster social reforms to promote economic development, such as the empowerment of women, building schools and health centers, provision of clean water and electricity, fighting disease, and protecting the environment.

Since 2000, the WB has been devoted to helping implement the Millennium Development Goals (MDGs), drafted by the United Nations at the Millennium World Summit. The MDGs are as follows:

1. Eradicate extreme poverty and hunger.
2. Achieve universal primary education.
3. Promote gender equality and empower women.
4. Reduce child mortality.
5. Improve maternal health.
6. Combat HIV/AIDS, malaria, and other diseases.
7. Ensure environmental sustainability.
8. Develop a global partnership for development.

The goals also have 18 specific targets and 48 performance indicators and are considered a step forward over previous development efforts, for they set specific targets and timetables for achievement, with 2015 as the major deadline. Commemorating the ten-year mark of when the MDG's were set, there was a major conference held at the UN headquarters in New York in September 2010 to review the progress made and the shortcomings of these projects. There is still great concern in the international community that nearly all of these goals are quite off-target, with the prospects of "eradicating extreme poverty and hunger" looking quite dismal.

While I do also share the goal of eradicating poverty, I also believe that the approach taken to poverty reduction is misguided. That is, the debate over poverty reduction has been developed within the two extreme schools of thought. The one lead by Jeffrey Sachs, adviser to the United Nations, relies upon the concept of "poverty trap" to explain poverty as a vicious cycle that can only be eradicated through the infusion of billions in US dollars provided by developed countries.[2] The other school, led by William Easterly, argues that aid is part of the poverty problem and not a solution.[3] Easterley's ideas have been, recently, echoed by Dambiso Moyo in her book, Dead Aid,[4] though for different reason—mass corruption perpetuated by leaders all around the developed countries. Between the two predominant schools of thoughts, a middle ground, led by Banerjee and Duflo,[5] seems to make its way by counter-balancing the aforementioned two "extreme schools of thought." The two authors recognized that many programs that were aimed at helping or alleviating the burden of poverty landed up in the wrong hands, but they argue that poverty eradication can be achieved through governance and policy improvements within attempting to supersede or replace the existing social and political structures of the developing countries.[6] The core finding of Barnejee and Esther is:

> If we resist the kind of lazy, formulaic thinking that reduces every problem to the same set of general principles; if we listen to poor people themselves and force ourselves to understand the logic of their choices; if we accept the possibility of error and subject every idea, including the most apparently common sensical ones, to rigorous empirical testing, then we will be able not only to construct a toolbox of effective policies but also to better understand why the poor live the way they do. Armed with this patient understanding, we can identify the poverty traps where they really are and know which tools we need to give the poor to help them get out of them.[7]

Unless radical change of mentality and thought is made, the WB group, and to some extent, the IMF, the Millennium Development Goals already count as failed vows, as no substantial results are visible as of the first half of 2015.

## REFORMING THE WB'S GOVERNANCE STRUCTURE

Like the IMF, the distribution of voting power in the WB is aligned to ownership shares. That system was set up to reflect state members' economic strength, based on a mix of reserves, international trade volumes, and national income. Despite the fact that the world economy has shifted eastward, the capital structure and the governance of the WB remains almost the same.

### Voting Rights

Under Article V, section 3 of the WB Agreement, each member state has 250 basic membership shares plus one additional vote for each share of stock held. The voting rights of state members have change a bit—last in 1995. The developing member countries, which are the main borrowers from the WB, retain only 38 percent of the overall votes. Such an inequity in voting power and representation has hindered developing countries from having an influence over the WB's policies.

### Representation to the Executive Board

The representation to the executive board of the WB is based on voting rights. The United States, Japan, Germany, France, and the United Kingdom, each have their own executive director on the board. Recently, China, Russia, and Saudi Arabia have also been allowed to each elect their own executive directors. The remaining executive directors are elected by different groups of countries, organized through "constituencies."

The biggest constituency is formed by forty-five sub-Saharan countries, with two executive directors. Given the fact that the WB works on a consensus basis with few decisions formally going to vote, the executive directors from developing countries are more or less merely "figurant." The assessment of developing countries is often conducted by the powerful executive directors from the G-7, without the involvement of their representatives.

## THE FINANCING OF THE WB

The WB's primary source of capital comes from contributions made by its shareholders and its capital reserves, accumulated over the years of its operations. The WB raises the bulk of its resources by selling bonds in international markets. With that capital, the WB lends, solely, to governments.

The IBRD issues bonds in international capital markets and provides long-term loans to middle-income countries. In fiscal 2013, IBRD raised US$22.1 billion by issuing bonds in 21 currencies. Its standing in the capital markets and its financial strength allowed IBRD to borrow these large volumes on very favorable terms, despite volatile market conditions.

The IBRD's equity primarily comprises paid-in capital and reserves. Under the terms of the general and selective capital increase resolutions approved by the board of governors on March 16, 2011, subscribed capital is expected to increase by $86.2 billion, of which $5.1 billion will be paid in over a five-year period. As of June 30, 2013, the cumulative increase in subscribed capital totaled $32.2 billion. Related paid-in amounts in connection with these capital increase resolutions were $1.9 billion.

## WB OPERATIONS

The WB's main activity consists of lending money to its members in order to sustain their development projects. Besides lending activities, the WB offers financial products that allow clients to efficiently fund their development programs and manage risks related to currency and interest rates, commodity prices, and natural disasters.

• Lending Activities

In 2013, new lending commitments by the WB were $15.2 billion for 92 operations all around the world. The following figures from the WB describe the lending by regions, sectors, and themes (figures 3.1–36).

• Financial Products Services

The WB's financial product services consist of hedging on behalf of member countries. It also executes swaps to provide catastrophe risk insurance. The WB also serves as an arranger for government bonds' issuance.[8]

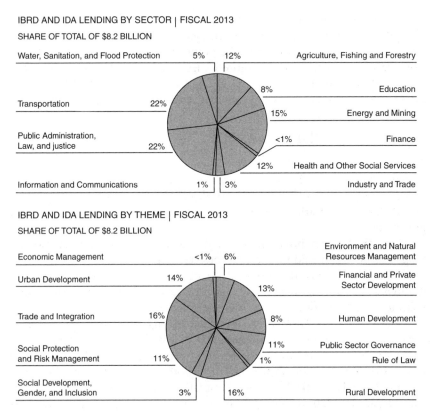

**Figure 3.1**   IBRD and IDA Lending in Africa.
*Source:* World Bank (2013).

## THE WB ASSESSMENT OF MEMBER STATES

To provide assistance to member states, the WB has developed metrics to assess the proper use of the aid, as well as the governance institutions put in place.

### The Work Bank Use of CPIA

CPIA, which stands for Country Policy and Institutional Assessment, assists the WB's staff in making professional judgments based on 16 criteria, grouped in four clusters.[9] The process begins with a benchmarking phase, which entails rating a small representative sample of countries drawn from all the regions. Then follows a rollout phase, during which the rest of the countries are rated. Both phases entail a multistep procedure:

- In the first step, the country teams generate a set of proposed ratings for their respective countries. The country economists usually lead this step, with the participation of sector specialists and country management.

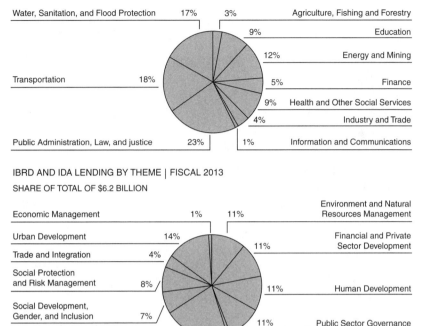

**Figure 3.2** IBRD and IDA Lending in East Asia and Pacific.
*Source*: World Bank (2013).

- In the second step, the Regional Chief Economist's offices review and revise the ratings for the countries within the respective regions, to ensure cross-country comparability within each region.
- In the third step, the network anchors and other central units review the ratings at the global level to ensure the cross-regional comparability of ratings.
- The fourth step is somewhat different for benchmarking, as opposed to the rollout phase. For the benchmarking phase, the fourth step entails a meeting of representatives from Operations Policy and Country Services (OPCS), the regions, networks, and central departments to review the proposed ratings for all of the criteria and for all of the benchmark countries, after which, the ratings are "frozen" and the rollout phase proceeds. For the fourth step of the rollout phase, most of the ratings are finalized through virtual communication because of the large number of countries involved.

Meetings are only held to discuss the few cases that have not been resolved by virtual communication.

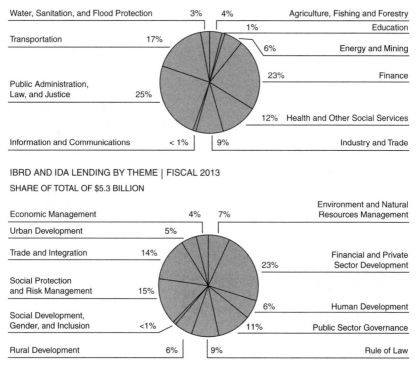

IBRD AND IDA LENDING BY SECTOR | FISCAL 2013

SHARE OF TOTAL OF $5.3 BILLION

Water, Sanitation, and Flood Protection  3%    4%   Agriculture, Fishing and Forestry

1%   Education

Transportation  17%

6%   Energy and Mining

23%   Finance

Public Administration, Law, and Justice  25%

12%  Health and Other Social Services

Information and Communications  < 1%    9%   Industry and Trade

IBRD AND IDA LENDING BY THEME | FISCAL 2013

SHARE OF TOTAL OF $5.3 BILLION

Economic Management  4%   7%   Environment and Natural Resources Management

Urban Development  5%

Trade and Integration  14%    23%   Financial and Private Sector Development

Social Protection and Risk Management  15%

6%   Human Development

Social Development, Gender, and Inclusion  <1%   11%   Public Sector Governance

Rural Development  6%    9%   Rule of Law

**Figure 3.3**  IBRD and IDA Lending in Europe and Central Asia.
*Source*: World Bank (2013).

## WB's Assessment of Country Governance

Given the importance of monitoring corporate governance implementation, the IMF and the WB are carrying out assessments of countries' corporate governance under the overall program of Report on the Observance
of Standards and Codes (ROSC).[10] The WB is mainly in charge of assessing
the achievements of member states in corporate governance, accounting and
auditing, and insolvency regimes and creditor rights. The assessment of corporate governance practices in a country measures the legal and regulatory
framework as well as the compliance-listed firms (if any) against the OECD
principles of corporate governance. Through the ROSC, the WB works with
member states to identify institutional weaknesses and vulnerabilities and
offers recommendations to help and strengthen the domestic institutions
of the assessed country. Countries' participation in the ROSC is voluntary,
though countries assessed noted that such participation brings several benefits compared to regular Article IV consultations. The WB is facing a huge
demand from both developing and emerging countries in their efforts to
enhance their corporate governance frameworks and practices. Following

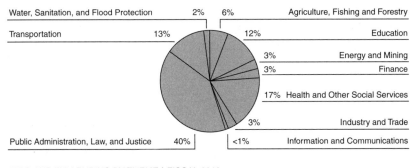

IBRD AND IDA LENDING BY SECTOR | FISCAL 2013

SHARE OF TOTAL OF $5.2 BILLION

| | |
|---|---|
| Water, Sanitation, and Flood Protection 2% | 6% Agriculture, Fishing and Forestry |
| Transportation 13% | 12% Education |
| | 3% Energy and Mining |
| | 3% Finance |
| | 17% Health and Other Social Services |
| | 3% Industry and Trade |
| Public Administration, Law, and Justice 40% | <1% Information and Communications |

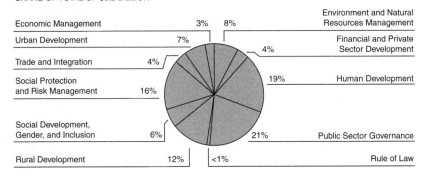

IBRD AND IDA LENDING BY THEME | FISCAL 2013

SHARE OF TOTAL OF $5.2 BILLION

| | |
|---|---|
| Economic Management 3% | 8% Environment and Natural Resources Management |
| Urban Development 7% | 4% Financial and Private Sector Development |
| Trade and Integration 4% | |
| Social Protection and Risk Management 16% | 19% Human Development |
| Social Development, Gender, and Inclusion 6% | 21% Public Sector Governance |
| Rural Development 12% | <1% Rule of Law |

**Figure 3.4**   IBRD and IDA Lending in Latin America and the Caribbean.
*Source*: World Bank (2013).

the ROSC, the WB remains involved with the authorities of the assessed country in supporting capacity building and policy development in the areas of regulation and supervision. The observance of the OECD corporate governance standards as revised in 2004 is analyzed, compared with the country practices. By and large, the ROSC is made of four components:

- an executive summary, which provides a clear assessment of the overall degree of observance that could be;
- a principle-by-principle summary of observance of the standard;
- A prioritized list of key recommendations.

The WB uses a consistent methodology for assessing national corporate governance practices. It also provides benchmark indices by which countries can evaluate themselves and gauge progress achieved. Often, the WB will commission a local consultant to complete a template designed to capture a country's corporate governance, legal, and regulatory framework, and information on corporate governance practices. Then afterwards, the WB "experts" visit the country and interact with the government officials, the

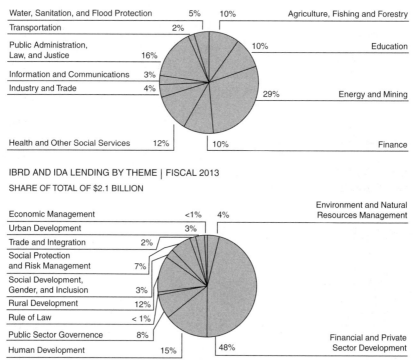

**Figure 3.5** IBRD and IDA Lending in Middle East and North Africa.
*Source*: World Bank (2013).

investors, and other participants in the country's economy. The process can be improved if the WB moves to work closely with regional experts instead of generalist-experts deprived of international backgrounds. The WB's assessment of any given country does not come with a rating. Some have argued that a rating would entice the country to improve if corporate governance if really on the top of the country's priorities.

## Toward a WB of Twenty-First Century

Like the IMF, the WB is losing its relevance. Developing countries are increasingly turning their backs to the institution due its lack of proper corporate governance. The WB's governance is seen as undemocratic, and its policies are criticized as inadequate. Some even argue that it has become a continuing factor for the poverty it is meant to fight against. To remain relevant, the WB needs to alter its Articles of Agreement in order to provide transparency and become more accountable to the developing countries. Several proposals are commonly argued, starting from (i) the protection of the borrower Countries (often from the south), (ii) the alteration of the voting rights and

IBRD AND IDA LENDING BY SECTOR | FISCAL 2013

SHARE OF TOTAL OF $4.5 BILLION

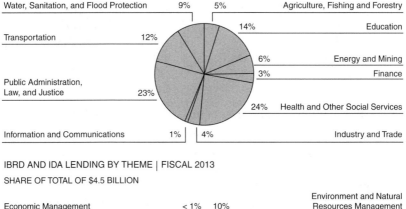

| | | |
|---|---|---|
| Water, Sanitation, and Flood Protection | 9% | 5% Agriculture, Fishing and Forestry |
| | | 14% Education |
| Transportation | 12% | |
| | | 6% Energy and Mining |
| | | 3% Finance |
| Public Administration, Law, and Justice | 23% | |
| | | 24% Health and Other Social Services |
| Information and Communications | 1% | 4% Industry and Trade |

IBRD AND IDA LENDING BY THEME | FISCAL 2013

SHARE OF TOTAL OF $4.5 BILLION

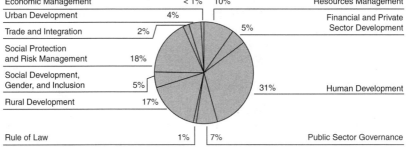

| | | |
|---|---|---|
| | | Environment and Natural Resources Management |
| Economic Management | < 1% | 10% |
| Urban Development | 4% | Financial and Private Sector Development |
| Trade and Integration | 2% | 5% |
| Social Protection and Risk Management | 18% | |
| Social Development, Gender, and Inclusion | 5% | 31% Human Development |
| Rural Development | 17% | |
| Rule of Law | 1% | 7% Public Sector Governance |

**Figure 3.6**   IBRD and IDA Lending in South Asia.
*Source*: Wrold Bank (2013).

the representation on the board of governors, (iii) the establishment of an "independent" Office of Independent Evaluation (OIE) detached from the WB, and (iv) the alteration of the auditing of the WB's activities.

## The Protection of the Minorities

The OECD corporate governance principles require that, in any structure—private or public—the rights of the minorities must be protected against the dominant shareholders. *The Report of the High--Level Commission on Modernization of World Bank Group Governance* found important shortcomings in three areas of the group's governance: strategy formulation, voice and participation, and accountability.[11] Given the dual attribute of the minority as shareholders and borrowers, the WB has to work out a mechanism that ensures its minority members a protection against any form of abuse by the dominant shareholders. This can be achieved by allowing the minority either to acquire or subscribe to additional capital in the WB's capital in order to rebalance the relation between the dominant shareholders' group and the minority shareholders' group.

### The Alteration of the Voting Rights

The board of governors, as the guardian and the interpreter of the WB's Articles, should amend the WB's constitution in order to accommodate the developing countries and enhance their voting rights within all decision-making institutions. The WB would gain more credibility if it aligns its voting rights principle to the UN General Assembly's principle of one country-one vote.

### The Establishment of an Independent "OIE"

Establishing an independent OIE would be helpful to developing countries, if such an office were composed primarily of outside executive directors, elected by both the dominant shareholders' group and the minority group based upon skills, independence, and openness. Furthermore, the current leeway granted to the board of governors to ignore certain recommendations from the OIE should be abolished. The board of governors would achieve a higher level of transparency and accountability if all the recommendations were made accessible to the general public.

### Changing the Auditing Process of the WB's Activities

Ex-post auditing of the WB's activities should be conducted not by an "independent auditor" hired by the board of governors, but rather, the external auditor of the WB's activities should be appointed by the minority group and held accountable to the minority group alone. Studies show that "independent auditors" hire by the dominant group are most often too cooperative with the hirer, and are eager to please in order to retain business.

## WB's CHALLENGES

The challenge for the WB is to identify and provide a competitive menu of development solutions for middle-income countries, involving customized services as well as finance.[12] With its undemocratic corporate governance structure, the WB has failed developing countries that rely upon its mandates. The bureaucratic administration of the institution has sustained ineffective and counterproductive policies toward poverty, without collaborating with local authorities. Most of the views express by the WB are inadequate to the needs of its members, mainly in developing countries. To face the challenges of the twenty-first century, the WB must adapt its governance, be more accountable and result oriented while including all its minority shareholders. As an international institution collectively owned by its member countries, the World Bank's governance should provide all members with a fair measure of voice and participation.[13]

# CHAPTER 4

# THE INTERNATIONAL FINANCE CORPORATION

## GENERAL

Established in 1956, the International Finance Corporation (IFC) is the largest public source of financial investment for private sector projects in developing countries. Unlike the grass-roots development efforts pursued by the IBRD and the International Development Association, the IFC's investments are often used for projects such as the building of hotels or power plants, where finance and trade are more heavily involved. IFC provides private sector investment, helps companies acquire additional financing in international markets, and provides technical advice and assistance. Membership to the IFC is reserved only to member countries of the International Bank for Reconstruction and Development (the World Bank). Currently, the IFC has 182 members and its employees come from 140 countries located in 102 offices in 92 countries. IFC operations are tailored to specific client needs and country circumstances, and cross a broad spectrum of sectors. The IFC has committed more than $32.4 billion of its funds, plus $7.5 billion in syndications for 1,490 companies in 122 countries. The IFC has increased its funds to $12.7 billion in 2010.

## IFC MANDATES

The IFC is mandated to further economic development by encouraging the growth of productive private enterprise in developing countries. It is the largest global development institution focused on the private sector. It offers its clients a combination of investment services, advisory services, and third-party equity fund management.

## ORGANIZATIONAL STRUCTURE OF THE IFC

The IFC is composed of the board of governors, the board of executive directors, and the president

## The Board of Governors

The IFC's corporate powers are vested in the board of governors. Each country member appoints one governor and one alternate governor. The board of governors essentially delegates its powers to the executive directors.

## The Executive Directors

The board of directors or the executive board is composed of 25 directors based in Washington, DC. Executive directors meet regularly to review and decide on investments and development projects and provide overall strategic guidance to the IFC management. Voting power is weighed according to the share capital owned by each director represents. Executive directors serve on one or more standing committees: the Audit Committee, the Budget Committee, the Committee on Development Effectiveness, the Ethics Committee, the Governance Committee, and the HR Committee.

## The President

The President of the IBRD (World Bank) is the de facto president of the IFC. He is assisted in his management by an executive vice president, and a chief executive officer.

# CORPORATE GOVERNANCE OF THE IFC

Contrary to the Multilateral Investment Guarantee Agency (MIGA), there is a voting power imbalance within the IFC. Developing countries hold only 33 percent of the total voting power. The remaining 67 percent is held by the developed countries: a group dominated by European countries. The imbalance of voting power within the IFC has no parallel within the World Bank Group (WBG) and undermines the actions of the IFC, perceived by many as a European old boys' club.

# FINANCING OF THE IFC

The IFC's investments are funded from the paid-in capital from member countries and retained earnings from its products and services. Its capital structure does not include the callable capital, which is a factor supporting the Aaa ratings of other MDBs. Rather, its high level of paid-in capital and retained earnings are key to its rating.

By the end of FY 2013, the total equity of the IFC amounted to $22.2 billion, up from the $20.6 billion reported in its FY2012. This was equal to 50.0 percent of disbursed assets and approved but undisbursed commitments—an un-weighted measure of broad economic exposure.[1] The IFC manages its capital adequacy using a risk-based economic capital framework that establishes a level of resources required to provide protection from risks stemming from all of its asset classes.

The IFC is conservatively leveraged, with a 2.6:1 ratio of outstanding borrowings and guarantees to capital. It has a leverage policy ceiling of 4.0:1; the ratio is calculated with outstanding debt (including derivatives and other liabilities as well as borrowings) and commitments to capital. The IFC manages its capital adequacy using a risk-based economic capital framework that establishes a level of resources required to protect it from risks stemming from all of its asset classes.[2]

In FY2013, the IFC reported a net income of US$ 1,010 million from its operations.[3] TheIFC's Aaa rating with a stable outlook is based on its robust capital adequacy and liquidity, preferred creditor status, and strong shareholder support.

## THE IFC'S SERVICES

The IFC mainly provides its services to IDA countries in the fields of investment services, advisory services, and asset management. Besides these three core lines of services, the IFC provide additional services.

### Investment Services[4]

IFC's investments continue to be significantly more concentrated in IDA countries than global foreign direct investment (FDI). There is a clear need for the IFC to continue investing and helping to create the business environment that will help IDA countries attract more FDI. In FY11, IFC invested in 251 projects in 56 IDA countries. Since FY2000, IFC investments in IDA have grown tenfold, totaling US$4.9 billion in FY11 alone. IFC employs a broad suite of financial services to help ease poverty and spur long-term growth, by promoting sustainable enterprises, encouraging entrepreneurship, and mobilizing resources that would not otherwise be available. Financing products include loans, equity, trade finance, syndications, structured finance, and client risk-management services. In recent years, the IFC has also been engaged in the provision of concessional financing, particularly to mobilize investments in the climate change space. IFC is currently working to develop appropriate principles, rules, and governance mechanisms for the provision of such concessional funding.

Financing products are tailored to meet the needs of each project. The IFC provides growth capital, while the bulk of funding comes from private sector owners who also bear leadership and management responsibility. In FY11, IFC invested US$12.2 billion in 518 projects, of which US$4.9 billion went to projects in IDA countries. The IFC also mobilized an additional US$6.5 billion to support the private sector in developing countries. New commitments reached US$18.7 billion in FY11, which is more than double the level of five years ago, and reflects an estimated project value of nearly US$100 billion.

## Advisory Services[5]

The IFC's Advisory Services provide advice, problem-solving methodologies, and training to companies, industries, and governments. It also helps investment clients improve corporate governance and become more sustainable. The IFC's advisory services are funded by donor partners, the IFC, and client contributions. IFC's advisory services operations are organized around four business lines:

### Access to Finance

IFC helps increase the availability and affordability of financial services for individuals and micro-, small-, and middle-size enterprises (MSMEs). It also helps clients provide broad-based financial services and promotes growth and employment generation by supporting sustainable lending, and building the necessary financial infrastructure, such as credit bureaus and collateral registries.

### Investment Climate

IFC aims to design and encourage regulatory reforms that support business and trade-friendly environments, while also helping resolve legal and policy weaknesses that prohibit investment.

### Public-Private Partnerships (PPPs)

The IFC helps governments design and implement PPPs in infrastructure and other basic public services. IFC helps governments to achieve long-term economic growth and better living standards by harnessing the potential of the private sector to increase access to public services such as electricity, water, health, and education, while enhancing their quality and efficiency.

### Sustainable Business

IFC supports the development of markets that are inclusive, sustainable, and efficient. Building on IFC's environmental and social performance standards, IFC promotes sustainable business practices in such sectors as agribusiness, infrastructure, oil, gas and mining, and manufacturing and services. Programs promote good corporate governance practices, build the capacity of small firms and small-scale farmers, advance women entrepreneurs, and engage the private sector in climate change solutions.

## IFC's Asset Management Company (AMC)[6]

The AMC, a wholly owned subsidiary of IFC, mobilizes and manages third-party funds for investment in developing and frontier markets. It was created in FY09 to expand the supply of long-term capital to these markets, enhancing IFC's development impact as well as investing profitably for others. AMC helps IFC achieve one of its core development mandates—mobilizing additional capital resources for investment in productive private enterprise in developing countries. It also enhances IFC's development impact by increasing both the size and number of investments IFC can transact. The AMC invested US$632 million in IFC projects in FY11, and has approximately US$4.1 billion in assets under management. It manages funds on behalf of a wide variety of institutional investors, including sovereign funds, pension funds, and DFIs. It is currently managing three funds: IFC Capitalization Fund; IFC African, Latin American, and Caribbean Fund; and the Africa Capitalization Fund. Others are under consideration, including a Climate Catalyst Fund to support PPPs in the climate space.

## ACTIVITIES OF THE IFC

Examples of IFC actions include:

- In Colombia, the IFC is financing the first stage of development of oil fields in Middle Magdalena Valley, providing loans totaling $30 million from its own account and organizing a combined loan of $25 million for a number of other private participants.
- In Azerbaijan, Georgia, and Turkey, the IFC is helping finance the construction of an oil pipeline to move up to a million barrels of oil per day from Baku, in Central Asia, to Ceyhan, on Turkey's Mediterranean coast.

## IFC REVIEW PROCESS

The IFC conducts a quality review of any project upon entry. IFC's initial assessment of the project includes a review of information in the public domain; a determination as to whether the impacts and outcomes have potential environment and social risks; and an examination of mitigation measures for such risks. In furtherance of its operations, the IFC expects clients to manage the social and environmental risks and impacts of their projects. This entails the client's assessment of these risks and impacts, and implementation of measures to meet the requirements of the performance standards. The IFC's role is to review the client's assessment and to assist the client in developing measures to avoid, minimize, mitigate, or compensate for social and environmental impacts consistent with the performance standard.[7] Then, the IFC discloses the on-going projects/ mission on its website. In determining whether any particular information is to be made available by IFC as a routine matter or upon request, IFC first considers whether such information falls within the scope of the IFC's responsibilities and, if so, whether there is any compelling reason not to disclose all or any part of such information. In making this determination, the IFC considers whether the disclosure of information is likely to cause harm to specific parties or interests that outweighs the benefit of disclosure, or whether the information contains or makes reference to information described in the list of exceptions set out in the policy. The exceptions include information that is commercially sensitive, confidential, or deliberative in nature, as well as staff personal information.[8]

## IFC COMPLIANCE PROCESS

The Office of the Compliance Advisor/Ombudsman (CAO) is the independent accountability mechanism for IFC and MIGA. Reporting directly to the WBG President, the office of the CAO responds to complaints from people affected by IFC and MIGA projects, with the goal of enhancing social and environmental outcomes and strengthening the public accountability of IFC and MIGA. Since CAO was established in FY00, it has helped address 82 complaints related to 55 different IFC projects in 29 countries. It has enabled IFC to respond quickly and effectively to citizens' concerns, and ensure that their voices are heard and acted upon.

The purpose of a CAO audit is to ensure compliance with policies, standards, guidelines, procedures, and conditions for IFC/MIGA involvement, and thereby improve the environmental and social performance of investments and activities backed by IFC/MIGA. Such an audit must remain within the scope of the original complaint or request. It cannot go beyond the confines of the complaint nor request that other issues be addressed. The CAO appraisals and audits consider how IFC/MIGA assured itself/themselves of compliance with national law, reflecting international legal commitments, along with their audit criteria. The CAO is neither a court of appeal nor a legal enforcement mechanism, nor is CAO a substitute for international court systems or court systems in host countries.

## IFC CHALLENGES

Though the IFC remains the largest source of finance for private sector projects in developing markets, the institution is facing mounting competition from regional development banks, G-20 bilateral financing and export credit facilities, mainly from China and other sovereign wealth funds. On the other hand, IFC investment projects often lack features that would enhance their impact, including clear strategies connecting interventions to intended outcomes and solid measurement systems. IFC needs to adapt its business model, risk tolerance, product mix, procedures, and processes to achieve its goal of increasing engagement in IDA countries and be more responsive to their social needs.[9]

# CHAPTER 5

---✦❧✦---

# THE INTERNATIONAL DEVELOPMENT
# ASSOCIATION

## GENERAL

The International Development Association (IDA) was organized by the WB in 1960 to provide additional financial assistance to the poorest developing countries. The IDA is the concessional arm of the Bretton Woods institutions, which plays a distinctive role in the development of finance systems, and provides a framework for performance, and financial and credit discipline in the developing world.[1] Property and assets of the IDA, wherever located and by whomsoever they might be held, shall be immune from search, requisition, confiscation, expropriation, or any other form of seizure by executive or legislative action.[2] Likewise, the archives of the IDA are also immune.[3]

In order to provide resources on better terms than those that are available from the WB, the IDA provides "special credits." These credits are zero-interest loans that have longer payment periods of 35–40 years and a grace period of ten years. These types of loans are offered to the poorest countries to help them pursue their development goals, sometimes despite disease and conflict. Currently, 169 of the UN members and Kosovo are members of the IDA. The IDA complements the WB's original lending arm—the International Bank for Reconstruction and Development (IBRD). IBRD was established to function as a self-sustaining business and provide loans and advice to middle-income and credit-worthy poor countries. The IBRD and the IDA share the same staff and headquarters, and evaluate projects with the same rigorous standards.

IDA is one of the largest sources of assistance for the world's 81 poorest countries, 39 of which are in Africa. It is the single largest source of donor funds for basic social services in these countries. The IDA-financed operations deliver positive change for 2.5 billion people, the majority of whom survive on less than $2 a day.

To be eligible to IDA resources, a member country must satisfy two criteria:

- relative poverty, defined as GNI per capita below an established threshold and updated annually (in fiscal year 2012: $1,175), and
- lack of creditworthiness to borrow on market terms and, therefore, needs concessional resources to finance the country's development programs.

Furthermore, the main factor that determines the allocation of IDA resources to an eligible country is the country's performance in implementing policies that promote economic growth and poverty reduction. This is assessed by the Country Policy and Institutional Assessment (CPIA), which, for the purposes of resource allocation, is referred to as the IDA Resource Allocation Index (IRAI). The IRAI and portfolio performance together constitute the IDA Country Performance Rating (CPR). In addition to the CPR, population and per capita income also determine the IDA's allocations. Beginning in 2005, the numerical IRAI as well as the CPR are disclosed every year. The IDA lends money on concessional terms. This means that IDA charges little or no interest and repayments are stretched over 25–40 years, including a 5–10-year grace period. IDA also provides grants to countries at risk of debt distress. In addition to concessional loans and grants, the IDA provides significant levels of debt relief through the Heavily Indebted Poor Countries (HIPC) Initiative and the Multilateral Debt Relief Initiative (MDRI). Since its inception, the IDA has supported activities in 108 countries. Annual commitments have increased steadily and averaged about US$15 billion over the last three years, with about 50 percent of that going to Africa. For the fiscal year ending on June 30, 2012, the IDA's commitments reached US$14.8 billion, spread over 160 new operations. 15 percent of the total was committed to grant terms.

## THE INTERNATIONAL DEVELOPMENT ASSOCIATION'S MISSIONS

The IDA helps developing countries with seeking additional assistance; it has established a framework that emphasizes six core principles.

(1) The IDA seeks to promote growth through macroeconomic policy, especially in rural and private sector development.
(2) The IDA concentrates on social issues such as gender equality and public health.
(3) The IDA works to improve governance by assisting in public management and in combating corruption.
(4) The IDA strives for sustainable development projects that help protect the environment.
(5) The IDA fosters recovery efforts in post-conflict countries.
(6) The IDA promotes economic integration through regional trade.

## THE IDA'S ORGANIZATIONAL STRUCTURE

The IDA comprises (i) a board of directors, (ii) an executive directorate, and (iii) a president. The IDA's staff is divided into four areas: operations, finance, policy, and planning and research. Fifty-two percent of the voting power is earmarked for developed countries and 48 percent for developing countries.

### Board of Governors

The board of governors is the highest body within the organizational structure. The directorate of the IDA is a permanently functioning executive body. Decisions of the board of governors are decided by a majority vote, and voting rights exist only if total subscriptions are paid into basic capital. The board of governors shall hold an annual meeting and such other meetings as may be provided for by the board of governors or called by the executive directors. Governors and alternate governors shall serve as such without compensation from the IDA.

The board of governors may delegate the authority to exercise any of its powers to the executive directors, except the power to:[4]

(i) admit new members and determine the conditions of their admission;
(ii) authorize additional subscriptions and determine the terms and conditions relating thereto;
(iii) suspend a member;
(iv) decide appeals from interpretations of the IDA agreement made by the executive directors;
(v) make arrangements pursuant to Section 7 of this Article to cooperate with other international organizations (other than informal arrangements of a temporary and administrative character);
(vi) decide to suspend permanently the operations of the IDA and to distribute its assets;
(vii) determine the distribution of the IDA's net income pursuant to Section 12 of this Article; and
(viii) approve proposed amendments to this agreement.

### Executive Directorate

The directorate of the IDA is a permanently functioning executive body. The directors of the WB serve as directors of the IDA as well. Executive directors are responsible for conducting the general operations of the IDA, and for this purpose shall exercise all the powers given to them by the agreement that created the IDA or delegated to them by the board of governors.[5] The quorum for any meeting of the executive directors is a majority of the directors exercising not less than one-half of the total voting power.

### President

The president of the WB acts as the president of the IDA. The president shall be chairman of the executive directors of the IDA, but shall have no vote except a deciding vote in case of an equal division. He may participate in meetings of the board of governors but shall not vote at such meetings.[6]

The actual governance of the IDA is inadequate in a sense that its current allocation of voting power grants larger power to former contributor members relative to new contributors. European countries are overrepresented in terms of the number of chairs they occupy within the executive board or directorate. Also, there is no a transparent and fair principle that governs the distribution of chairs on the board.[7]

## REFORMING THE IDA'S GOVERNANCE STRUCTURE

For better coordination with regional development banks in providing concessional aids and other assistance, the proper governance of the IDA would need to include, at least one representative for each regional development bank. That is because regional development banks and other creditors rely and often depend on the policy work and programs of the IDA to create the development framework and performance track records on which to base their country programs. By bringing in the IDA's governance, those representatives would enable both the IDA and the regional development banks to work together, tailoring policies and programs that respond to the very needs of their recipients. Such a reform is more urgent today when the IDA faces new challenges, including promoting development in an environment of conflict, post conflict, and severe social dislocation; addressing the AIDS/HIV epidemic and the rise of other communicable diseases; confronting issues of corruption and supporting improved governance; and redressing long-term social and economic inequities.[8] Though the IDA has the expertise, it may lack the underpinning culture of the recipients of its aid. Those Regional Development Bureau (RDB) representatives will sit on a specific committee within the board of executives. The Committee's core mission would be to advise and elaborate policy and framework for their member states by providing their cultural experience within the policy process. In so doing, the IDA would retain the leading role and the RDB, the implementation within the ground. A reformed corporate governance such as the one described above would provide more relevance, legitimacy, and accountability.

## THE IDA FINANCING

The IDA's funds are replenished every three years by its 40 donor country members. Additional funds are generated through repayments of principal on its 35–40-year no-interest loans. Donor contributions account for over 70 percent of all resources available to the IDA (providing about $138 billion). The remainder is funded by internal IDA resources (primarily principal repayments from IDA borrowers) and transfers from the IBRD's net income.[9] The five largest contributors to the IDA are the United States with 39.5%, with Japan, Germany, the United Kingdom, and France contributing between 7.11 percent and 13.78 percent of the total.

The bulk of IDA funding comes from three sources: member country contributions, supplementary funds provided by the International Bank for Reconstruction and Development and, supplementary funds from the International Finance Corporation. Thirty-four member states had agreed to provide US$18 billion during the tenth undertaking of IDA (IDA-10), held in 1993–1996, in order to strengthen efforts to combat poverty, fuel economic reform, improve management, and promote environmentally sustainable development.

## IDA RESOURCE ALLOCATION

The CPIA assesses the conduciveness of a country's policy and institutional framework to poverty reduction, sustainable growth, and the effective use of development assistance. Two premises underlie the use of CPIA as an indicator in the allocation of IDA resources: (i) IDA resources are important in supporting the world's poorest countries in their efforts to boost economic growth, lower poverty, and improve the living conditions of people; and (ii) such resources could only be used effectively in the presence of sound policies and institutions that are assessed under the CPIA.[10] CPIA criteria have evolved since their inception to cover 16 criteria in four clusters—each with equal weightage given in the overall rating. Although most of the metrics and indicators specified for the assessment are policies and institutions, a few criteria-outcome indicators have been included, in particular for the financial sector and the project fostering gender equality.[11]

For such an assessment, the IDA takes into account the specificity of the assessed country, such as the size of its economy and the stage of development.[12]

IDA presupposes that growth leads to poverty reduction, whereas a large body of empirical literature on the relationship between growth and changes in inequality finds no statistical correlation between the two. For such a correlation to exist, policies need to be designed to further the distributional impact of economic growth.[13]

### The CPIA Criteria

The allocation of IDA's resources is determined primarily by each recipient's rating in the annual CPIA. The CPIA assesses each country's policy and institutional framework and consists of 16 criteria grouped into four equally weighted clusters: (i) economic management; (ii) structural policies; (iii) policies for social inclusion and equity; and (iv) public sector management and institutions.[14]

## Criticisms of the CPIA Criteria

CPIA criteria have been often criticized by authors as relying too much on current growth for the allocation of development aid, and as tending to neglect or ignore a country's efforts toward sustainable future growth. Therefore, some have argued that the CPIA is not a good indicator of future growth.[15] Cage argued that CPIA criteria induced some "hidden conditionality."[16] She went on further to enumerate some caveats of the CPIA, inter alia, (i) it relies on policies rather than on outcomes, (ii) it relies too much on a "one-size-fits-all" approach, failing to include and address the specificities of the assessed country, (iii) it does not reflect the reality of development. In the same vein, Van Waeyenberge argues that CPIA perpetuates the traditional biases of the Washington consensus, without real correlation to aid allocation.[17]

# IDA's ACTIVITIES

The IDA credits are meant for the poorest and least creditworthy countries and are allocated based on the size of the country, the annual income per capita, and the effectiveness of its economic policy. Only countries with an annual per capita income of less than US$1,305 are eligible for IDA loans. Most IDA credits are granted to countries with an annual per capita income of US$800 or less.

In general, the IDA's financing comes mainly in the form of loans. IDA lends money on concessional terms. That is, IDA credits have a zero or very low interest charge. The terms of these loans vary for the different members of the IDA, reflecting their income levels and debt status. However, the IDA may provide other financing: either

(i)   out of funds subscribed pursuant to Article III, Section 1, and funds derived therefrom as principal, interest, or other charges, if the authorization for such subscriptions expressly provides for such financing; or

(ii)  in special circumstances, out of supplementary resources furnished to the IDA, and funds derived therefrom as principal, interest, or other charges, if the arrangements under which such resources are furnished expressly authorize such financing.[18]

In addition, the IDA may:[19]

(i)    borrow funds with the approval of the member in whose currency the loan is denominated;

(ii)   guarantee securities that it has invested in so as to facilitate their sale;

(iii)  buy and sell securities it has issued or guaranteed or in which it has invested;

(iv)   in special cases, guarantee loans from other sources for purposes not inconsistent with the provisions of these articles;

(v)    provide technical assistance and advisory services at the request of a member; and

(vi)   exercise such other powers incidental to its operations as shall be necessary or desirable in furtherance of its purposes.

Repayment of loans begins after the ten-year grace period, and they are available for 35 or 40 years without interest. Each project has been funded by the IDA's political and economic expertise to the most effective use of the financial assistance. Loans are provided in the national currency of the country or territory.

The IDA's operations place a special emphasis on four thematic areas: gender equality, climate change, fragile and conflict affected countries, and crisis response. In Africa, the program is especially supported by sub-Saharan countries with low income and high debt. Examples of IDA projects include the following:

- In Tanzania, since 1995, the IDA has allocated US$3.2 billion, which has caused an annual increase of an average of five and six percent in the GDP, and the GDP per capita has doubled. All of this has greatly improved the standard of living.
- In Bhutan, the IDA gave a ten-year, $31 million credit for construction of rural schools and curricula development.

## IDA CHALLENGES

While the IDA's success is far over-reaching, it needs to do more in order to deliver integrated solutions to member countries by leveraging private investment, public resources, and knowledge in a more result-oriented and cost-effective way. To that end, a close cooperation with Regional Development Banks would enhance the IDA performance through the benefit of local expertise.

# CHAPTER 6

---⟨◈⟩---

# THE INTERNATIONAL CENTER FOR SETTLEMENT OF INVESTMENT DISPUTES

## GENERAL

The World Bank established the International Center for Settlement of Investment Disputes (ICSID) in 1966 to encourage investors and governments to undertake and receive foreign direct investments, by providing a neutral dispute resolution system. ICSID provides arbitration services that are entered into on a voluntary basis, but once two parties agree to submit issue resolution to ICSID, they are required to follow ICSID procedures until the verdict is rendered. Furthermore, all member countries of the ICSID are bound to recognize and enforce the rulings that are made. In 2011, ICSID concluded 225 cases, and 128 cases are still pending. Although it is technically a separate entity, ICSID is chaired by the president of the WB, and the two organizations are well integrated, with their annual meetings being held in concert, and with ICSID's operating expenses coming from the WBG's budget. Currently 143 UN member nations and Kosovo are members of the ICSID.

## ICSID's PURPOSES

The purpose of the ICSID is to provide facilities for conciliation and arbitration of investment disputes between contracting states and nationals of other contracting states in accordance with the provisions of the convention that conceived the ICSID.[1]

## THE ORGANIZATIONAL STRUCTURE OF ICSID

The ICSID consists of (i) an administrative council, (ii) a secretariat, and (iii) a president.[2]

ICSID has also a panel of conciliators and a panel of arbitrators.

## The Administrative Council

The administrative council is composed of one representative of each con-tracting state. An alternate may act as representative in case of his principal's absence from a meeting or inability to act. In the absence of a contrary designation, each governor and alternate governor of the WB appointed by a contracting state shall be its ex officio representative and alternate respec-tively.[3] The president of the WB presides over the administrative council of the ICSID. However, he has no voting rights. During his absence or inabil-ity to act and during any vacancy in the office of president of the WB, the person for the time being acting as president acts as chairman of the admin-istrative council.[4]

The administrative council holds an annual meeting and such other meet-ings as may be determined by the council, or convened by the chairman, or convened by the secretary-general at the request of not less than five mem-bers of the council. Each member of the administrative council has one vote and, except as otherwise herein provided, all matters before the council shall be decided by a majority of the votes cast. The quorum for any meeting of the administrative council is a majority of its members.[5] Members of the administrative council and the chairman serve without remuneration from the ICSID.[6]

The administrative council is vested with the following powers:[7]

- adopt the administrative and financial regulations of the ICSID;
- adopt the rules of procedure for the institution of conciliation and arbitra-tion proceedings;
- adopt the rules of procedure for conciliation and arbitration proceedings;
- approve arrangements with the WB for the use of its administrative facil-ities and services;
- determine the conditions of service of the secretary-general and of any deputy secretary-general;
- adopt the annual budget of revenues and expenditures of the ICSID;
- approve the annual report on the operation of the ICSID.

The administrative council shall also exercise such other powers and per-form such other functions that it shall determine to be necessary for the implementation of the provisions of this convention.

## The Secretariat

The secretariat of ICSID consists of a secretary-general, one or more deputy secretary-generals and their staffs.[8] The secretary-general is the legal rep-resentative and the principal officer of the ICSID and is responsible for its administration. He performs the function of registrar and has the power to authenticate arbitral awards rendered pursuant to the ICSID conven-tion, and to certify copies thereof.[9] The secretary-general and any deputy secretary-general are elected by the administrative council by a majority of two-thirds of its members upon the nomination of the chairman for a term of service not exceeding six years. He or she is eligible for re-election. After consulting the members of the administrative council, the chairman proposes one or more candidates for each such office.[10] The offices of the secretary-general and deputy secretary-general are incompatible with the exercise of any political function. Neither the secretary-general nor any deputy secretary-general may hold any other employment or engage in any other occupation except with the approval of the administrative council.[11]

## The President

The president of the WB is, the de facto president or chairman of the ICSID administrative council, but has no voting rights.[12]

Beside the aforementioned organs, ICSID is made of conciliator and arbitrator panels composed of qualified persons. Each contracting state may designate up to four persons who may or may not be its nationals.[13] The chairman may designate ten persons to each panel. The persons so designated to a panel shall each have a different nationality.[14] Panel members shall serve for renewable periods of six years. In case of death or resignation of a member of a panel, the authority which designated the member shall have the right to designate another person to serve for the remainder of that member's term.[15]

## CORPORATE GOVERNANCE OF THE ICSID

The ICSID governance is biased in favor of rich countries. The ICSID is known as a secretive court as no arbitration has permitted public attendance, and lacks formal appeal processes. Instead, there is a review committee that lacks the power to overturn judgments made by the original panel. The proportion of cases filed against G7 countries is 1.4 percent, all of which have been filed by US investors. Cases against middle-income countries account for 74 percent of all ICSID cases, and 17 percent are against low-income countries. Twenty per cent of the ICSID cases are brought by companies that rank within the top 500 globally; seven of these companies have revenues that exceed the GDP of the country against which they are bringing a case. Seventy percent of the ICSID cases have favored the investor. The legal fees and arbitration costs are borne by the losing party. The implications for developing countries are substantial, in respect to the technical capacity to handle investment disputes, the effect of the award on the national budget, and the resultant damaged investment reputation to the country.

The ICSID's role in settling disputes that have arisen out of the measures a government has taken to shield its citizens from economic crisis is controversial, and it remains to be seen how the global crisis of 2008 has affected the institution.

# THE ICSID's FINANCING

The ICSID's administrative expenditures in FY2012 were covered by the International Bank for Reconstruction and Development (IBRD), pursuant to the Memorandum of Administrative Arrangements concluded between the IBRD and ICSID, and also by fee income. It is therefore not necessary to assess any excess expenditures on contracting states pursuant to Article 17 of the convention. Expenditures relating to pending arbitration proceedings are borne by the parties in accordance with ICSID's administrative and financial regulations.

# ICSID ACTIVITIES

The ICSID conducts several activities pertaining to its core missions, including:

## The ICSID Disputer Settlements

The ICSID does not conciliate or arbitrate disputes; it provides the institutional and procedural framework for independent conciliation commissions and arbitral tribunals constituted in each case to resolve the dispute. The ICSID has two sets of procedural rules that govern the initiation and conducting of proceedings under its auspices. These are (i) the ICSID's convention, regulations, and rules; and (ii) the ICSID's additional facility rules.

### ICSID Convention, Regulations, and Rules

The ICSID convention provides the basic procedural framework for conciliation and arbitration of investment disputes arising between member countries and investors that qualify as nationals of other member countries. This framework is supplemented by detailed regulations and rules adopted by the ICSID administrative council pursuant to the convention.

A principal feature of conciliation and arbitration under the ICSID convention is that they are based on a treaty establishing an autonomous and self-contained system for the institution, conducting, and conclusion of such proceedings.

Arbitration and conciliation under the convention are entirely voluntary, but once the parties have given their consent, neither may unilaterally withdraw it. A further distinctive feature is that an arbitral award rendered pursuant to the convention may not be set aside by the courts of any contracting state, and is only subject to the post-award remedies provided for in the convention. The convention also requires that all contracting states, whether or not they are parties to the dispute, recognize and enforce ICSID convention arbitral awards.

There are several essential jurisdictional conditions for access to arbitration or conciliation under the ICSID convention:

- The dispute must be between an ICSID contracting state and an individual or company that qualifies as a national of another ICSID contracting state. (ICSID contracting states may designate constituent subdivisions and agencies to become parties to ICSID proceedings).[16]
- The dispute must qualify as a legal dispute arising directly out of an investment.
- The disputing parties must have consented in writing to the submission of their dispute to ICSID arbitration or conciliation.[17] A contracting state may require the exhaustion of local administrative or judicial remedies as a condition of its consent to arbitration under this convention.[18]

Under the ICSID convention, the secretary-general is vested with the limited power to "screen" requests for the initiation of ICSID conciliation and arbitration proceedings, and to refuse registration if, on the basis of the information provided in the request, the secretary-general finds that the disputes is manifestly outside the jurisdiction of the ICSID.

### ICSID's Additional Facility Rules

Besides providing facilities for conciliation and arbitration under the ICSID convention, the ICSID has since 1978 had a set of additional facility rules authorizing the ICSID secretariat to administer certain types of proceedings between states and foreign nationals that fall outside the scope of the convention.

These include:

- Conciliation and arbitration proceedings for the settlement of disputes arising directly out of an investment where either the state party or the home state of the foreign national is not an ICSID contracting state.
- Conciliation and arbitration proceedings between parties, at least one of which is a contracting state or a national of a contracting state, for the settlement of disputes that do not directly arise out of an investment.
- Fact-finding proceedings.

### Other Dispute Settlement Activities of the ICSID

Additional activities of ICSID in the field of the settlement of disputes have included the secretary-general of ICSID agreeing to act as the appointing authority of arbitrators in ad hoc (i.e., non-institutional) arbitration proceedings. This is most commonly done in the context of arrangements for arbitration under the arbitration rules of the United Nations Commission on International Trade Law (UNCITRAL), which are specially designed for ad hoc proceedings. At the request of the parties and the tribunal concerned, ICSID may also agree to provide administrative services for proceedings handled under the UNCITRAL's arbitration rules. The services rendered by the ICSID in such proceedings may range from limited assistance with the organization of hearings and fund-holding to full secretarial services in the administration of the case concerned.

## Institutional Arrangements

As a general rule, ICSID proceedings are held at its headquarters in Washington, DC. However, parties may agree to hold their proceeding at any other place, subject to certain conditions. The ICSID convention contains provisions that facilitate advance stipulations for such other venues when the place chosen is the seat of an institution with which the ICSID has an arrangement for this purpose.

To date, ICSID has concluded such arrangements with the:

- Permanent Court of Arbitration at The Hague;
- Regional Arbitration Centres of the Asian-African Legal Consultative Committee at Cairo, Kuala Lumpur and Lagos;
- Australian Commercial Disputes Centre at Sydney;
- Australian Centre for International Commercial Arbitration at Melbourne;
- Singapore International Arbitration Centre;
- Gulf Cooperation Council Commercial Arbitration Centre at Bahrain;
- German Institution of Arbitration;
- Maxwell Chambers, Singapore;
- Hong Kong International Arbitration Centre;
- Centre for Arbitration and Conciliation at the Chamber of Commerce of Bogota; and
- China International Economic and Trade Arbitration Commission.

## ICSID's Basis of Consent for Proceedings

Arbitration and conciliation under the ICSID convention and additional facility rules are entirely voluntary. The basis of the parties' consent to ICSID jurisdiction can be found in a variety of sources, including investment laws, contracts concluded between a foreign investor and the host state of the investment. Of the new cases registered in FY2012, the vast majority (28 cases) asserted ICSID jurisdiction on the basis of a bilateral investment treaty (BIT). In five cases, the parties invoked ICSID arbitration clauses in multilateral investment agreements such as the Oman-US Free Trade Agreement, the North American Free Trade Agreement, and the Energy Charter Treaty. Investors claimed under investment contracts in five further cases, and three cases relied on investment laws. One of these cases invoked both a BIT and a law as bases of consent and another invoked both a law and a contract and bilateral or multilateral treaties. State parties involved in ICSID disputes registered in FY2012 remained diverse and included states from every region of the world. In 2012, Eastern Europe and Central Asia were the regions with the greatest numbers of states involved in newly registered ICSID cases.

## ICSID's Arbitration Process[19]

ICSID convention's arbitration is initiated by the submission of a request for arbitration to the secretary-general. The request is filed by the potential claimant and outlines the basic facts and legal issues to be addressed. The request must be registered unless the dispute is manifestly outside the jurisdiction of ICSID. In the past year, Requests for arbitration were processed on average within 25 days of being filed at ICSID.

The next procedural step is the constitution of the arbitral tribunal. The tribunal shall consist of a sole arbitrator, or any odd number of arbitrators, appointed as per the agreement of the parties.[20] The ICSID's arbitration rules allow significant flexibility regarding the number of arbitrators and the methods of their appointment. In most instances, the tribunals consist of three arbitrators: one arbitrator appointed by each party, and the third, presiding, arbitrator appointed by agreement of the parties or the party-appointed arbitrators. The parties may ask the ICSID to assist with the appointment of arbitrators, either in accordance with a previous agreement or pursuant to the default provisions in the ICSID Rules. In FY2012, ICSID made such appointments on average within 38 days of receiving the request to appoint.

Proceedings are deemed to have begun once the tribunal is constituted. The tribunal holds a first session within 60 days of its constitution. Preliminary questions of procedure are dealt with in the first session. Subsequently, the proceeding usually comprises two distinct phases: a written procedure followed by in-person hearings. After the parties present their cases, the tribunal deliberates and renders its award. Once an ICSID convention award is rendered, it is binding and not subject to any appeal or other remedy except those provided by the convention. The convention allows the parties to request a supplementary decision or rectification of the award, or to seek the post-award remedies of annulment, interpretation, or revision.

Arbitration under the ICSID additional facility is similar in process to ICSID's conventional arbitration, with some notable differences. In particular, parties must obtain approval of access to the additional facility prior to instituting proceedings, and post-award remedies under the additional facility rules are limited to interpretation, correction, and supplementary

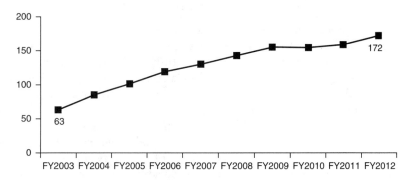

**Figure 6.1**   ICSID—Arbitration Cases.

decisions by the original tribunal. Holiday Inns versus Occidental Petroleum was the first dispute submitted to the ICSID, in 1972 (figure 6.1).[21]

### Economic Sectors Involved in New Proceedings

The investment disputes commenced in FY2012 involved a variety of economic sectors. Based on WB industry sector codes, the oil, gas, and mining sector remained dominant, with 25 percent of cases registered in FY2012. However, this fiscal year has seen an increase in the diversity of other industries represented, with 25 percent of cases involving pharmaceuticals, chemicals, gaming, textiles, and food production. The number of cases registered concerning transportation increased from 6 percent in FY2011 to 15 percent in FY2012. Ten percent of the new cases concerned the information and communication sector. The segment of the new cases relating to electric power and other energy decreased to 8 percent and the number of cases involving the construction industry increased slightly to 8 percent. The remaining cases involved tourism; services and trade; and water, sanitation, and flood protection.

## CONSTITUTION OF TRIBUNALS AND AD HOC COMMITTEES IN ICSID CASES

In the course of the fiscal year, 37 tribunals, 8 ad hoc Committees, and 1 conciliation commission were constituted or reconstituted in proceedings pending before the ICSID. A total of 131 individual appointments were made by the parties and by ICSID. This is the most appointments made in a single fiscal year. Overall, 82 individuals from 33 different countries were appointed to serve as arbitrators, conciliators, or ad hoc Committee members in ICSID cases in FY2012. In that same year, the pool of arbitrators, conciliators, and ad hoc Committee members continued to expand. In terms of diversity, 31 percent of the new appointees were nationals of developing countries, and 9 percent of the new appointees were women.

## CASES CONCLUDED IN FY2012

Thirty-one proceedings were concluded in the course of the fiscal year. Twenty-two of these were arbitration cases, seven were annulment proceedings, and two were revision proceedings. In the 22 concluded arbitration proceedings, 15 disputes were decided by a tribunal, and seven cases were discontinued or settled. Of the 15 cases decided by a tribunal, three award cases declined ICSID jurisdiction, and three member countries' tribunals rejected the ICSID awards. Of the seven arbitration cases that were discontinued or settled, four were discontinued following agreement by the parties, one was discontinued at the request of one party, and one was discontinued for lack of payment of the required advances. In one further case, the parties' settlement agreement was embodied in an award. Both of the revision proceedings that concluded during FY2012 were also discontinued following agreement by the parties. The majority of arbitrations concluded in FY2012 lasted between three to four years from the date of the tribunal's constitution. The ICSID has recently adopted a number of new practices in an effort to reduce the length and cost of arbitrations while respecting the due process rights of the parties. These include (i) requiring arbitrators to provide calendars indicating their long term availability, (ii) updating parties on a regular basis concerning the costs expended to date, (iii) encouraging tribunal members to establish a budget at the outset of a case outlining anticipated arbitrator fees and expenses, (iv) encouraging tribunal consultations immediately prior to hearings, and deliberations immediately after hearings, and (v) requiring tribunals to report to the parties on the timing of outstanding decisions or awards.

Seven annulment proceedings were concluded in FY2012. In three cases, the ad hoc Committee rejected the application for annulment of the award. Three annulment proceedings were discontinued at the request of one or both parties, and one case was discontinued for failure to pay the required advances.

No awards were annulled in FY2012.

The average duration of annulment proceedings concluded in FY2012 was shortened by about a third, from an average duration of 25 months in FY2011, to an average of 17 months from the date of registration of the application.

In FY2012, ICSID continued to develop partnerships with other arbitration institutions to enhance its ability to offer hearings in locations around the world. In the past year, ICSID entered its first facilities cooperation agreement with an arbitration center in Latin America—the Centre for Arbitration and Conciliation at the Chamber of Commerce in Bogota, Colombia. ICSID now has 12 such agreements in place, including agreements with the Australian Centre for International Commercial Arbitration in Melbourne; the Australian Commercial Disputes Centre in Sydney; the German Institution of Arbitration; the Gulf Cooperation Council Commercial Arbitration Centre in Bahrain; the Hong Kong International Arbitration Centre; Maxwell Chambers in Singapore; the Permanent Court of Arbitration in The Hague; the Regional Arbitration Centres of the Asian-African Legal Consultative Committee in Cairo, Kuala Lumpur, and Lagos; and the Singapore International Arbitration Centre. ICSID continued its collaboration with other multilateral institutions on issues pertinent to international investment law and dispute settlement during FY2012. For example, ICSID participated in several conferences organized by UNCITRAL, which addressed transparency in treaty-based investor-state arbitration.

ICSID's administrative expenditures in FY2012 were covered by the IBRD, pursuant to the Memorandum of Administrative Arrangements concluded between the IBRD and ICSID, and also by fee income. It is therefore not necessary to assess any excess expenditures on contracting states pursuant to Article 17 of the convention. Expenditures relating to pending

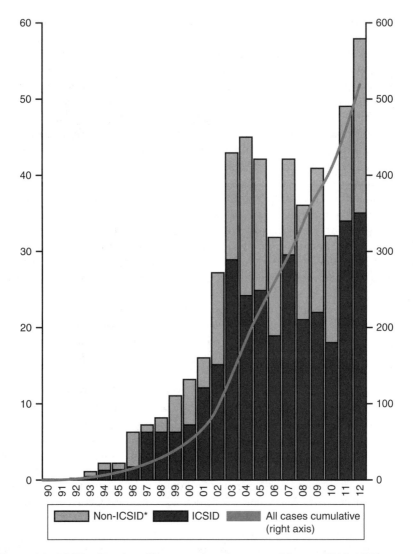

**Figure 6.2**   ICSID—Number of Investor—State Investment Disputes (1990–2012).
*Source*: UNCTAD, World Investment Report 2013.

arbitration proceedings are borne by the parties in accordance with ICSID's Administrative and Financial Regulations (figure 6.2).

## ICSID's Challenges

ICSID faced several challenges, including competition from other dispute settlement institutions and a dramatic expansion of ICSID's caseload.[22] Furthermore, ICSID needs to diversify its panel of arbitrators in order to avoid group-thinking resolutions among "super-elitists attorneys." The current composition of the panel, overrepresented by lawyers, many without any business background, remains a concern to some. Finally, ICSID must allow experts from all around the world to represent *pro hac vice* clients before its jurisdiction. In so doing, the procedure would become accessible to developing countries lacking the financial resources to hire costly US lawyers. Finally, ICSID needs to find ways to work closely with its member states concerning the enforcement of its resolutions. Unless these steps are taken, the legitimacy of the ICSID will also be challenged.

# CHAPTER 7

---⋆‑)⊚(‑⋆---

# THE MUTUAL INVESTMENT
# GUARANTEE AGENCY

## GENERAL

The Multilateral Investment Guarantee Agency (MIGA) was created in 1988 to provide risk-balancing insurance services to foreign direct investment projects in developing countries. Since its inception in 1988, MIGA has issued guarantees worth more than $21 billion for more than 600 projects in 100 developing countries. In Fiscal Year 2010, MIGA issued $1.5 billion in guarantees, up from $1.4 billion in FY2009.

The typical service offered by MIGA is political risk insurance, which insulates investors against government expropriations and the consequences of conflict, terrorism, and similar threats. This allows both investors and lenders to undertake commitments to such projects without the overwhelming downside risk that would otherwise exist. It also enables developing countries to attract and maintain private investment in their countries, which is essential to sustained development. Membership in MIGA is offered to all member countries of the WBG, and that currently numbers 175 countries.

The result of all of MIGA's activities is that, with the potential reduction of risks through insurance, developing countries are encouraged to adopt policies that promote investment. This combination of reform at the domestic level and insurance coverage for investors is another important tool in the drive to reduce poverty by the WBG.

## PURPOSES OF MIGA

The purpose of MIGA is to encourage investment for productive purposes in member states, especially in developing countries.

MIGA's functions are:

- To increase the potential of other insurers through coinsurance and reinsurance.
- Insurance investment in countries not subject to such insurance other insurers because of past policies.
- Maintenance of investors who do not have access to other officially recognized insurers.
- Provision of guarantees for investors of different nationalities belonging to a multinational syndicate, which creates favorable conditions for the conclusion of insurance contracts and the settlement of claims.

## THE ORGANIZATIONAL STRUCTURE OF MIGA

The organizational structure of MIGA is three-tiered with (i) the board of governors, (ii) the directorate, and (iii) the executive vice president.

### Board of Governors

The board of directors is the supreme body of MIGA. It has vested authority upon the admission of new members, the suspension of membership, and the increase or reduction of capital. Unless specifically assigned to the council, it may delegate its authority to the directorate. The board (or council) is composed of the governors and their deputies (one from each member state). The chairman of the board is elected from among the governors.

### Directorate, Chairman of the Directorate

The directorate is made of 20 directors (each with one substitute) and is responsible for the overall operations of MIGA. The chairman of the WB presides over the directorate.

### Executive Vice President

The executive vice president of MIGA is appointed by the chairman of the directorate and performs its functions under the general supervision of the directorate. He is responsible for the organization of work as well as the appointment and dismissal of staff.

## THE CORPORATE GOVERNANCE OF MIGA

Voting power is weighed according to the share of capital each director represents. The principle behind the parity in MIGA's voting system is split 50–50 between developed countries and developing countries.[1] The directors meet regularly at the WBG headquarters in Washington, DC, where they review and decide upon investment projects and oversee general management policies.

## THE FINANCING OF MIGA

MIGA derives its financial resources primarily from the capital it receives from its shareholders and its retained earnings. The MIGA convention established authorized capital stock (membership shares) at 100,000 shares—equivalent to $1,082 million—with authorized capital stock automatically increasing upon the admission of a new member. The subscribed capital and retained earnings determine MIGA's statutory underwriting capacity, and the board of governors and the board of directors have set the maximum amount of contingent liability that may be assumed by MIGA as 350 percent of the sum of its unimpaired subscribed capital and reserves and retained earnings, 90 percent of reinsurance obtained by MIGA with private insurers, and 100 percent of reinsurance obtained with public insurers. MIGA provides financial support in a range of sizes, but the average size of political risk insurance throughout the life of the organization is $40 million. Its current outstanding guarantees portfolio stands at $9.1 billion.[2]

## MIGA's OPERATIONS

MIGA's operational strategy plays to our foremost strength in the marketplace—attracting investors and private insurers into difficult operating environments. It focuses on insuring investments in the areas where it can make the greatest difference mostly in countries eligible for assistance from the International Development Association (the world's poorest countries).

As a multilateral development agency, MIGA only supports investments that are developmentally sound and meet high social and environmental standards. MIGA applies a comprehensive set of social and environmental performance standards to all projects and offers extensive expertise in working with investors to ensure compliance with these standards.

MIGA has issued $2.7 billion of guarantees in support of investments in developing countries. MIGA welcomed two new members, Niger and South Sudan, during the fiscal year. MIGA is committed to promoting projects that promise a strong development impact and are economically, environmentally, and socially sustainable. In all the projects involved, MIGA has shown its ability to catalyze private sector investment into high-priority areas and to draw on the complementary strengths of the WBG—leveraging products and services across institutions for the benefit of host countries and private investors.

MIGA also strengthened its commitment to development in sub-Saharan Africa, one of the fastest-growing developing regions, with huge opportunities. In fiscal year 2012, MIGA's projects in the region accounted for 24 percent of the volume—twice the level of the previous year. Another area of focus for support was to the Middle East and the Northern African region, where the need for investments that create jobs and opportunity is greater than ever (figure 7.1).

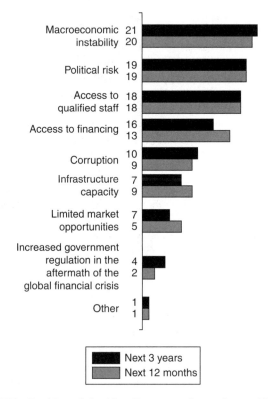

**Figure 7.1** MIGA—Ranking of the Most Important Constraints to FDI in Developing Countries.

*Source*: MIGA-EIU Political Risk Survey 2013. http://www.miga.org/documents/WIPR13.pdf.

MIGA maintains important partnerships with other institutions including other multilateral and bilateral development institutions, many of the world's export credit agencies, other insurers, and industry organizations such as the Berne Union. These partnerships play an important role in helping MIGA identify and underwrite good projects, while collaboratively managing risk.

MIGA complements the existing insurers' investment through coinsurance and reinsurance. MIGA offers four main types of guarantees:

- Currency inconvertibility: provides protection against losses arising from the inability to convert local currency into foreign to be transferred outside the country of residence.
- Expropriation: consists of protection against losses caused by the actions of the government of the host country to limit or eliminate the right of ownership or control over it, and the right to investment is insured.
- War and civil unrest: Consists of protection against damages caused by war or civil unrest, leading to the destruction of or damage to physical assets of the enterprise or the obstruction of its activities.

- Breach of contract: provides protection against losses related to the fact that an investor cannot enforce a decision of a court or arbitral tribunal and its implementation against the host country, as well as contracts that are cancelled or in breach of an investment contract.

MIGA projects are examined in the course of the application process in order to ensure their financial, economic, and environmental soundness and their useful contribution to meeting the development needs of the host country.

MIGA provides a variety of services to provide technical assistance to support the efforts of member countries to encourage foreign direct investment. In 1994, MIGA provided a range of services, from consulting services for improving investment policy regimes to aid in increasing the flow of foreign investment and legal advice relating to foreign investment.

The most important source of funding is the main capital of MIGA. The MIGA convention stipulates that industrialized countries must pledge 10 percent of its hard currency. Another 10 percent of each country contributes in the form are not traded on the open market interest bearing debt. The remainder is a capital reserve. Up to 25 percent of the contributions of developing countries may be added in their own currency.

## Risk Covered

*Currency Inconvertibility and Transfer Restriction*
MIGA coverage protects against losses arising from an investor's inability to legally convert local currency (capital, interest, principal, profits, royalties, and other remittances) into foreign exchange for transfer outside the host country. However, currency depreciation is not covered (figure 7.2).[3]

*Expropriation*
Expropriation protection covers losses arising from certain government actions that may reduce or eliminate ownership of, control over, or rights to the insured investment. In addition to outright nationalization and confiscation, "creeping" expropriation—a series of acts that, over time, have an expropriatory effect—is covered. Coverage is also available on a limited basis for partial expropriation (e.g., confiscation of funds or tangible assets).[4] In case of total expropriation of equity investments, compensation for the insured party is based on the net book value of the covered investment. For expropriation of funds, MIGA pays the insured portion of blocked funds. For loans and loan guaranties, MIGA can insure the outstanding principal and any accrued and unpaid interest. Compensation is paid upon assignment of the investor's interest in the expropriated investment (e.g., equity shares or interest in a loan agreement) to MIGA.

*War, Terrorism, and Civil Disturbance*
MIGA's War, Terrorism, and Civil Disturbance policy protects against loss due to the destruction, disappearance, or physical damage to tangible assets

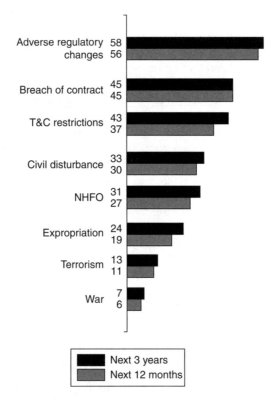

**Figure 7.2** MIGA—Types of Political Risks of Most Concern to Investors in Developing Countries.

*Source*: MIGA-EIU Political Risk Survey 2013. http://www.miga.org/documents/WIPR13.pdf.

or total business interruption (the total inability to conduct operations essential to a project's overall financial viability) caused by politically motivated acts of war or civil disturbance in the country, including revolution, insurrection, coups d'état, sabotage, and terrorism. The policy separates the policy into three categories: tangible asset losses, total business interruption, and temporary business interruption.

(i) For tangible asset losses, MIGA would pay the investor's share of the lesser of the replacement cost and the cost of repair of the damaged or lost assets, or the book value of such assets if they were not being replaced or repaired.

(ii) For total business interruption that results from a covered war and civil disturbance event, compensation would be based, in the case of equity investments, on the net book value of the insured investment or, in the case of loans, the insured portion of the principal and interest payment in default. This coverage encompasses not only violence in a host country directed against the host country's government, but also against foreign governments or foreign investments, including the investor's government or nationality.

(iii) Temporary business interruption may also be included upon a request from the investor and would cover a temporary but complete cessation of operations due to loss of assets or unreasonably hazardous conditions in the host country that result in a temporary abandonment or denial of use. For short-term business interruption, MIGA pays unavoidable continuing expenses and extraordinary expenses associated with the restarting of operations and lost business income or, in the case of loans, missed payments.[5]

*Breach of Contract*

For MIGA, breach of contract cover protects against losses arising from a government's (including, in certain cases, state-owned enterprises) breach or repudiation of a contract with an investor, but requires that the investor invoke the dispute-resolution mechanism (e.g., an arbitration) set out in the underlying contract.[6]

This coverage protects against losses arising from the government's breach or repudiation of a contract with the investor (e.g., a concession or a power purchase agreement). Breach of contract coverage may be extended to the contractual obligations of state-owned enterprises in certain circumstances. If, after a specified period of time, the investor has been unable to obtain an award due to the government's interference with the dispute resolution mechanism (denial of recourse), or has obtained an award but the investor has not received payment under the award (non-payment of an award), MIGA provides compensation. If certain conditions are met, MIGA may, at its discretion, make a provisional payment pending the outcome of the dispute and before compensation for non-payment of an award is paid (figure 7.3).

*Non-Honoring of Sovereign Financial Obligations*

This policy protects against losses resulting from a government's failure to make a payment when due under an unconditional financial payment obligation or guarantee related to an eligible investment. The policy does not require the investor to obtain an arbitral award. This coverage is applicable in situations when a sovereign's financial payment obligation is unconditional and not subject to defenses. Compensation would be based on the insured outstanding principal and any accrued and unpaid interest.

## Types of Investments Covered

MIGA insures cross-border investments made by investors in a MIGA member country into a developing member country. In certain cases, MIGA may also insure an investment made by a national of the host country, provided the funds originate from outside said country. Corporations and financial institutions are eligible for coverage if they are either incorporated in, and have their principal place of business in, a MIGA member country or if they

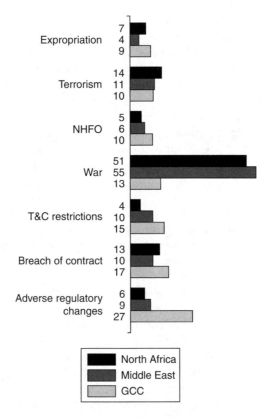

**Figure 7.3**  MIGA—Ranking of the Most Important Political Risks in MENA.
*Source*: http://www.miga.org/documents/WIPR13.pdf.

are majority-owned by nationals of member countries. A state-owned company is eligible only if it operates on a commercial basis. Similarly, an investment made by a non-profit organization may be eligible only if it is carried out on a commercial basis.[7]

The types of foreign investments that can be covered include:

- Equity
- Shareholder loans
- Loan guarantees
- Loans from financial institutions
- Non-shareholder loans
- Non-equity direct investment

Other forms of investment such as technical assistance and management contracts, asset securitizations, capital market bond issues, leasing, services, and franchising and licensing agreements may also be eligible for coverage.

## Guarantee Pricing

MIGA prices its guarantee premiums based on a calculation of both country and project risk. Fees average approximately one percent of the insured amount per year, but can be significantly lower or higher. Generally speaking, the rates offered by MIGA are less expensive than political risk insurance offered by private providers.[8]

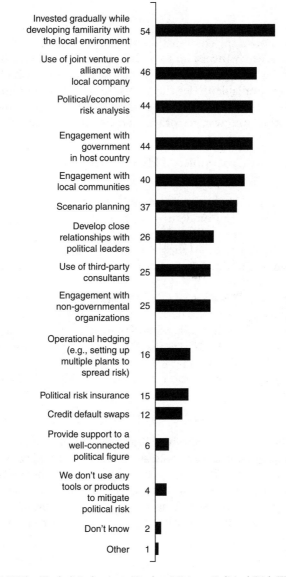

| | |
|---|---|
| Invested gradually while developing familiarity with the local environment | 54 |
| Use of joint venture or alliance with local company | 46 |
| Political/economic risk analysis | 44 |
| Engagement with government in host country | 44 |
| Engagement with local communities | 40 |
| Scenario planning | 37 |
| Develop close relationships with political leaders | 26 |
| Use of third-party consultants | 25 |
| Engagement with non-governmental organizations | 25 |
| Operational hedging (e.g., setting up multiple plants to spread risk) | 16 |
| Political risk insurance | 15 |
| Credit default swaps | 12 |
| Provide support to a well-connected political figure | 6 |
| We don't use any tools or products to mitigate political risk | 4 |
| Don't know | 2 |
| Other | 1 |

**Figure 7.4**  MIGA—Tools/Mechanisms Used to Mitigate Political Risk When Investing in Developing Countries.

*Source*: MIGA-EIU Political Risk Survey 2013. http://www.miga.org/documents/WIPR13.pdf.

## MIGA's Guarantee Duration

Coverage is for up to 15 years (possibly 20, if justified by the nature of the project). MIGA cannot terminate the contract unless the investor defaults on its contractual obligations, but the investor may reduce or cancel coverage without penalty on any contract anniversary date starting with the third anniversary.[9]

## MIGA's Coverage

Investors may choose any combination of the five types of coverage offered by MIGA. MIGA may insure up to $220 million per project, and if necessary, more can be arranged through syndication of insurance. Other coverage can be made available under the Small Investment Program—investors are offered a package covering currency inconvertibility and transfer restriction; expropriation; and war, terrorism, and civil disturbance (figure 7.4).[10]

## Examples of MIGA's Projects

- In Azerbaijan, MIGA provided insurance to protect Turkish investors in a project to expand and modernize a flourmill to produce and distribute flour sold in Azerbaijan and Georgia.
- In Ecuador, MIGA is supporting investors in the construction of a new airport to serve the capital of Quito to improve and expand economic development and trade.
- In the Democratic Republic of Congo (DRC) MIGA provided insurance to cover equity and shareholder loan investments by Global Broadband Solution Inc (GBS) of the United States in its subsidiary Global Broadband Solution SPRL (GBS-DRC) in DRC. The investor applied for MIGA guarantees of $11.1 million for a period of up to ten years against the risks of transfer restriction, expropriation, and war and civil disturbance.

## MIGA's CHALLENGES

MIGA needs to find or work out political risk-mitigation instruments for countries where no sound risk-tools are available.[11] Besides, MIGA needs to be more focused on efficiently delivering products and having a better understanding of investors from both developed and developing member countries.[12] Furthermore, MIGA needs to enhance its brand, for it is seen by some investors as a bureaucratic entity—a market perception that needs to be overcome.

# CHAPTER 8

---※◎※---

# THE BANK FOR INTERNATIONAL SETTLEMENT

## GENERAL

Established in 1930 by the Hague agreement among the ten founding central banks,[1] the Bank for International Settlements (BIS) is an intergovernmental body. The BIS is the world's oldest international financial institution and remains the principal center for international central bank cooperation. The BIS is protected by the 1987 Headquarters Agreement with the Swiss government, which has no jurisdiction over the BIS premises. The BIS and its employees are both exempt from Swiss taxes.[2] Further, the BIS assets are immune from all jurisdictions under Swiss law. That is, they cannot be seized. In July 1944, the United Nations Bretton Woods Conference adopted a resolution calling for the liquidation of the BIS, on the grounds of its supposed domination by the Axis Powers during war and because its traditional field of activity would henceforth be largely covered by the soon to be created IMF and IRBD. However, in 1946 the governors of the European Bank started to reconvene again at Basel, and in 1948, the liquidation resolution was officially revoked.[3] While the suspicious Congress of the United States forbad the US Federal Reserve from joining the BIS formally, the New York Federal Reserve and its allied Morgan interests were able to work closely with the BIS, and the BIS treated the New York Federal Reserve as if it were the central bank of the United States.[4] With the collapse of the Bretton Woods system, in the 1970s, the BIS's role became even prominent. The BIS aims to foster international monetary and financial cooperation and serves as a bank for central banks. The BIS offers a framework for discussion and decision making among central banks. It is a limited liability company, incorporated under Swiss law, with an issued share capital. The BIS's shares are traded on stock markets, and it is held by private shareholders. Membership of the BIS is still a privilege rather than a right.

As of march 2007, the BIS had total assets of $409.15 billion, including its 150 tons of fine gold. The BIS carries out its work through its Annual General Meeting of all members.

## THE BIS OBJECTIVES

Under Article 3 of its statutes, the objects of the BIS are (i) to promote cooperation among central banks, (ii) to provide additional facilities for international financial operations; and (iii) to act as trustee or agent in regard to international financial settlements entrusted to it under agreements with the parties concerned. Besides its core objectives, the BIS buys and sells gold and foreign exchange for its clients, provides asset management, and arranges short-term credit to central banks.[5] While not clearly stated under Article 3 of its statutes, the BIS's objectives have evolved to include the supervision of commercial banks through the Basel Committee on Banking Supervision.[6]

## ORGANIZATIONAL STRUCTURE OF THE BIS

The organizational structure of the BIS has undergone considerable change since its creation in 1930. The BIS is governed by three decision-making bodies: (i) the governors, (ii) the board of directors, and (iii) the BIS management.

### The Governors

This is the first decision making body, composed of representatives or governors of the 55 member central banks. These representatives meet every two months to discuss and vote on key banking and regulatory issues.

### The Board of Directors

The board of directors determines and conducts the strategic direction of the BIS. The board is composed of the governors of the central banks of Belgium, France, Germany, Italy, and the United Kingdom, and the chairman of the board of governors of the US Federal Reserve system. The board elects its chairman and vice chairman, and meets at least six times a year.

### The BIS Management

The BIS management carries out the policies determined by the board and oversees the daily operations of the BIS. The management consists of a general manager—who acts as the BIS's chief executive officer—the department heads, other senior officials, and chief representatives from the two representative offices.

Besides the aforementioned, the BIS has three main departments: (i) the Banking Department; (ii) the Monetary and Economic Department (MED); and (iii) the General Secretariat.

• The Banking Department

The Banking Department is responsible for carrying out banking transactions on behalf of central bank customers, including the investment of central bank foreign exchange on the market.

• The Monetary and Economic Department (MED)

While monetary policy is determined by each member state, the MED of the BIS conducts economic and monetary research and compiles and shares relevant statistics with its members (and non-members). The MED produces the BIS Annual Report and liaises with member central banks. It prepares and hosts many of the central bank expert meetings taking place at the BIS.

• The General Secretariat

The General Secretariat provides administrative support and is responsible for the BIS's internal administration.

It is also worth noting that the BIS hosts six committees dealing with either global banking (the Basel Committee on Banking Supervision, the Committee on the Global Financial System, the Committee on Payment and Settlement Systems, and the Irving Fisher Committee[7]) and two other committees working on insurance and the Financial Stability Board.

## THE BIS's FINANCING

The BIS's initial share capital was set at 500 million Swiss francs, divided into 200,000 shares of 2,500 gold francs. The BIS's main shareholders are central banks. However, some of its original shareholders (the US, France, Belgium) sold portion of their holdings within the BIS. As of today, 14 percent of the BIS's capital (72,648 shares) is held by private institutions. The BIS is committed to redeeming all these privately held shares.

## THE BIS GOVERNANCE

The activities of the BIS are highly secretive. The minutes of meetings, and agenda of the BIS are unknown to the general public, while its press releases offer almost no information to the average person.[8] The BIS's archives are open to the public, and researchers are allowed to consult its documents that are over 30 years old, known as the 30-year rule.[9] The BIS is not accountable to anyone, save its shareholders, and remains unaccountable and socially irresponsible as to the effects of its activities.[10]

Table 8.1 BIS Reporting Banks—Summary of International Positions (in Billions of US Dollars)

| Positions | Amounts Outstanding | | | | Estimated Exchange Rate Adjusted Changes | | | | | |
|---|---|---|---|---|---|---|---|---|---|---|
| | December 2008 | December 2009 | September 2010 | December 2010 | 2009 | 2010 | Q1 2010 | Q2 2010 | Q3 2010 | Q4 2010 |
| **A. Total assets** | **35,363.1** | **33,832.4** | **34,897.7** | **33,938.1** | **-2,348.70** | **974.1** | **666.3** | **-15.2** | **776.7** | **453.6** |
| claims on banks | 22,275.6 | 21,078.7 | 21,709.1 | 20,963.7 | -1,732.4 | 470.4 | 376.7 | 125.2 | 345.8 | -377.3 |
| claims on non-banks | 13,087.4 | 12,753.7 | 13,188.5 | 12,974.5 | -616.4 | 503.7 | 289.6 | -140.5 | 430.9 | -76.3 |
| **B. External assets** | **31,288.1** | **30,073.7** | **31,016.4** | **30,117.1** | **-1,957.6** | **860.5** | **614.7** | **16.9** | **651.6** | **-422.6** |
| claims on banks | 20,286.3 | 19,244.9 | 19,843.9 | 19,121.0 | -1,531.2 | 418.7 | 379.2 | 134.1 | 283.5 | -378.1 |
| claims on non-banks | 11,001.8 | 10,828.7 | 11,172.5 | 10,996.1 | -426.4 | 441.8 | 235.5 | -117.2 | 368.1 | -44.6 |
| **1. Loans and deposits** | **22,902.5** | **21,656.1** | **22,360.4** | **22,004.3** | **-1,721.1** | **931.7** | **447.9** | **179.8** | **391.1** | **-87.0** |
| claims on banks | 16,589.7 | 15,654.7 | 16,058.9 | 15,634.0 | -1,262.9 | 532.0 | 321.1 | 155.6 | 188.4 | -133.1 |
| claims on non-banks | 6,312.7 | 6,001.4 | 6,301.4 | 6,370.3 | -458.2 | 399.7 | 126.7 | 24.2 | 202.7 | 46.0 |
| **2. Holdings of securities and other assets** | **8,385.7** | **8,417.5** | **8,656.0** | **8,112.8** | **-236.5** | **-71.1** | **166.8** | **-162.8** | **260.4** | **-335.5** |
| claims on banks | 3,696.6 | 3,590.2 | 3,785.0 | 3,487.1 | -268.3 | -113.3 | 58.0 | -21.5 | 95.1 | -244.9 |
| claims on non-banks | 4,689.1 | 4,827.3 | 4,871.0 | 4,625.7 | 31.8 | 42.2 | 108.8 | -141.4 | 165.3 | -90.6 |
| **C. Local assets in foreign currency** | **4,074.9** | **3,758.7** | **3,881.3** | **3,821.1** | **-391.2** | **113.6** | **51.6** | **-32.2** | **125.1** | **-31.0** |
| claims on banks | 1,989.3 | 1,833.7 | 1,865.2 | 1,842.7 | -201.2 | 51.7 | -2.5 | -8.9 | 62.3 | 0.8 |
| claims on non-banks | 2,085.6 | 1,925.0 | 2,016.1 | 1,978.4 | -190.0 | 61.9 | 54.1 | -23.3 | 62.8 | -31.7 |

| | | | | | | | | | |
|---|---|---|---|---|---|---|---|---|---|
| **D. Total liabilities** | **33,981.3** | **32,335.6** | **33,444.2** | **32,738.6** | **−2,486.7** | **1,078.4** | **474.0** | **42.0** | **853.3** | **−290.8** |
| Liabilities on banks | 24,337.8 | 23,173.9 | 23,881.1 | 23,132.6 | −1,903.3 | 502.1 | 323.2 | 12.5 | 538.7 | −372.3 |
| Liabilities on non-banks | 9,643.6 | 9,161.7 | 9,563.1 | 9,606.0 | −583.4 | 576.4 | 150.7 | 29.5 | 314.6 | 81.5 |
| **E. External liabilities** | **29,170.7** | **28,127.5** | **29,100.4** | **28,461.5** | **−1,797.3** | **928.1** | **505.1** | **34.6** | **654.6** | **−266.2** |
| Liabilities on banks | 21,464.1 | 20,845.9 | 21,492.8 | 20,832.7 | −1,305.2 | 501.7 | 378.8 | 12.9 | 419.4 | −309.3 |
| Liabilities on non-banks | 7,706.6 | 7,281.6 | 7,607.6 | 7,628.8 | −492.1 | 426.4 | 126.3 | 21.7 | 235.2 | 43.2 |
| **1. Loans and deposits** | **24,442.5** | **23,113.5** | **23,566.2** | **23,228.3** | **−1,859.5** | **772.1** | **374.1** | **22.5** | **370.3** | **5.1** |
| Liabilities on banks | 17,442.6 | 16,523.6 | 16,663.2 | 16,239.1 | −1,358.0 | 293.8 | 246.9 | -8.4 | 160.6 | −105.4 |
| Liabilities on non-banks | 6,999.9 | 6,589.9 | 6,903.0 | 6,989.2 | −501.6 | 478.3 | 127.2 | 30.9 | 209.7 | 110.5 |
| **2. Own issues of securities and other liabilities** | **4,728.2** | **5,014.0** | **5,534.1** | **5,233.1** | **62.2** | **156.0** | **131.0** | **12.1** | **284.3** | **−271.4** |
| Liabilities on banks | 4,021.5 | 4,322.3 | 4,829.6 | 4,593.5 | 52.7 | 207.9 | 131.8 | 21.3 | 258.8 | −204.0 |
| Liabilities on non-banks | 706.7 | 691.7 | 704.6 | 639.6 | 9.5 | −51.9 | −0.8 | -9.2 | 25.5 | −67.4 |
| **F. Local liabilities in foreign currency** | **4,810.7** | **4,208.1** | **4,343.8** | **4,277.1** | **−689.4** | **150.4** | **−31.1** | **7.4** | **198.7** | **−24.6** |
| Liabilities on banks | 2,873.7 | 2,328.0 | 2,388.3 | 2,299.9 | −598.1 | 0.3 | −55.5 | 0.4 | 119.3 | −63.0 |
| Liabilities on non-banks | 1,937.0 | 1,880.1 | 1,955.5 | 1,977.2 | −91.3 | 150.0 | 24.4 | 7.8 | 79.4 | 38.4 |

*Source:* www.bis.org/statistics/bankstats.htm.

## THE FUNCTIONS OF THE BIS

### Central Bank Function

The BIS performs as the central bank for central banks. It organizes regular meetings of central bank governors and officials to debate over international banking issues. The BIS receives deposits from central bank members. The B IS extends loans and received deposits from central banks, and assists central bank members in their management of external reserves. In support of this cooperation, the BIS has developed its own research in financial and monetary economics and makes an important contribution to the collection, compilation, and dissemination of economic and financial statistics. Besides monetary policy cooperation, the BIS performs "traditional" banking functions for the central bank community (e.g., gold and foreign exchange transactions), as well as trustee and agency functions. Finally, the BIS also provides or organizes emergency financing to support the international monetary system whenever needed. More recently, the BIS has provided finance in the context of IMF-led stabilization programs (e.g., for Mexico in 1982 and Brazil in 1998).

The BIS operations thereon must be conducted in compliance with Article 19 of its statutes, which states:

> The operations of the Bank shall be in conformity with the monetary policy of the central banks of the countries concerned.

Central banks make deposits to the BIS, which invests the money deposited in high-quality short-term government securities and highly rated commercial banks.[11] Further, the BIS extends credit facilities to central banks as short-term advances. The BIS also hold international positions as illustrated below (table 8.1).

### Investment Services Advisory

The BIS assists central banks in managing their liquidity positions on their foreign assets. It also offers investment instruments with maturities up to five years for central banks in need of long-term reserve management.[12]

**Table 8.2** BIS Gold Safekeeping Services

| As at 31 March SDR millions | 2010 | 2009 |
| --- | --- | --- |
| Gold bars held at central banks | 41,596.9 | 22,616.5 |
| Total gold loans | 1,442.9 | 2,799.7 |
| Total gold and gold loan assets | 43,039.8 | 25,416.2 |
| Comprising: | | |
| Gold investment assets | 2,811.2 | 2,358.1 |
| Gold and gold loan banking assets | 40,228.6 | 23,058.1 |

*Source*: www.bis.org/statistics/bankstats.htm

### Gold Safekeeping Services

The BIS takes deposits of gold from central banks as a safe-keeper and intermediary seller/purchaser before letting the gold into the market, as illustrated below (table 8.2).

### Insurance Supervisor

Given the fact that insurance has become a part of international bank services, the BIS is more involved in developing standards for global supervision of insurance.[13] In the United States, for instance, since the repealing of the Glass-Steagall Act, banks are allowed to offer insurance products and services. The Financial Services Modernization Act of 1998 allows banks, through their holdings, to engage in insurance and real estate. While the international banking sector operates under strict rules and regulations, the international insurance industry still operates in a vacuum. The BIS has stepped in to provide adequate standards in the insurance arena in order to harmonize the practices within the banking industry.

## THE BIS'S MONETARY AND BANKING POLICIES

In the 1970s and 1980s, the BIS's monetary policy was focused on managing the cross-border capital flows following the oil crises and the international debt crisis.

The 1970s crises drove the BIS to consider the issue of regulatory supervision of internationally active banks. Since then, the promotion of international financial stability has been a primary concern of the BIS.[14]

Furthermore, the BIS has been really effective in the banking system through the Basel 1, 2, and 3. However, the Basel system is geared toward the stability of individual financial institutions, and does little to take account of their interactions with their environment and its stability. On the other hand, the IMF has developed a set of "Financial Soundness Indicators" (FSI) as a key tool for macro-prudential surveillance.

## THE BIS'S CHALLENGES

The benefits of services rendered by the BIS are quite obvious. Since the 2007–2009 financial crises, many have come to consider the BIS as a substitute for the IMF, or at least have advocated the merger of the two institutions. The expertise of the BIS is unparalleled relative to the IMF. Whether such a vital reform would occur is not certain. IMF reforms are more important than the succession of its disgraced managing director, Dominique Strauss-Khan.

Though quite important, the BIS needs to improve its corporate governance, particularly its board of directors being in the hands of a handful developed countries. Some critics view the BIS as an elitist organization through which the wealthy control the world. With the world's wealth shifting eastward, some argue that the BIS should have formal representation from developing countries, which have assumed growing importance in the global economy (i.e., China, India). Another major criticism of the BIS is its obscurity and secrecy. For an international financial institution of its level, the BIS should take a greater leadership role in increasing transparency in other financial and banking transactions across the world. The BIS, with its affiliations with other multilateral financial institutions such as the IMF, the WB, and the Organization for Economic Cooperation and Development (OECD), can set an enhanced example of corporate governance.

# PART II

---✦---

# THE REGIONAL DEVELOPMENT BANKS

Regional development banks play key roles in their respective jurisdictions. As partners of development, regional development membership is not restricted to countries from the region, but includes other countries from different parts of the world. Regional development banks have adapted their modus operandi to play a key role in financing the new sustainable development agenda. They perform three functions: (i) to mobilize resources from private capital markets and from official resources to make loans to developing countries on better conditions that the markets set up; (ii) to generate knowledge on and provide technical assistance and advice for economic and social development; (iii) to furnish a range of complementary services, such as international public goods.

Regional development banks use, for the most part, the Country Policy and Institutional Assessment developed by the World Bank Group as a tool to tailor their assistance within their respective regions.

CHAPTER 9

# THE INTER-AMERICAN
# DEVELOPMENT BANK

## GENERAL

Established in 1959, the Inter-American Development Bank (IDB) is composed of 48 member countries, including donor nations in Europe, North America, and Japan. The IDB is the largest among regional development banks, lending more than US$9 billion annually. The IDB promotes economic development throughout Latin America. Among other objectives, the IDB is engaged in poverty reduction, social equity, and environmentally sustainable growth. The IDB's activities are organized in four priority areas: (i) fostering competition to increase the potential for development in an open global economy; (ii) modernizing the state by strengthening the efficiency and transparency of public institutions; (iii) investing in social programs that expand opportunities for the poor; and (iv) promoting regional integration. The IDB has its headquarter in Washington, DC, and it has 26 offices in all 26 Latin American and Caribbean borrowing countries, as well as in Paris and Tokyo.

## ORGANIZATIONAL STRUCTURE OF THE IDB

### The Board of Governors

The board of governors is the highest authority in the IDB and all powers not delegated remain with the board of governors. The board of governors is composed of representatives from each member country's government, generally, the minister of finance or the president of the central bank. Each member country appoints one member to the board of governors for a five-year term. The board of governors may delegate nearly all powers to the executive directors.

### The Board of Executive Directors

The board of executive directors is responsible for the day-to-day conduct and operations of the IDB. The board of executive directors is authorized

The governor conducts the CEB's financial policy in accordance with the administrative council's guidelines, and represents the CEB in all its transactions. He/she examines the technical and financial aspects of the requests for financing submitted to the CEB and refers them to the administrative council.

## The Auditing Board

The powers of the auditing board are described in Article XII of the Articles of Agreement. The auditing board is composed of three members appointed by the governing board. It checks the accuracy of the annual accounts after they have been examined by an external auditor.

In accordance with Article XIII of the Articles of Agreement, the secretariat of the organs of the CEB is provided by the "Secretariat of the Partial Agreement on the Council of Europe Development Bank," Council of Europe, Strasbourg.

# THE CEB'S FINANCING

The CEB bases its activity on its own funds and reserves and receives no aid or subsidy from its member states. In 2004, the CEB's total assets amounted to €16.4 billion, and its own funds stood at €4.5 billion.

# THE CEB'S ACTIVITIES

CEB provides long-term lending to its 40 member states' local or regional governments, entities, or financial institutions (public or private), provides technical assistance for project preparation and intervention strategies, and facilitates co-financing.[3] The CEB has three sectoral action lines: (i) strengthening social integration, (ii) managing the environment, and (iii) developing human capital. Projects presented to the CEB should be:

- eligible for CEB financing (i.e., meet sectorial, geographic, and social criteria);
- technically sound;
- financially viable; and
- comply with CEB's environmental and procurement regulations.

## Borrowing from the CEB

The CEB can grant loans (but not subsidies) to its 40 member states[4] to finance projects corresponding to a certain number of sectoral, geographic, social, and financial criteria defined in the CEB's Articles of Agreement and policy for loan and project financing. Potential borrowers (Governments, local or regional authorities, as well as public or private financial institutions) by the board of governors to establish operational policies, approve loans, set interest rates, authorize borrowings in capital markets, and approve the organization's budget. The board of governors elects its president for a five-year term, who, along with the executive vice president, oversees the organizations' operations. Each country's executive director maintains an office at the IDB's Washington, DC headquarters. Voting power within the IDB is based on each country's subscription to the IDB's ordinary capital.

## The President

The president of the IDB, under the guidance of the executive directors, conducts the ordinary affairs of the IDB and is the chief of staff of the IDB for a five-year term. The president is elected by the board of governors. The president presides over board meetings but does not have voting power. There are also vice presidents and various other offices that coordinate certain sectors within the IDB.

The IDB currently employs about 2,030 staff members, including 120 managers, and the IDB estimates that some of those staff members might quit or be fired because of the new realignment strategy, which places less emphasis on seniority and nationality indicators. The IDB also will be offering buyouts for some veteran managers as the organization seeks to have the proper personnel for its new initiatives. On June 6, 2007, the Employees Association of the IDB called a special assembly to respond to the IDB's realignment initiative. The assembly responded with general approval of the realignment plan, but noted that the process in which the realignment was taking place was "erratic, non-participatory, and obscure" and that the IDB's lack of information among the employees did not enable them to make sounds judgments about the merits of the realignment. Notwithstanding complaints about the process in which the realignment was taking place, the employees expressed support for the realignment's strengthening of merit, transparency, and competitiveness involved in the processes of selection, promotion, and retention of IDB personnel.

The employees' support for the new employment philosophy represents dissatisfaction with the IDB's previous lack of emphasis on merit in the hiring and promotion process. The IDB's 2006 *Development Effectiveness Overview* states that, as part of the realignment, there will be a focus on performance incentives and accountability and that these changes will be initiated as part of the IDB's greater emphasis on results-based effectiveness. Therefore, the IDB appears to be moving toward a more transparent as well as competitive process for employee retention and merit-based promotions.

## IDB GOVERNANCE

An important facet of governance is the level of control over the IDB exercised by its various member countries. Voting, for many important functions of the IDB, is determined by the amount of shares a member country possesses. The amount of shares belonging to each country was established by the 1959 agreement creating the IDB, and is based on contributions. Although the precise amounts of capital stock have changed since that time, the overall percentages remain similar. The borrowing member group of the IDB is made up of the countries of Latin America and the Caribbean. These countries are the targets and recipients of IDB projects and loans, and they hold over 50 percent of the voting power of the IDB. The borrowing-member majority at the IDB is in contrast to, for example, the EBRD, where non-borrowing members hold a substantial voting majority. At the IDB, in the borrowing member group, Argentina (10.7%), Brazil (10.7%), Mexico (6.9%), and Venezuela (5.7%) hold the largest percentages of voting power.

Otherwise, the United States holds roughly 30 percent of the voting power, while Japan holds 5 percent and Canada 4 percent. Most of the 21 non-borrowing members are from Europe. Italy's voting power, for example, is around 1.9 percent of the total. This is greater than borrowing members Paraguay, Panama, Nicaragua, and Honduras combined. Non-regional members have relatively large stakes in the IDB because they are the biggest contributors and therefore provide the IDB with much of its capital. Although the borrowing members hold over one-half of the voting power, voting rules of the IDB often require more than a simple majority of stock. Therefore, any important action within the IDB is often controlled by the United States as largest shareholder, or, in any case, cannot be undertaken solely by the borrowing members of the IDB. Many voting rules require an absolute majority of member countries, but require a higher percentage of total voting power. This skews power toward those members holding higher percentages of voting power, principally, toward the United States for holding 30 percent of total voting power. For instance, a quorum for a meeting of the board of governors is an absolute majority of the total number of governors, representing no less than two-thirds of the total voting power. Amending the IDB's charter requires two-thirds of the total number of governors but also three-fourths of the total voting power. The United States' influence over the IDB, which is headquartered in Washington, DC, is evident. The United States automatically gets to appoint one member to the board of directors (as the largest shareholding member) while the other members are appointed by the board of governors. Moreover, although the president is elected by a majority of the voting power as well as with a majority of member countries' approval, current president Moreno was the US-supported candidate when he was elected in 2005. Moreno was Colombia's former ambassador to the United States and was a leading proponent of the US free trade agreement with Colombia. One outgrowth of criticism of the IDB and other financial organizations is the recent establishment of the Bank of the South. The Bank of the South was created to counter the traditional Bretton Woods institutions and the power that western countries (such as the US) exercise in those institutions. The Bank of the South will lend money for infrastructure projects and social programs. Most countries in South America are planning to participate in the Bank of the South. The Venezuelan finance minister stated that the Bank of the South would be unique because no one member will have disproportionate power. This criticism of the IDB is articulated despite the IDB borrowing members' possession of over 50 percent of the voting power, a deliberate decision to give borrowing countries more power. Therefore, there is a potential for inequity within the IDB because those receiving the IDB's funding, and complying with the conditionality attached to that funding, hold a bare majority of overall voting power and, on many important decisions, need the support of the United States or any other non-Latin American member for decision-making power. The US, Canada, and Japan control a sizable portion of voting power within the IDB, but are not subject to the IDB's conditionality requirements for lending because they are non-borrowing members. Furthermore, the voting power percentages are roughly the same today (with the exception of the entrance of Canada and Japan into the IDB) as they were when the IDB was formed in 1959.

## THE IDB FINANCIAL RESOURCES

The IDB has an authorized and subscribed capital stock of US$101 billion. Besides the authorized capital, the IDB has a US$9.6 billion Fund for Special Operations (FSO).

## THE IBD ACTIVITIES

Within the IDB, projects and thus, IDB staff, are divided into Region I (Bolivia, Brazil, Argentina, Chile, Paraguay, and Uruguay; Region II (Mexico, Central America, the Dominican Republic, and Haiti); and Region III (the English-speaking Caribbean, Colombia, Ecuador, Peru, and Venezuela). Each region has a team that prepares project loans, evaluates, and implements projects.

Other Important departments within the IDB include:

- The Private Sector Department (PRI) oversees loans to the private sector throughout the region. The PRI primarily makes loans for transportation, energy, water and sanitation, communications, and capital markets. The PRI also contains an environmental and social unit that works to ensure that all PRI projects are designed and implemented in accordance with environmental, social, health and safety, and labor concerns. However, many PRI projects, such as the Cana Brava dam project in Brazil, have failed to meet minimum environmental and social standards, resulting in environmental destruction, forced displacement without sufficient compensation, and highly inadequate civil society consultation.
- The Sustainable Development Department (SDD) deals with a wide range of social and environmental issues. SDD contains the Committee on Environment and Social Impact (CESI), which is responsible for evaluating all IDB operations to address their environmental and social impact and to advise project teams and country governments on preventive and "mitigating" strategies.

**IDB Loans**

The IDB makes several types of loans:

- Investment loans for specific projects in sectors, such as agriculture, credit, education, energy, environment, health, planning and reform, pre-investment, sanitation, social programs, transportation, and urban development
- Structural adjustment loans to support the liberalization of a country's economy in order to adapt it to the free market and neo-liberal macroeconomic policies.
- Sectoral adjustment loans address the microeconomic details of structural adjustment loans, leading to the privatization of public services and the reform of public sector operations.

## THE IDB CHALLENGES

Despite the flow of money spent within the region, the real impact remains unseen. Some long-standing challenges need to be tackled, raising the quality of education, reducing informality, and increasing productivity. In the absence of these actions, growth may not be sustained, and the region will continue to depend on the vagaries of international finance.

# CHAPTER 10

---

# THE EUROPEAN BANK FOR
# RECONSTRUCTION AND
# DEVELOPMENT

## GENERAL

The European Bank for Reconstruction and Development (EBRD) was established in 1990 and began operations in 1991. The EBRD was created during the disintegration of the Soviet Union and its mission was directly related to the USSR's demise. The agreement establishing the EBRD states that the purpose shall be "to foster the transition towards open market-oriented economies and to promote private and entrepreneurial initiative in the Central and Eastern European countries" and work toward three important principles: multiparty democracy, pluralism, and market economics. While the primary goal of the EBRD is to help Central and Eastern European countries move toward market-oriented economies after decades of state-run economies, the agreement makes it clear that the EBRD is also committed to promoting the rule of law, respect for human rights, and the strengthening of democratic institutions. The EBRD, which some have described as "stand[ing] out" because of the specific political goals in its charter, has been criticized at times for holding its annual meetings in dictator-run countries and not applying pressure for democratic change. Since its creation in 1990, the EBRD's objectives have always been different from the objectives pursued by other international financial institutions. The EBRD aims to foster the transition of its countries of operations to open-market economies. The EBRD is owned by 61 countries and two intergovernmental institutions. It has an excellent credit rating of AAA from Standard & Poor, Aaa from Moody's and AAA from Fitch (figure 10.1).

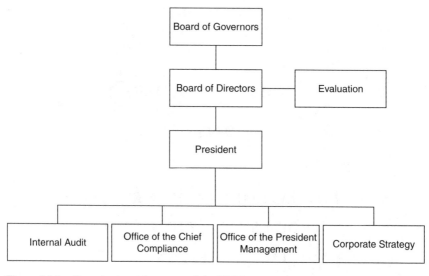

**Figure 10.1**  Organizational Structure of the EBRD.
*Source*: http://www.ebrd.com/downloads/orgcharts/ebrd.pdf.

## ORGANIZATIONAL STRUCTURE OF THE EBRD

### The Board of Governors

The board of governors is composed of representatives from each member state. Each member state appoints one governor and one alternate governor to the board. Alternate governors vote only in the absence of their principal. At each of its annual meetings, the board shall elect one of the governors as chairman, who would then hold office until the election of the next chairman. Governors and alternates serve as such without remuneration from the EBRD. All the powers of the EBRD are vested in the board of governors, which may delegate some to the board of directors, except the power to:

- admit new members and determine the conditions of their admission;
- increase or decrease the authorized capital stock of the EBRD
- suspend a member;
- decide appeals from interpretations or applications of this agreement given by the board of directors;
- authorize the conclusion of general agreements for co-operation with other international organizations;
- elect the directors and the president of the Bank;
- determine the remuneration of the directors and alternate Directors and the salary and other terms of the contract of service of the President;
- approve, after reviewing the auditors' report, the general balance sheet and the statement of profit and loss of the Bank;
- determine the reserves and the allocation and distribution of the net profits of the Bank;

- amend the EBRD Agreement;
- decide to terminate the operations of the Bank and to distribute its assets; and
- exercise such other powers as are expressly assigned to the Bbard of Governors in this Agreement.

The board of governors retains full power to exercise authority over any matter delegated or assigned to the board of directors. The board of governors holds an annual meeting, and such other meetings as may be provided for by the board or called by the board of directors. Meetings of the board of governors are called by the board of directors, whenever requested by not less than five members of the EBRD, or members holding not less than one quarter of the total voting power.

Two-thirds of the governors constitute a quorum for any meeting of the board of governors, provided such majority represents not less than two-thirds of the total voting power of the members. Unless otherwise stated, each governor is entitled to cast the votes of the member he or she represents. The board of Governors may, by regulation, establish a procedure allowing the board to obtain a vote of the governors on a specific question without calling a meeting of the board of governors. The board of governors, and the board of directors to the extent authorized, may adopt such rules and regulations and establish such subsidiary bodies as may be necessary or appropriate to conduct the business of the EBRD.[1]

## The Board of Directors

The board of directors is responsible for the direction of the general operations of the EBRD and, for this purpose, shall, in addition to the powers assigned to it expressly by the agreement, exercise all the powers delegated to it by the board of governors, and in particular:[2]

- prepare the work of the board of governors;
- in conformity with the general directions of the board of governors, establish policies and take decisions concerning loans, guarantees, investment in equity capital, borrowing by the EBRD, the furnishing of technical assistance, and other operations of the EBRD;
- submit the audited accounts for each financial year for approval of the board of governors at each annual meeting; and
- approve the budget of the EBRD.

The board of directors is composed of twenty-three members who shall not be members of the board of governors, and of whom:[3]

(i) 11 are elected by the governors, representing Belgium, Denmark, France, the Federal Republic of Germany, Greece, Ireland, Italy, Luxembourg, the Netherlands, Portugal, Spain, the United Kingdom, the European Economic Community, and the European Investment Bank; and

ii) 12 are elected by the governors representing other members, of whom:

- (a) four (4), by the governors representing those countries listed in Annex A as Central and Eastern European countries eligible for assistance from the EBRD;
- (b) four (4), by the governors representing those countries listed in Annex A as other European countries;
- (c) four (4), by the governors representing those countries listed in Annex A as non-European countries.

Directors, as well as representing members whose governors have elected them, may also represent members who assign their votes to them.

The board of governors may increase or decrease the size or revise the composition of the board of directors in order to take into account changes in the number of members of the EBRD, by an affirmative vote of not less than two-thirds of the governors, representing not less than three-fourths of the total voting power of the members. Each director appoints an alternate with full power to act for him/her when he/she is not present. Directors hold office for a term of three (3) years and are re-eligible. A majority of the directors constitutes a quorum for any meeting of the board of directors, provided such majority represents not less than two-thirds of the total voting power of the members. The voting power of each member is equal to the number of its subscribed shares in the capital stock of the EBRD.[4]

## The President

The president is the legal representative of the EBRD.[5] He/she is responsible for the organization, appointment, and dismissal of the officers and staff in accordance with regulations to be adopted by the board of directors.[6] The president is elected by a majority vote of the board of governors. The president shall not be a governor or a director, or an alternate for either post.[7] The president is elected for a four-year term, and can be reelected.[8] The president can be terminated when the board of governors so decides by an affirmative vote of not less than two-thirds of the governors, representing not less than two-thirds of the total voting power of the members. If the office of the president for any reason becomes vacant, the board of governors shall elect a successor for up to four (4) years.[9]

## Vice President(s)

One or more vice presidents are appointed by the board of directors on the recommendation of the president. A vice president holds office for such term, exercises such authority, and performs such functions in the administration of the EBRD as may be determined by the board of directors. In the absence or incapacity of the president, a vice president exercises the authority and performs the functions of the president.[10] A vice president may participate in meetings of the board of directors but has no vote at such meetings, except that he or she may cast the deciding vote when acting in place of the president.[11]

## CORPORATE GOVERNANCE OF THE EBRD

Membership of the EBRD is comprised of mostly European and Central Asian countries and a small number of other countries. Similar to other regional development banks, voting power in the EBRD is proportionate to the number of shares held by the member country. The largest sharehold-ers in the EBRD are the United States (10% of voting power), the United Kingdom (8.5%), Italy (8.5%), Japan (8.5%), France (8.5%), and Germany (8.5%). Russia, Spain, and Canada also have large subscriptions. The US and other non-regional members are some of the biggest contributors to the EBRD, and therefore their membership is crucial to the EBRD's operations and financial mission. Although there is no explicit distinction between borrowing and non-borrowing countries in the EBRD, the voting power held by the de facto non-borrowing countries (Western Europe and non-European) far outweighs the voting power held by the borrowing countries (Eastern European and Central Asian). Although the EBRD's charter allows addition capital stock to be authorized and issued, the charter requires a majority of stock (and therefore voting power) to belong to countries that are members of the European Economic Community (mostly Western Europe). This provision was included because of the desire for the EBRD to be a fun-damentally "European" bank. Further, the EBRD charter explicitly grants Western European and non- European countries the ability to elect a major-ity of the board of governors. The board of governors elects the president and board of directors of the EBRD. Thus, decision-making power remains firmly in the hands of the non-borrowing members of the EBRD. This is in contrast to organizations like the IDB, where borrowing members hold a 51 percent voting power majority over non-borrowing members. Further, many of the voting requirements in the EBRD's charter favor the EBRD's non-borrowing members. For example, certain operational decisions require two-thirds of the vote from the board of governors, but three-fourths of the total voting power of the members. The president must be elected by a majority of the board of governors, but also by a majority of the total voting power. There is also an informal agreement at the EBRD that the president will be either from France or from Germany, irrespective of his/her skills or qualifications. Since the EBRD was formed in 1990, there have been three French presidents and one German president. However, this arrangement has recently been opposed by several of the EBRD's borrowing member countries. The Bank's Board of Governors elected Sir Suma as President of the EBRD for the next four years, from July 3, 2012. He replaces Thomas Mirow, the President since 2008. Thus, the power within the EBRD to make important policy decisions rests in the hands of its non-borrowing members. Although these non-borrowing members control the voting power of the

EBRD, make project decisions, and determine the loan conditions, they are not subject to any of the terms of the EBRD's loans. Therefore, the potential for inequity exists, as well as what could be termed a democracy deficit, as the borrowing members (those using the EBRD) have comparatively less power to control the EBRD's policies.

## THE EBRD'S FINANCING

The EBRD's initial capital base was European Currency Unit (ECU)10 billion (over US$11.5 billion) with a paid-in capital requirement of 30 percent (ECU3 billion or US$3.4 billion), making it the MDB with the most expensive budget for member governments to have financed in recent times. The Articles of Agreement of the EBRD require the European Union (EU) and the European Investment Bank (EIB) to always hold the combined majority of issued and subscribed capital stock.

The EBRD has a subscribed capital totaling €20 billion (€5 billion paid-in and €15 billion callable).

## THE EBRD'S CORE MISSIONS

To foster the transition toward open market-oriented economies and to promote private and entrepreneurial initiative in the central and Eastern European countries (including Mongolia and even member countries of the southern and eastern Mediterranean) committed to and applying the principles of multiparty democracy, pluralism, and market economics, the EBRD assists the recipient member countries to implement structural and sectoral economic reforms—including de-monopolization, decentralization, and privatization—to help their economies become fully integrated into the international economy by measures:

  (i)  to promote, through private and other interested investors, the establishment, improvement, and expansion of productive, competitive, and private sector activity, in particular, small and medium-sized enterprises;

  (ii)  to mobilize domestic and foreign capital and experienced management to the end described in (i);

  (iii)  to foster productive investment, including in the service and financial sectors, and in related infrastructure where investment is necessary to support private and entrepreneurial initiatives, thereby assisting in making a competitive environment and improving productivity, the standard of living, and conditions of labor;

  (iv)  to provide technical assistance for the preparation, financing, and implementation of relevant projects, whether individual or in the context of specific investment programs;

  (v)  to stimulate and encourage the development of capital markets;

  (vi)  to give support to sound and economically viable projects involving more than one recipient member country;

(vii)   to promote, in the full range of its activities, environmentally sound and sustainable development; and

(viii)  to undertake such other activities and provide such other services as may further these functions.

## The EBRD's New Mandates

The EBRD is moving toward a big expansion in its economic assistance to North Africa and the Middle East. The EBRD has recently included Egypt, Jordan, Morocco, and Tunisia within its new mandates. The EBRD's board of governors—the leading authority—has approved amendments to EBRD statutes that will allow it to invest in the southern and eastern Mediterranean region.

Virtually all the EBRD members have voted to expand its new mandate; still, their votes would require approval from national governments.

## EBRD's Activities

Initially set up to build market economies on Western Europe's borders while instilling progress in Eastern Europe and the former Soviet Union through entrepreneurship, the missions or mandates of the EBRD have evolved with time. Today, the EBRD focuses more on fostering stability in the Balkan countries, Georgia and the other countries of the Caucasus, and Central Asia. To that end, the EBRD is helping countries such as Ukraine and Russia stay the course as market-oriented economies. The EBRD offers loan and equity finance, guarantees, leasing facilities, trade finance, and professional development through support programs. Direct investments range from €5 million to €230 million. Smaller projects are financed both directly by the EBRD and through "financial intermediaries."

The EBRD finances projects in sectors including agribusiness, energy efficiency, financial institutions, manufacturing, municipal infrastructure/public works (which includes transport, schools, water supply, waste disposal, and pollution control services), natural resources, power and energy, property, tourism, telecommunications, and information technology.

To be eligible for EBRD funding, "a project must be located in an EBRD country of operations, have strong commercial prospects, involve significant equity contributions in-cash or in-kind from the project sponsor, benefit the local economy and help develop the private sector and satisfy banking and environmental standards."

### Project Financing

The EBRD offers a wide range of financial instruments and takes a flexible approach in structuring its financial products. The principal forms of direct financing that the EBRD may offer are loans, equity, and guarantees.

### The EBRD Loans

The EBRD's loans are structured with a high degree of flexibility to provide loan profiles that match client and project needs. The basis for a loan is the expected cash flow of the project and the ability of the client to repay the loan over the period agreed upon. The credit risk can be taken entirely by the Bank or may be partly syndicated to the market. A loan may be secured by a borrower's assets and/or it may be converted into shares or be equity-linked. EBRD loans have some specific features:

- Minimum €5–15 million, although this can be smaller in some cases.
- Fixed or floating rate.
- Senior, subordinated, mezzanine, or convertible debt.
- Denominated in major foreign or local currencies.
- Short to long-term maturities, from 5–15 years.
- Project-specific grace periods may be incorporated.

EBRD's interest rates for its loans are based on current market rates and are priced competitively. EBRD's financial terms can be discussed in detail with banking staff. The EBRD does not subsidize projects, nor does it offer soft loans.

The EBRD offers both fixed and floating interest rates:

- Fixed rate basis, linked to a floating rate such as LIBOR.
- Floating rate basis with a cap[12] or a collar.

As the type rate directly affects profitability, a project's financial structure should preferably include both floating and fixed rate loans. The mix is evaluated with respect to client and project sensitivities to interest rate movements.

A margin fees and charges are added on to the base rate. The margin is a combination of country risk and project-specific risk. This information is confidential to the client and the EBRD. In addition to the margin, the EBRD may charge some of the following fees and commissions:

- Front-end commission, paid up-front.
- Commitment fee, payable on the committed but undisbursed loan amount.
- Loan conversion fee, paid at the time of interest rate or currency conversion on the amount that is to be converted.
- Prepayment, cancellation, and late payment fees are also charged if necessary.

In line with commercial practice, sponsors will be obliged to reimburse the EBRD for out-of-pocket expenses, such as fees for technical consultants, outside legal counsel, and travel expenses.

Other Lending Terms
A complete set of lending terms are negotiated with the client for each project.

Recourse
Recourse to a sponsor is not required. However, the EBRD may seek specific performance and completion guarantees plus other forms of support from sponsors of the kind that are normal practice in limited-recourse financing.

Insurance
The Bank requires project companies to obtain insurance against normally insurable risks. Examples of such risk insurances include theft of assets, outbreak of fire, and specific construction risks. The EBRD does not require insurance against political risk or non-convertibility of the local currency.

Security
The EBRD usually requires the companies it finances to secure the loan with project assets. These can include:

- Mortgage on fixed assets, such as land, plants, and other buildings.
- Mortgage on movable assets, such as equipment and other business assets.
- Assignment of the company's hard currency and domestic currency earnings.
- Pledge of the sponsor's shares in the company.
- Assignment of the company's insurance policy and other contractual benefits.

Covenants
Typical project-financing covenants are required as part of the loan package. Such covenants—limiting indebtedness and specifying certain financial ratios and various other issues, will be negotiated.

Loan Repayment
Repayment is normally in equal, semi-annual instalments. Longer maturities may be considered on an exceptional basis—for example, up to 15 years for large infrastructure operations.

Hedging Possibilities
The EBRD can help manage financial risks associated with a project's assets and liabilities. This covers foreign exchange risk, interest rate risk, and commodity price risk. Risk hedging instruments include currency swaps, interest rate swaps, caps, collars and options, and commodity swaps.

The EBRD also participates in investment funds, which, in turn, invest in medium-sized companies that need to expand their business. Equity funds are focused on a specific region, country, or industry sector; have local presences; and are run by professional venture capitalists. Their main investment criteria are consistent with the EBRD's overall investment policy.

Terms and Conditions

The terms and conditions of the EBRD's investments depend on risks and prospective returns associated with each project. They are also affected by the financial/ownership structure of the project company.

The EBRD does not take up long-term equity investments or controlling interests, nor does it assume direct responsibility for managing the project company.

*Equity Financing*

The EBRD's equity financing ranges from €2 million to €100 million in industry, infrastructure, and the financial sector.

The EBRD uses innovative approaches and instruments and expects an appropriate return on investment. Equity and quasi-equity instruments used are:

- Ordinary shares.
- Preference shares.
- Subordinated loans.
- Debentures.
- Income notes.
- Redeemable preference shares.
- Listed and unlisted.
- Underwriting of share issues by public or privately-owned enterprises.
- Financing the transfer of shares in existing enterprises. This form is only used in cases of privatization, where such a transfer will definitely improve efficiency—for example, through better management, rehabilitation, or expansion under new ownership or synergy with the acquirer's operations.
- Other forms can be discussed with EBRD banking staff.

Equity finance is available from EBRD-supported private equity funds, donor-supported equity funds, and directly from the EBRD. Equity funds support all kinds of investments including business start-ups, expansions, and acquisitions. Some funds specialize in financing companies in need of restructuring, in distressed situations, or mezzanine capital for a later stage. Fund investments generally have a higher prospective return and require longer-term risk capital than standard EBRD projects.

Investment criteria are consistent with EBRD policy, but investment decisions are made by fund managers.

*The EBRD Guarantees*

Through the program ("Trade facility Programme"), the EBRD provides guarantees to international confirming banks, taking the political and commercial payment risk of international trade transactions undertaken by banks in the countries of operations (the issuing banks). The EBRD also provides short-term loans to selected banks and factoring companies for on-lending to local exporters, importers, and distributors. The program can guarantee any genuine trade transaction to, from, and among the countries of operations. In so doing, the program strengthens the ability of local banks to provide trade financing and, through these banks, gives entrepreneurs throughout its countries of operations the support they need to increase their access to their import and export trade.

## THE EBRD's CHALLENGES

Since its inception, the EBRD has performed under the assumption that access of countries to shared prosperity and sustainable development is only possible through market economies, and has neglected to include the legal and social infrastructures in its mandates. In order to remain a trusted partner, the EBRD needs to ensure that its investments are going to countries committed to multiparty democracy. Furthermore, given that most of its borrowing members are now middle-income economies, the EBRD needs to expand its region of operation to more needy countries in order to be more relevant. Last but not least, the EBRD needs to correct its democracy deficit and end the informal agreement between France and Germany as to the choice of its president.

CHAPTER 11

---❈❖❈---

# THE COUNCIL OF EUROPE
# DEVELOPMENT BANK

## GENERAL

Established on April 16, 1956, the Council of Europe Development Bank
(CEB) is a multilateral development bank with a social vocation. Initially
set up to as one of the solutions to the problems of refugees, the CEB is
the oldest pan-European supranational financial institution. All its 40 member states are member of the Council of Europe.[1] Its scope of action has
progressively widened to other sectors of action, directly contributing to
strengthening social cohesion in Europe. The CEB is a major instrument
of the policy of solidarity in Europe, in order to help its 40 member states
achieve sustainable and equitable growth. Since 2012, two of the three rating agencies downgraded the CEB from AAA to AA+, as a consequence of
the downgrading of many CEB member countries and borrowers.[2]

## CORE MISSIONS

The CEB contributes to the implementation of socially oriented investment
projects through three sectoral lines of action, namely:

- strengthening social integration

   For the CEB, to contribute to strengthening social integration and thus to
attack the roots of exclusion means, at an operational level, acting in favor of refugees, migrants, and displaced persons; promoting social housing, job creation,
and preservation; and improving living conditions in urban and rural areas.

- managing the environment

   To contribute to managing the environment means not only systemati-
cally responding to emergency situations in the event of natural or ecological

disasters, but also promoting protection of the environment and preservation of historic and cultural heritage.

- supporting public infrastructure with a social vocation

Supporting the development of public infrastructure with a social vocation in the key sectors of health, education, vocational training, and administrative and judicial public services, in the long term, facilitates more dynamic and more equitable economic and social growth, thus promoting individual fulfilment and collective wellbeing. The CEB enjoys a unique and original position in Europe, both on account of the nature of the projects it finances, the sectors in which it undertakes its action, and the geographic scope of its shareholder base.

## THE ORGANIZATIONAL STRUCTURE OF THE CEB

Under Article VIII of the Articles of Agreement, the CEB is organized, administered, and controlled as follow:

### The Governing Board

The powers of the governing board are described in Article IX of the Articles of Agreement. It consists of a chairman, and one representative for each member state. The governing board sets out the general orientations for the CEB's activity, lays down the conditions for CEB membership, decides on capital increases, and approves the annual report, the accounts, and the CEB's general balance sheet. It elects its own chairman and the chairman of the administrative council and appoints the governor and the members of the auditing board.

### The Administrative Council

The powers of the administrative council are described in Article X of the Articles of Agreement. The administrative council consists of a chairman, elected by the governing board; and one representative for each member state.

The administrative council exercises the powers delegated to it by the governing board, establishes and supervises operational policies, and approves investment projects submitted by the governments. It votes on the CEB's operating budget.

### The Governor

The powers of the governor are described in Article XI of the Articles of Agreement. The governor is the CEB's legal representative. He/she is the head of the CEB's operational services and is responsible for its staff, under the general supervision of the administrative council.

The governor conducts the CEB's financial policy in accordance with the administrative council's guidelines, and represents the CEB in all its transactions. He/she examines the technical and financial aspects of the requests for financing submitted to the CEB and refers them to the administrative council.

### The Auditing Board

The powers of the auditing board are described in Article XII of the Articles of Agreement. The auditing board is composed of three members appointed by the governing board. It checks the accuracy of the annual accounts after they have been examined by an external auditor.

In accordance with Article XIII of the Articles of Agreement, the secretariat of the organs of the CEB is provided by the "Secretariat of the Partial Agreement on the Council of Europe Development Bank," Council of Europe, Strasbourg.

## THE CEB'S FINANCING

The CEB bases its activity on its own funds and reserves and receives no aid or subsidy from its member states. In 2004, the CEB's total assets amounted to €16.4 billion, and its own funds stood at €4.5 billion.

## THE CEB'S ACTIVITIES

CEB provides long-term lending to its 40 member states' local or regional governments, entities, or financial institutions (public or private), provides technical assistance for project preparation and intervention strategies, and facilitates co-financing.[3] The CEB has three sectoral action lines: (i) strengthening social integration, (ii) managing the environment, and (iii) developing human capital. Projects presented to the CEB should be:

- eligible for CEB financing (i.e., meet sectorial, geographic, and social criteria);
- technically sound;
- financially viable; and
- comply with CEB's environmental and procurement regulations.

### Borrowing from the CEB

The CEB can grant loans (but not subsidies) to its 40 member states[4] to finance projects corresponding to a certain number of sectoral, geographic, social, and financial criteria defined in the CEB's Articles of Agreement and policy for loan and project financing. Potential borrowers (Governments, local or regional authorities, as well as public or private financial institutions) prepare their loan requests in close collaboration with the CEB's services. Although the borrowers are generally the beneficiaries of the financings, they can also act as project promoters on behalf of one or several final beneficiaries. The CEB does not directly finance individuals. It evaluates the debt sustainability of the borrower and, where necessary, of the guarantor. On the basis of the loan request formulated by the borrower, the CEB evaluates the project and its financing plan. Thus, a careful analysis is performed of the socioeconomic impact, technical aspects, costs, institutional and management capacity of the project, as well as of its effects on the environment.

The loan request is then submitted to the administrative council for approval.

Once the project has been approved by the administrative council, a framework loan agreement is signed with the borrower.

The CEB pays particular attention to the quality of the projects it finances, with an aim to optimizing their social impact. Therefore, assistance and monitoring throughout the whole project cycle constitute key factors in the effective implementation of these projects. Once the project's financing has started, the CEB's services carry out regular monitoring and on-site visits in order to verify the physical progress of the works, compliance with costs, implementation of procurement procedures, and achievement of the anticipated social objectives. A completion report is drawn up when the project is concluded.

## Examples of Conducted Projects

The CEB has conducted several projects, among others:

• In Poland[5]

Development of the rental-housing sector, and construction and modernization of 12,500 dwellings for low and middle-income families. Objective: to provide access to dwellings for 41,000 persons, with Bank Gospodarstwa Krajowego (BGK, the state development bank of Poland).

• In Latvia[6]

Improvement of the quality of the Latvian housing stock and increasing the availability of long-term loans for housing. Loans are granted for legal housing entities, private persons or social-housing providers, for the renovation of multistory apartment buildings, repair or purchase of housing, and completion of unfinished buildings for social housing purposes.

• In Bulgaria[7]

Construction of 75 houses for 200 low-income Roma families (1,600 persons), in the district of Slatina in Sofia. The area is underdeveloped, and the majority of houses in this district are illegal, from a regulatory point of view.

## THE CEB's CHALLENGES

The CEB needs to make more precise social targeting of projects feasible, with emphasis on project quality, the blending of grants and loans, as well as good management of risks and uncertainties.[8] It has to entail enhanced co-operation on capacity building with both borrowers and financing partners. Finally, the CEB needs to revisit its organizational structure to bring it in line with its core strategies.

# CHAPTER 12

---⛭---

# THE ASIAN DEVELOPMENT BANK

## GENERAL

The Asian Development Bank (ADB) is an international development finance institution headquartered in Manila, Philippines. Established in 1966, the ADB is owned and financed by its 67 members, of which 48 are from the region and 19 are from other parts of the globe. Georgia joined the ADB in 2007 to become its sixty-seventh member. Its main partners are governments, private sector, non-government organizations, development agencies, community-based organizations and foundations.

## CORE MISSIONS

Under the Agreement which set up the ADB in 1966, the main purposes of the ADB shall be to foster economic growth and co-operation in the region of Asia and the Far East and to contribute to the acceleration of the process of economic development of the developing member countries in the region. As the Asian-Pacific region has so dramatically changed over the next decades, the ADB adjusted its mandate as well. The ADB's mission extends to helping its developing member countries reduce poverty and improve the living conditions and quality of life of their people. Its vision is "An Asia and Pacific Region Free of Poverty." Strategy 2020, launched in 2008, sets ADB's new strategic course emphasizing that poverty reduction can only be sustained if more people are economically productive, economic growth takes place alongside well-managed natural environment, and neighbouring economies work together within larger and freer markets to achieve common interests through common efforts. Strategy 2020 focuses on three distinct but complementary development agendas of the region: inclusive economic growth, environment sustainable growth, and regional integration.

## BASIC STRUCTURE OF THE ADB

The organizational structure of the ADB is made of a board of governors, a board of directors, a president, four vice presidents, and a managing director-general.

### The Board of Governors

The board of governors is the highest level of policy-making body. It is composed of one governor and one alternate governor from each of the 67 member countries. The board of governors holds all the powers of the ADB. Each governor and his alternate represent the member country that selected them for their respective posts. These individuals are usually high-ranking officials from the economic or finance ministries, or central banks, of their appointing member country. The Governors attend an Annual General Meeting held by the board to exercise their decision-making powers.

The board of governors possesses a wide range of non-delegable powers. It is the only authoritative body of the ADB allowed (1) to decide on matters of membership and capital stock; (2) to review the interpretations or applications of the ADB's charter by the board of directors and consider any amendments to that document; (3) to enter into agreements with other international organizations on behalf of the ADB; (4) to elect directors and the president, and determine the terms of their employment; and (5) to manage the ADB's finances.

### The Board of Directors

The board of directors is the second-highest authority at the ADB. Stationed at the ADB headquarters in Manila, Philippines, the board oversees the day-to-day workings of the ADB. The board consists of twelve directors, eight of whom are elected by the governors of the regional member countries. The remaining four directors are selected by the governors of the non-regional member countries. Each director is allowed to select an alternate, provided the alternates are nationals of different member countries.

### The President

The president chairs the board of directors. The president is the highest-ranking member of the ADB's management team, and serves as the its legal representative. Like the directors, the president is elected by the board of governors and can be reelected. The president's main responsibility is to ensure that the ADB follows the decisions of the board of directors in its operations. Four vice presidents and one managing director-general assist the president on the management team.

## ENHANCING THE ADB's ORGANIZATIONAL STRUCTURE

While the structure of the ADB does not differ from other development banks or even the Bretton Woods institutions, it still needs to be enhanced in order to better face the global challenges. The structure of the ADB would be better if its Operation Evaluation Department (OED) becomes part of the organizational structure as an ad hoc committee within the board of directors. Such a committee can welcome a permanent expert from either the IFA or the IDA for better coordination. That is, contrary to the IMF and the WBG, projects funded by the ADB would be better tailored to the needs or projects supported, and a quick correction can be made if the project veers off track. Furthermore, given that the OED, in its current format, reports directly to the board of directors and not the ADB's management, its conversion to an ad hoc committee should not be hard to accommodate. In so doing, the ADB will be more accountable to its constituents and assumes success or failures.

## FINANCING OF THE ADB

ADB's funds come from member contributions, issuance of bonds on the world's capital markets, retained earnings from lending operations, and the repayment of loans. Besides, the ADB administers special funds (Japan Special Funds, PRC Regional Cooperation, and Poverty Reduction Fund). The ADB provides concessional loans and grants the same to its member countries. The bulk of its loans are made to public sectors: health, education, and poverty.

## THE ACTIVITIES OF THE ADB

ADB finances loan projects and programs in the territories of its Development Member Countries (DMCs). It also provides technical assistance, grants, guarantees, and equity investments. From the time of its establishment until December 31, 2011, ADB had approved loans, net of terminations and reductions, aggregating $136,999.5 million in its ordinary operations. As of December 31, 2011, the total amount of ADB's loans outstanding, undisbursed balances of effective loans, and loans not yet effective in its ordinary operations was $78,079.3 million.[1]

Since the tripling of its capital base in 2009, the ADB has conducted several operations on infrastructure and trade-related projects and has expanded into trade finance, guarantees, private sector investments, and technical assistance programs. The ADB has also offered a Countercyclical Support Facility (CSF) of $3 billion to fund fast-disbursing crises and offset the diminished external credit available to DMCs; sustain growth; and improve macroeconomic assistance and maintain credit flows into the real economy. The CSF aims to achieve these targets by expanding domestic demand and production, strengthening social protection, facilitating trade, and protecting employment from fresh external shocks.[2] Specific realizations include:[3]

## Almaty–Bishkek Regional Road Rehabilitation

This project aims to develop an integrated and efficient transport system to support sustainable economic growth and poverty reduction. The 245-km road between Almaty, Kazakhstan and Bishkek, Kyrgyz Republic is a key link between the respective business centers of the two countries. The project rehabilitated 204 km of the road in Kazakhstan, and 41 km in the Kyrgyz Republic, supported improvements to customs facilities at the Akzhol–Chu border crossing, and purchased road maintenance equipment for Kazakhstan.

The improvements have reduced travel times by half: what used to be a six-hour journey in summer, and even longer in winter, now takes between 2.5 and three hours. Easier access to Almaty, a bustling regional finance hub, creates new opportunities for the citizens and businesses of Kyrgyz Republic. During the summer of 2006, about one million international tourists visited Issyk-Kul Lake in the Kyrgyz Republic, up from about 300,000 the previous year. More importantly, trade between Kazakhstan and the Kyrgyz Republic at the Akzhol–Chu border crossing on the Almaty–Bishkek road increased by an average annual rate of 38 percent from 2000 to 2007.

## Regional Trade Facilitation and Customs Modernization

In October 2002, ADB approved two loans ($15 million for the Kyrgyz Republic and $10 million for Tajikistan) as part of the Regional Trade Facilitation and Customs Cooperation Program. This program contributed to institutional development in both countries through the improved organizational structure of customs administration, better human resource policies, and the introduction of feedback mechanisms for the public. Additional support was also granted to the Kyrgyz Republic and Tajikistan in the form of project loans amounting to the equivalent value of $7.5 million and $10.7 million, respectively. The core components of these loans are to develop a unified automated information system and border-post infrastructure for the customs administrations of the two countries.

## Southern Transport Corridor Road Rehabilitation Project

This project rehabilitates sections of road between the cities of Osh, Sary Tash, and Irkeshtam in the Kyrgyz Republic. The improvements will revitalize the transport network from the PRC's rapidly expanding economy, through the Kyrgyz Republic, and on to Uzbekistan. The project will reduce the cost of road transport and promote economic growth by increasing opportunities for regional trade and cooperation. The Osh–Sary Tash–Irkeshtam road connects to the Osh– Bishkek road, which is a vital national transportation corridor for the Kyrgyz Republic, as well as to a link to the Bishkek–Almaty road. These interconnecting projects highlight the building block approach and regional perspective of the CAREC Program.

### Regional Power Transmission Interconnection Project

This project will tap Tajikistan's power surplus to meet serious shortfalls in neighboring Afghanistan. The project involves the construction of a 220 kilovolt (kv) double-circuit transmission line linking the hydropower stations on Tajikistan's Vakhsh River to Kunduz in Afghanistan and, ultimately, Kabul. The total net economic benefits from the project are estimated to be $114 million, split almost evenly between the two countries.

## ADB CHALLENGES

The ADB needs to restructure its human resource capital and focuses on economically sound-projects with correct assessment measurements. Its staff performance evaluation system needs to be revised accordingly to include greater emphasis on project implementation, client orientation, innovation and knowledge development, and leveraging of resources.[4] The ADB shall adopt a strategic approach that takes into account the diversity of their development needs and expectations.

# CHAPTER 13

———◦≫◉≪◦———

# THE AFRICAN DEVELOPMENT BANK

## GENERAL

The African Development Bank (AfDB) came into existence on September 10, 1964, founded as part of the pan-African movement at the beginning of decolonization in the mid-twentieth century. Initially headquartered in Khartoum, Sudan, the AfDB was created to "contribute to the development and unity of Africa." The African Development Bank Group consists of (1) the AfDB; (2) the African Development Fund (ADF); and (3) the Nigeria Trust Fund (NTF). The AfDB is owned and overseen by its 79 members (Luxembourg became the seventy-ninth member in May 2014). As of May 31, 2013, there were 53 regional members[1] that held 59.712 percent of the voting power and 26 non-regional members.[2]

## ORGANIZATIONAL STRUCTURE

The organizational structure of the AfDB is composed of (i) the board of governors; (ii) the board of directors, (iii) the president, and (iv) specific departments.

### The Board of Governors

All the powers of the AfDB are vested in the board of governors. In particular, the board shall issue general directives concerning the credit policy of the AfDB.[3] However, the board of governors may delegate to the board of directors all its statutory powers, except the powers to:[4]

a. Decrease the authorized capital stock of the AfDB;
b. Establish or accept the administration of special funds;
c. Authorize the conclusion of general arrangements for cooperation with the authorities of African countries that have not yet attained independent

status, or of general agreements for cooperation with African governments that have not yet acquired membership with the AfDB, as well as of such agreements with other governments and with other international organizations;

d. Elect the president of the AfDB, suspend or remove him from office, and determine his remuneration and conditions of service;

e. Determine the remuneration of directors and their alternates;

f. Select outside auditors to certify the general balance sheet and the statement of profits and losses of the AfDB, or select such other experts as may be necessary to examine and report on the general management of the AfDB;

g. Approve, after reviewing the report of the auditors, the general balance sheet and statement of profit and loss of the AfDB; and

h. Exercise such other powers as are expressly provided for the board in the agreement.

The board of governors retains full powers to exercise authority over any matter delegated to the board of directors.

Each member of the AfDB is represented on the board of governors, and appoints one governor and one alternate governor. Each governor and alternate shall serve for five years, subject to termination of appointment at any time, or to reappointment, at the will of the appointing member.[5] The board meets once a year to review the implementation of past policy decisions and to deliberate on new policy issues initiated by them or by the institution's management. Other meetings of the board of governors shall be called, by the board of directors, whenever requested to by five members of the AfDB, or by members having one-quarter of the total voting power of all members.[6] The quorum for any meeting of the board of governors is the majority of the total number of governors (or their alternates), representing not less than seventy percent of the total voting power of the members.

There are two boards of directors at the AfDB: (i) one for the AfDB, and (ii) another for the ADF.[7]

## The Board of Directors

The AfDB's board of directors consists of twenty individuals, thirteen of whom are selected by the regional (i.e., African) member states of the AfDB. The remaining seven directors are selected by the AfDB's non-regional member states.[8] Individuals elected to serve on the AfDB's board of directors cannot also hold a position on the board of governors. The AfDB's directors are elected for a three-year term, and are reeligible to serve a maximum of two terms.[9] Like the board of governors, the AfDB's board of directors also allows for alternates. Alternate directors are selected by the directors, provided they are not of the same nationality (except for the American director and his or her alternate).

## The African Development Fund Board

The ADF has twelve Directors on its board, all of whom also serve on the AfDB's board. TheADF's Board is comprised of (1) the six directors of the AfDB's board that were selected by the non-regional (i.e., non-African) member states; and (2) half of the remaining twelve directors on the AfDB's Board. The regional directors of the AfDB's Board select the six directors that will serve on the ADF's board from among themselves. The AfDB's president serves as the chairman for both boards of directors.

## The President

The president of the AfDB is elected by a majority of the total voting power of the members, including a majority of the total voting power of the regional members,[10] and shall not be a governor, a director, or alternate for either. The term of office of the president is five years, renewable once.

The president can be suspended or removed from office if the board of governors so decides, by a majority of the total voting power of the members, including a majority of the total voting power of the regional members.

The AfDB president is also the president of the ADF as well as the chairman of the board of directors. In that capacity, he/she determines the organizational structure, functions, and responsibilities, as well as the regional and country representation offices. The president also proposes the appointment of the vice presidents who assist in the day-to-day management of the bank group AfDB to the board of directors.

## PURPOSES OF THE INSTITUTION

The core mission of the AfDB is to contribute to the sustainable economic development and social progress of its regional members either individually or jointly.[11] To implement its purpose, it is allowed to:[12]

- use the resources at its disposal for the financing of investment projects and programs relating to the economic and social development of its regional members,
- undertake, or participate in, the selection, study, and preparation of projects, enterprises, and activities contributing to such development;
- mobilize and increase within Africa, as well as outside Africa, resources for the financing of such investment projects and programs;
- promote public and private capital investment in projects or programs in Africa that are designed to contribute to the economic development or social progress of its regional members;
- provide such technical assistance as may be needed in Africa for the study, preparation, financing, and execution of development projects or programs; and
- undertake such other activities and provide such other services as may advance its purpose.

## CORPORATE GOVERNANCE: VOTING POWER OF MEMBER COUNTRIES

Each AfDB member country has an equal number of basic votes in addition to a number of votes proportionate to its paid-in shares. No member country holds veto powers and, in general, board decisions are made through open discussion and consensus, and less on the exercise of voting powers.

The AfDB Articles of Agreement require a two-thirds majority vote for decisions by the board of governors and the AfDB's board of directors. Should a member country believe an issue presented to either of the boards to be of great importance to it, the agreement allows the member to request that the decision require a 70 percent majority vote. These voting rules appear to empower the regional member countries. As in other RDBs, regional member countries receive economic assistance from the AfDB, while the non-regional member countries contribute the funds that allow the AfDB to render assistance in the first place. The AfDB's voting rules are designed to allow regional member countries shape the assistance they receive from the AfDB to fit their interests and needs, rather than those of the non-regional donor countries. The regional member countries hold two-thirds of the voting power in both the board of governors and the AfDB's board of directors. The rules also require non-regional member countries to cooperate with the regional member countries in order to influence decisions at the AfDB. Additionally, the rules enable regional member countries to unite against an unfavorable proposal by a non-regional member country.

Vote allocation at the AfDB is also unique because it is designed to prevent a single governor or director from controlling the outcome of the decision-making process. Put differently, the AfDB voting arrangement differs from that of the WB. Within the AfDB, countries appear to have less ownership of development assistance: the United States holds 16.41 percent of the voting power, followed by Japan at 7.87 percent, Germany at 4.49 percent, and France and United Kingdom at 4.31 percent. Despite the fact that non-regional member states are the minority shareholders of the AfDB, they nevertheless hold considerable influence over its activities. Not only do they make the key capital contributions as donors, but they often have greater capacity as developed countries to collect more information on AfDB projects than do the representatives of the regional, developing member states on the three AfDB Boards.

### Transparency and Accountability

The AfDB has conducted several reforms to enhance its governance. It has set up (i) the Office of the General Auditor; (ii) the Operation Evaluation Department; and (iii) the Independent Review Mechanism (IRM).

*The Office of the Auditor General*
The overall responsibility is to provide independent, objective assurance and consulting services designed to add value and improve the AfDB's operations.

The Office of the Auditor General is responsible for planning, organizing, directing, and controlling a broad, comprehensive program of auditing both internally and externally including, without limitation, all projects and programs of the AfDB group. The office provides all levels of management with periodic, independent, and objective appraisals and audits of financial, accounting, operational, administrative, and other activities, including identifying possible means of improving accountability, efficiency of operations, and economy in the use of resources.[13] The auditor general reports directly to the president, carries out his/her functions in total independence, and may not be influenced directly or indirectly in how he/she conducts his/her works. The president appoints and removes the auditor general in consultation with the board of directors. The term of his office is five years, renewable once, and he/she shall not be eligible for staff appointment thereafter. The auditor general meets and reports regularly to the president, the Audit and Finance Committee, and the board, on the activities of the office and on the sufficiency of resources.

### The Operations Evaluation Department

The Operations Evaluation Department (OPEV) of the AfDB is an independent unit that reports to the AfDB's Committee on Operations and Development Effectiveness (CODE)—a committee of the AfDB's boards of directors. OPEV serves the AfDB by undertaking independent evaluations of the group's operations, policies, and procedures to ensure learning and accountability and promote development effectiveness. OPEV's independent status helps to ensure the credibility of its work.[14] However, OPEV also seeks to be relevant, responsive, and useful to the AfDB's senior management, technical departments, and country teams, as well as to its regional and nonregional clients and partners.

OPEV undertakes evaluations of completed projects, sector policy reviews, country assistance evaluations, business process reviews, and other studies relevant to theAfDB's policies, operations, and results. Additionally, OPEV is tasked with oversight of the overall evaluation system within the AfDB; internal and external communication of evaluation findings and lessons; and promotion of evaluation capacity development. To ensure that OPEV is operationally independent of management, its director reports directly CODE. CODE maintains oversight of OPEV's work and approves OPEV's work plans. OPEV's budget, once approved by the board, is 'ring fenced' (that is, not subject to the influence or control of the management).

### The Independent Review Mechanism

The IRM's mandate is to provide people adversely affected by a project financed by the AfDB with an independent mechanism through which they can request the AfDB to comply with its own policies and procedures. The IRM intervenes when affected people or communities submit a complaint. In this way, the IRM can be considered as a recourse instrument for project-affected people who have previously been unable to resolve their problems with the AfDB's management. The compliance review is undertaken by an independent group of experts.[15] The CRMU undertakes the problem-solving exercises and out-reach activities to fulfill its mandate and contribute to the AfDB's overall objectives. For public sector projects, the IRM can review compliance with all operational policies and procedures. For the private sector, compliance reviews shall only be undertaken for social and environment policies.

### Combat against Corruption

The AfDB has joined a concerted effort by, the EBRD, the EIB Group, the IMF, the IDB Group, and the WBG to establish a Joint IFI's anti-corruption task force to work toward a consistent and harmonized approach to combat corruption in the activities and operations of the member institutions.[16]

## THE AfDB'S FINANCING

The AfDB's funds are derived from the subscriptions of member countries, borrowings on financial markets, and loan repayments. Its resources also come from special funds including the ADF and the NTF sources. The AfDF provides concessionary resources to low-income regional member countries (numbering 37 in April 2012) with concessionary resources, to boost their productivity and economic growth. Its resources are derived directly from special contributions from states participants, especially non-regional member countries.

Similarly, the NTF, established by the Nigerian Government in 1976, helps the AfDB's most underprivileged member countries by providing them with 2–4 percent interest rate loans repayable in 25 years.

AfDB resources and projects are intended for RMCs. The establishment of the AfDB's new credit policy in 1995 classified RMCs under three categories (A, B, C) on the basis of their country-creditworthiness and GDP-related considerations.

- The first category (A) comprises countries with a per capita GDP of less than US$540 and are only eligible for concessionary resources from the ADF.
- The second category (B) comprises countries with a GDP per capita of between US$540 and US$1,050 and allowed access to a blend of AfDB and ADF resources.
- The third category (C) is made up of middle-income countries with access to only AfDB loans. These countries have a GDP per capita higher than US$1,050.

## THE AfDB ACTIVITIES

The AfDB group finances projects, programs, and studies in multiple sectors such as infrastructure, agriculture, health, education, higher education and training, public utilities, environment, climate change, gender, telecommunications, industry, and the private sector.

Since 1983, the AfDB has also been financing non-project operations, including structural adjustment loans, policy-based reforms and various forms of technical assistance and policy advice. The AfDB has also widened the scope of its activities to cover initiatives such as the New Partnership for Africa's Development (NEPAD), water and sanitation, green growth and HIV/AIDS. The AfDB group is also involved in important initiatives on RMCs debt reduction. It also helps African Countries manage mining contracts through the legal arrangements set up by the AfDB, and improve their governance. A bank staff's "Guidance Note on Governance Rating" has been developed to guide the Bank's country economists and country teams in formulating their assessment of the GR, through the provision of a menu of available sources of information and indicators to inform the assessment of each area.

In line with its long-term strategic vision 2013–2022, the AfDB Group's core operations are focused on the strategic sectors of infrastructure, governance, private sector development, higher education, and regional integration. The creation and dissemination of knowledge-based activities in Africa, the environment climate change and gender equality, which are crosscutting activities, are also taken into consideration in all its operations.

## THE AfDB CHALLENGES

While the overall continent is experiencing a sustainable economic growth, the lack of infrastructures could still erode the progress achieved. To that end, the AfDB has to accompany member countries in their infrastructure-building effort to close the gap. The AfDB has little invested in infrastructure. With the support of non-continent members, the Bank should design a long-term strategy to cope with the infrastructure investment gap.

# Chapter 14

———◆———

# The Latin America
# Development Bank

## General

Established in 1970, the Latin America Development Bank also known as the Corporación Andina de Fomento (CAF) is an international financial institution that promotes a model of sustainable development through credit operations, grants and technical support, and financial structuring to public and private sector projects in Latin America. The Latin American Development bank is composed of eighteen countries in Latin America, the Caribbean and Europe,[1] and fourteen private banks from the Andean region. CAF is based in Caracas, Venezuela, and has offices in Buenos Aires, La Paz, Brasilia, Bogota, Quito, Madrid, Panama City, Lima, and Montevideo. The Institution's shareholders are Argentina, Bolivia, Brazil, Chile, Colombia, Costa Rica, Dominican Republic, Ecuador, Jamaica, Mexico Panama, Paraguay, Peru, Portugal, Spain, Trinidad & Tobago, Uruguay, Venezuela, and 14 private banks within the region.

## The CAF's Core Missions

CAF's activities consist of providing and/or supporting the development of vital physical infrastructure in order to handle the basic needs of its shareholder countries. CAF also supports the processes of integration and international competitiveness in the region, especially aimed at the areas of roadwork, energy, telecommunications, and Latin American river integration.

CAF's participation has led to the rendering of technical assistance and/or financial advice to governments to facilitate the project construction process, by funding key projects that would boost national and regional development, and implementing co-financing and A/B Loans (with the participation of private financiers) to attract more resources toward the sector.

CAF's Comprehensive Development Agenda is aimed at achieving a high level of growth that is sustained, sustainable, and of quality. In terms of infrastructure that agenda is strengthened through the following programs and projects discussed further below.

## ORGANIZATIONAL STRUCTURE OF THE CAF

### The Shareholders' Assembly

The shareholders' assembly is CAF's supreme authority. It meets in regular sessions—once a year, within ninety days after the end of the fiscal year—and in special sessions, if and when needed. The assembly is comprised of series A, B, and C shareholders. It approves the annual report of the board of directors, the audited financial statements, and the allocation of net income. In addition, it elects board members according to the provisions set forth in the Articles of Agreement, appoints external auditors, and examines other issues expressly submitted for its consideration.

### Board of Directors

The board of directors is comprised of representatives of series A, B, and C shareholders. The board establishes CAF's policies, appoints the CEO, and approves credit operations and the annual expense budget. It also approves guarantees, investments and other operations within CAF's mandate. However, approval of certain operations can be delegated to the Executive Committee or the executive president, according to criteria set forth by the board.

### The Executive Committee

The Executive Committee was established by the board of directors in 1971. It is comprised of directors appointed by the shareholders of series A, B, and C and is chaired by the executive president. It approves financial operations within the limits established by the board.

### The Audit Committee

The Audit Committee was established by the board of directors in July 1996. It is comprised of the chairman of the board, who presides over the committee, as well as directors who are elected by the board of directors for a period of two years, and CAF's executive president. The committee recommends the selection and hiring of external auditors and reviews their annual work plan. It also reviews the institution's annual report and financial statements, with the corresponding external auditors' opinion, before their submission to the board and the Shareholders' Assembly, reviews the reports presented by the internal auditors on the structure of internal control systems, the annual portfolio risk management program, and the annual report of its implementation.

## CAF's Corporate Governance

Unlike other regional financial institutions (i.e. Inter-American Development Bank), CAF does not require member countries to be part of the Organization of American States. Latin America country members hold a large majority of shares and voting rights. The voting system is "one director, one vote" regardless of the members' contributions to the capital of the Bank. Therefore decision-making process is more balanced, and less prone to political influence. A plural number of persons representing at least 80 percent of Series "A" shares and 50 percent of the other shares constitute the required quorum for both the regular and special shareholders' meeting.

Another aspect in the governance of the CAF is the delegation of powers between the management and the committees on issues related to lending, operations, and administration. Although CAF directors are statutorily vested with the power to establish and conduct the financial, credit and economic policies of the Bank, they often delegate their powers to ad hoc committees. Crucial among these committees is the ethics committee, which receives and channels complaints related to fraudulent acts related to projects in which CAF participates or its financial operations. All officers, employees and service providers within the organization must remain compliant to the Ethical Conduct Guidelines. Chairman of the Ethics Committee ensures the confidentiality of all submitted information submitted including its source. All deliberations are book recorded.

Moreover, although the President is elected by a majority of the voting power as well as with the approval of the majority of member countries, current president Moreno was the US-supported candidate when he was elected in 2005. Moreno was Colombia's former ambassador to the United States and was a leading proponent of the United States' free trade agreement with Colombia.

## CAF's Financing

CAF obtains most of its funding from global financial markets. The institution promotes sustainable development and regional integration through credit operations, grants and technical support, and offers financial structuring to public and private sector projects in its member countries.

CAF borrows in international capital markets through a funding strategy that aims to diversify the sources of financing and mitigate interest rate and currency risks, while matching the average maturity of its assets and liabilities to maintain sufficient liquidity in its portfolio. CAF obtained its first credit ratings in 1993 from the three main rating agencies, and these have steadily increased, even during several economic crises that hit the region. Currently, CAF is the highest-rated frequent bond issuer in Latin America. Prudent financial policies have made CAF a profitable institution that reinvests, through grants and technical cooperation, in programs and projects to support its member countries. Today, CAF has become the main source of multilateral financing for infrastructure and energy in the region, with approvals of close to US$10 billion at the end of 2012, which represents around 30 percent of the total multilateral lending for Latin America.

## CAF's Core Activities

CAF provides sustainable development and regional integration through an efficient mobilization of resources for a timely provision of multiple financial services—with high value added—to clients in the public and private sectors of the shareholder countries. CAF provides loans and other products or services in the normal course of its activities:

### Loans

Loans represent CAF's main financial tool, and can be short term (one year), medium term (1–5 years), and long term (over five years). There are also different types of loans: commercial loans (pre-shipment and post-shipment) and working capital loans, for projects and limited guarantee loans. The range of projects that CAF may fund varies, and includes plans related to infrastructure for roads, transportation, telecommunications, power generation and transmission, water, and sanitation, as well as those that encourage border development and physical integration between shareholder countries. Eligible transactions for funding by CAF are those that are submitted by the governments of shareholder countries, as well as private or mixed capital sector projects from a wide range of economic sectors.

CAF is also involved in syndicated loans, and co-financing.

### Financial Consultancy

CAF provides financial advisory services to national and regional governments and clients in the private, public, or mixed sectors. The range of advisory services that CAF offers involves defining and structuring financing plans for projects or companies, assisting the public sector in the design and implementation of public bidding processes for construction, operation, and management of infrastructure or public services (public-private partnerships, concessions), assisting the private sector in preparing bids to take part in said public bidding processes, assisting in mergers and acquisitions and company appraisals, among other activities.

### Credit Lines

A credit line allows CAF's customers to request funding for various similar and independent projects during the term thereof. The amount of the credit line and terms of each transaction is established by CAF during the evaluation process. Credit Lines can be short term (one year), medium term (from 1 to 5 years) and, as an exception, long term (more than five years). CAF also acts as a second tier bank, providing credit lines to development finance institutions, private commercial banks, or qualified companies in the productive sectors of the region, so that they can offer funding to specific groups, such as small and medium enterprises (SMEs).

## Structured Financing

CAF's Project Financing is aimed at entities seeking financing operations related to the infrastructure sector that generally come from concession contracts granted by governments. Likewise, these funds are often used to finance mining projects as well as oil and gas exploitation. By adopting these types of financing methods, the organizations promoting the project minimize the impact the project debt would otherwise cause on their financial statements.

## Guarantees and Collaterals

CAF guaranties part of the credit risk of a client's obligation to a third party under the Partial Credit Guarantee (PCG) program, by using sureties and guarantees. Partial guaranties contribute to improving debt issue and loan ratings, and to shaping structured trusts that support the development of capital markets in CAF's shareholder countries.

## Treasury Services

The close relationship that CAF maintains with customers allows it to provide treasury services to meet their needs. The following treasury services are offered by CAF in Latin America:

- checking accounts
- time deposits
- funds management.

## Equity Investments

CAF equity investments take various forms:

- Through investment funds aimed at the acquisition, possession, management, and sale of fixed or variable income securities of companies or infrastructure projects represented in shares or participation certificates issued by those companies.
- Directly through corporate capital to support the production of goods or the delivery of services.
- Through quasi-capital investments, such as subordinate loans, preferred shares, and loans with an option to be converted into shares.

## CAF CHALLENGES

CAF's main challenge remains to be ensuring that its project reach out to the main beneficiaries. To that end, close cooperation with civil society would assist CAF in the targeting and implementation of the projects. CAF needs also to provide assistance or training among its members in order to increase their productivity, since the goal is not only economic growth, but also achieving it in the most efficient and fairest way possible.

# CHAPTER 15

———— ✦※✦ ————

# THE CARIBBEAN DEVELOPMENT BANK

## GENERAL

Established by an agreement signed on October 18, 1969, the Caribbean Development Bank (CDB) is a regional financial institution headquartered at Wildey, St. Michael, Barbados. The CDB entered into operation on January 26, 1970, and came into existence with the aim of contributing to the harmonious economic growth and development of the member countries in the Caribbean, and promoting economic cooperation and integration among them.

## THE CDB's MISSIONS

The CDB pursues several functions, inter alia:

- to assist the borrowing member countries to optimize the use of their resources, develop their economies, and expand production and trade;
- to promote private and public investment, encourage the development of the financial upturn in the region, and facilitate business activity and expansion;
- to mobilize financial resources from both within and outside the region for development;
- to provide technical assistance to its regional borrowing members;
- to support regional and local financial institutions and a regional market for credit and savings;
- to support and stimulate the development of capital markets in the region.

## THE ORGANIZATIONAL STRUCTURE OF THE CDB

The CDB is headed by a board of governors, which delegates oversight of CDB operations to the board of directors, chaired by the president. The president is assisted by two vice presidents.

## The Board of Governors

The board of governors is the highest policymaking body of CDB. That is, all of the powers of CDB are in the hands of the board of governors, which can, unless otherwise provided for, delegate its powers to the board of directors. The board of governors meets once a year in one of its member countries. Matters such as the admission of new members, the change in capital stock, the election of directors and the president, amendments to the charter, and the termination of the operations of the CDB cannot be delegated.

## The Board of Directors

The board of directors is composed of 18 directors who represent the regional members of CDB[1] and six who represent the non-regional members.[2]

Directors hold office for a term of two years and are eligible for selection for a further term or terms of office. Each director appoints an alternate director, who acts on his/her behalf when the director is not present.

The board of directors is responsible for the general policy and direction of the operations of CDB. The board makes decisions concerning loans, guarantees, and other investments by CDB, borrowing programs, technical assistance, and other operations of the CDB. It also approves the administrative budget of the Bank and submits accounts for each financial year for approval by the board of governors. It appoints the Audit and Post-Evaluation Committee, consisting of four of its members, for a term of two years.

## The President

The president is chairman of the board of directors and chief executive officer of the CDB. He conducts, under the direction of the board of directors, the current business of the CDB. The Internal Audit Unit, Office of Risk Management, and the Office of Independent Evaluation are attached to the office of the president.

## The Vice President and Secretary

The vice president (Corporate Services) and bank secretary is responsible for the effective planning, development, and provision of advice and services relating to the Legal Department, Finance and Corporate Planning Department, Information and Technology Solutions Department, Human Resources and Administration Department, and the Bank Secretariat. External relations with member countries, donors, and other international organizations are also within the purview of the vice president (Corporate Services) and bank secretary.

## THE CDB's GOVERNANCE

Each member country nominates one governor and one alternate governor. Each governor casts the votes of the member territory that he/she represents. However, the British overseas territories of Anguilla, British Virgin Islands, Cayman Islands, Montserrat and Turks, and Caicos Islands are regarded together as one member.

## THE CDB's FINANCING

A major responsibility of CDB as a multilateral development bank is the mobilization of investment capital from the international financial community and official development assistance agencies for on-lending to its BMCs. International capital sourcing has a clear justification in terms of aggregate savings-investment gaps. Further justification resides in the superior terms and conditions of CDB's external borrowing as compared with those faced by individual BMCs in international financial markets. In addition to the benefits of a superior loan size, the CDB, with an asset portfolio consisting of credits to individual Caribbean countries, is a de facto country risk pooling entity, thereby minimizing the sum of individual country risks and reducing the risk premium (Bourne 1996). Reduced market interest rates—with long grace periods and maturities—translate into significant cost savings to borrowing members. Moreover, CDB, by virtue of its superior knowledge of local conditions and influence on national economic policies, has become the preferred conduit of donor funds in many instances.

### The CDB's Resource Base

CDB's financial strength has grown considerably since its inception. Its capital base consists of members' subscriptions that are divided into paid up and callable portions. At its inception, the CDB's ordinary capital resources were US$50 million (10,000 shares) evenly divided between paid up and callable capital. Since then, the CDB has had three general capital increases and several special capital increases that were associated with the admission of new members. At the end of 2000, the CDB's subscribed capital amounted to 107,971 shares with a value of US$705 million. Callable-shares represented 78.0 percent while paid-up share capital stood at 22.0 percent.

The CDB's charter stipulates that not less than 60 percent of its total authorized share capital should be held by its regional members and not more than 40 percent by its non-regional members. This was used as the basis for the initial subscription of its regional and non-regional members. Despite these defining parameters regarding ownership structure, it is interesting to note that, in terms of contributions to the CDB's resources, regional members are in the minority.

In terms of the CDB's lending patterns, there has been a deliberate bias in favor of the LDCs. This distribution of funds is consistent with the CDB's mandate, which requires that special attention be paid to less developed countries in the region. On a cumulative basis, LDCs have received a total of 52.7 percent ($1,015.6 million) of total loans, contingent loans, equity, and grants during 1970–2000.

## THE OPERATIONS OF THE CDB

The CDB has a number of policies for each of the sectors in which it operates.[3]

### Poverty Reduction Action Plan

The Poverty Reduction Action Plan (PRAP) is the BMC's approach to the use of Basic Needs Trust Fund (BNTF) grant resources for alleviating, mitigating, and/or reducing poverty in the short to medium term. It details the BMC's poverty level based on an analysis of new or existing data and based on the country's national development priorities and available resources; it indicates priorities and strategies that will be implemented using these resources. The PRAP is the reference document when assessing applications for the disbursement of funds for subprojects under the BNTF. BNTF is a Category "B" project based on CDB's *Environment and Social Review Guidelines*. Under the BNTF, all sub-project applications submitted to CDB include a completed and signed copy of the environmental screening form.

### Disaster Risk Management

The Caribbean region is vulnerable to many different natural hazards, including floods and droughts; tropical storms and hurricanes; landslides; earthquakes; tsunamis and volcanic events. These natural hazards change the natural environment and result in social and economic disruption, trauma, property damage, and loss of life. Climate change resulting from global warming is ongoing, and the Fourth Assessment Report of the Intergovernmental Panel on Climate Change predicts rising temperatures, accentuated sea level rise, changing precipitation patterns, ocean acidification, and more extreme weather events (including stronger hurricanes) for the Caribbean region.

Since 1974, the CDB has been responding to requests from its member countries for assistance with post-disaster rehabilitation. The Disaster Management Strategy and Operational Guidelines, 2009, provide a comprehensive approach to disaster risk management and climate change adaptation.

### Basic Need Trust Fund

The BNTF program provides resources to poor communities to improve access to basic infrastructure services, provide temporary employment, enhance economic activity through skills enhancement, and reduce the economic and social vulnerability to risks that impact on the income and well-being of the beneficiaries. The program is able to respond quickly and through participatory methods that can effectively engage poor communities to assess their assets and determine their priority needs for grant funding.

## THE CDB'S ACTIVITIES IN 2013

In 2013, the CDB recorded a strong recovery in loan approvals and disbursements, due to sustained improvements in global growth, the strengthening of regional economic performance as well as improved efficiencies, and strengthening of internal controls.

Loan approvals totalled US$139 million, a 34 percent increase from US$104 million in 2012. Similarly, total disbursements amounted to US$186 million in 2013, approximately 60 percent above disbursements of US$116 million in 2012.

For Fiscal Years 2013 and 2014, the CDB has granted loans and/or grants to the following member states or the institutions within their control:

- US$16.18 million loan to the government of Barbados in order to improve the international competiveness of Barbados in the area of air cargo;
- US$13.497 million loan and US$114 grant to the government of Antigua and Barbuda in order to improve the access to, quality, and effectiveness of early childhood development and basic education;
- US$2.9 million loan and US$22.1 million grant to the government of the Cooperative Republic of Guyana in order to strengthen its sea and rivers defense systems;
- US$13 million loan and US$160,000 grant to the University of the West Indies (with the guarantee of the Government of St. Lucia) in order to provide greater access and enhance the quality of its tertiary education.

## THE CDB CHALLENGES

CDB needs to foster a climate that is favorable to investments in its sphere of activities, and assist country members design programs that promote macroeconomic stability and private sector growth. This requires an investment in human capital (i.e., skills). It has to revisit some of its priorities and allocate more grants to education and security among its member countries.

# CHAPTER 16

———❦———

# THE ISLAMIC DEVELOPMENT BANK

## GENERAL

The Islamic Development Bank Group (IDB Group) is a multilateral development financing institution comprising five entities:

(i) Islamic Development Bank (IDB); (ii) Islamic Research and Training Institute (IRTI); (iii) Islamic Corporation for the Insurance of Investment and Export Credit (ICIEC); (iv) Islamic Corporation for the Development of the Private Sector (ICD); and (v) International Islamic Trade Finance Corporation (ITFC). This chapter covers only the IDB.

The IDB is an international financial institution established in pursuance of the Declaration of Intent issued by the Conference of Finance Ministers of Muslim Countries held in Jeddah in Dhul Q'adah 1393H, corresponding to December 1973. It is composed of 56 member countries from four continents.[1] The basic condition for membership is that the prospective member country should be a member of the Organisation of Islamic Cooperation (OIC), pay its contribution to the capital of the IDB, and be willing to accept such terms and conditions as may be decided upon by the IDB's board of governors. The IDB's principal office is in Jeddah, in the Kingdom of Saudi Arabia. Four regional offices were opened in Rabat, Morocco (1994), Kuala Lumpur, Malaysia (1994). Almaty, Kazakhstan (1997), and Dakar, Senegal (2008). The IDB also has field representatives in twelve member countries. These are Afghanistan, Azerbaijan, Bangladesh, Guinea Conakry, Indonesia, Iran, Nigeria, Pakistan, Sierra Leone, Sudan, Uzbekistan, and Yemen.

The official language of the IDB is Arabic, but English and French are additionally used as working languages.

## CAPITAL STRUCTURE

Up to the end of 1412H (June 1992), the authorized capital of the IDB was two billion Islamic Dinars (ID).[2] Since Muharram 1413H (July 1992), in accordance with a resolution of the board of governors, it became ID six billion, divided into 600,000 shares having a par value of ID 10,000 each. Its subscribed capital also became ID four billion, payable according to specific schedules and in freely convertible currency acceptable to the IDB. In 1422H, the board of governors, at its annual meeting held in Algeria, decided to increase the authorized capital of the IDB from ID 6 billion to ID 15 billion and the subscribed capital from ID 4.1 billion to ID 8.1 billion. According to the Directive of the Third Extra-Ordinary Session of the OIC Islamic Summit Conference held in Makkah Al-Mukarramah on December 7 & 8, 2005, the capital stock of the IDB was to see a substantial increase, in order to enable it to strengthen its role in providing financial support and technical assistance to its member countries. The board of governors of the IDB, in its thirty-first Annual General Meeting in Kuwait, decided to increase the authorized capital stock of IDB by ID 15 billion to become ID 30 billion and the subscribed capital by ID 6.9 billion to become ID 15 billion.

## ORGANIZATIONAL STRUCTURE

The organizational structure of the IDB is made of (i) the board of governors, (ii) the board of executive directors, (iii) the president, and (iv) the vice presidents.

### The Board of Governors[3]

Each member country is represented on the board by a governor and an alternate governor. Each member has five hundred basic votes plus one vote for every share subscribed. Generally, decisions are taken by the board of governors based on a majority of the voting power represented at the meeting. The board of governors meets once every year to review the activities of the IDB for the previous year and to decide on future policies. In its annual meeting, the board designates a chairman, who holds office until the election of another chairman at the next board meeting. The board of governors is the highest policymaking body. It can delegate powers to the board of executive directors for the general operation of the IDB. However, only the board of governors can deal with issues relating to membership, increase or decrease in the IDB's authorized capital, authorize cooperation agreements with international and regional organizations, election of the president and executive directors, and decide their remuneration.

### The Board of Executive Directors[4]

The board of executive directors (BED) is the body responsible for the direction of the general operations and policies of the IDB and, for this purpose, shall, in addition to the power assigned to it expressly by the Articles of Agreement, exercise all powers delegated to it by the board of governors.

In the current term, the BED is composed of eighteen members: nine executive directors appointed by their countries, which are the main shareholders, while nine others are elected by the governors from other countries. The term of office in the BED is a renewable period of three years.

### The President[5]

The president is the chairman of the Board of Executive Governors. He is elected and ousted from office by a majority vote of the total number of governors, representing no less than two-thirds of the total voting power of the members. The president is elected for five year and may be re-elected. He is the chief executive officer and the legal representative of the IDB.

## THE VICE PRESIDENT(S)[6]

One or more vice presidents are appointed by the BED upon the president's recommendation. In the case of vacancy or incapacity of the president, the vice president or the ranking vice president shall exercise the authority and functions of the president.

## CORPORATE GOVERNANCE

The voting power of each governor is linked to the country's contribution to the IDB's capital stock, with each having 500 votes plus one additional vote for every subscribed share. Any decision of the board of governors and the BED requires a simple majority. No member state holds a veto power. However, Saudi Arabia enjoys an enormous advantage in every decision making process, as it owns almost half of the voting power required for a resolution to be accepted. Saudi Arabia does have a de facto veto, as it is somehow very difficult to approve any project it opposes. Its formal influence in the governance of the IDB is reflected by the fact that the president has always been a Saudi national.

## THE ACTIVITIES OF THE IDB

The IDB exclusively offers financial instruments that are consistent with Sharia law, the most common being interest-free loans, instalment sales, leasings, and financial services referred to as *istisna'a*.

The IDB is mandated by its charter to foster the socioeconomic development of its member countries and Muslim communities in non-member countries, in accordance with the principles of *Shari'ah* (Islamic Law). The IDB is rated "AAA" by Standard and Poors. The IBD Group uses Shariah-compliant modes of finance in project and trade financing operations. The IDB's loan and LDMCs loans modes of financing are highly concessionary. In addition, concessionality on ordinary financing extended to the LDMCs is achieved through combination with Loan or LDMCs Loans mode of financing. After extensive consultation with member countries, the IDB revised the terms and conditions of its ordinary modes of financing in order to reduce cost of financing for beneficiaries in member countries by:

- extending the repayment period for ordinary modes of financing (*Ijara,* Instalment Sale, *Istisna'a*) from 15 years to a maximum of period of 20 years, including a gestation period of 5 years.
- increasing the current financing ceiling per project from ID 35 million to ID 80 million ($114 million) for ordinary modes of financing.
- reducing the current annual markup for ordinary financing from 6 percent to 5.1 percent and to discontinue the rebate for timely repayment, which, in practice, member countries have difficulty qualifying for.

Beside these changes, the IDB provides various services to its members.

## Technical Cooperation Program

The Technical Cooperation Program (TCP) is devoted to the promotion of human resources development in member countries/institutions through the following vehicles:

- exchange of expertise among member countries/institutions,
- organization of familiarization visits for senior officials and study visits to augment their experiences,
- organization of seminars, workshops, and conferences on technical issues related to socioeconomic development, and
- enhancing the skills of technicians, professionals, and officials in mid-level management by providing on-the-job training possibilities in order to enhance their performance and increase their technical and professional capacities.

In general, the TCP is a tripartite cooperative scheme that endeavors to match the capacity needed with the capacity available within the member countries through exchange of skills, expertise, and know-how, by using three-dimensional cooperation, wherein IDB plays the role of financier and coordinator to the provision of capacity needed by the beneficiary country and the capacity available in the provider country.

## Financing of Science and Technology

The IDB announced a new policy in 1426H (2005), under which it would consider approving at least 10 percent of a member country's annual program in the science and technology sector. The IDB supports scientific and technological development in member countries in three distinct areas: (i) assistance to build physical facilities and infrastructures; (ii) forge collaboration and exchange of knowledge through activities such as short-term exchange of experts, on-the-job training, and conferences; and (iii) financing research and development projects by designated centers of excellence.

## Poverty Reduction

The IDB views poverty as having four dimensions that go beyond the scope of income of a nation comprising:

Opportunities—lack of access to the labor market, employment opportunity, mobility problems, and time burdens;

Capabilities—lack of access to public services such as health and education;

Security—vulnerability to economic risks and to civil and domestic violence; and

Empowerment—being without voice and without power at the household, community, and national levels.

While the IDB recognizes the complex issues in defining poverty, it takes the view that the eight Millennium Development Goals (MDGs) agreed upon at the United Nations Millennium Summit in September 2000 are helpful in defining and identifying poverty. These MDGs are now at the center of national development plans and poverty reduction programs, reflecting national ownership and consensus building. The MDGs are also directly compatible with the IDB's 1440H vision. This was in fact amply illustrated through the IDB's participation in one of the thematic debates of the UN General Assembly held in 2006, where it announced the launching of the specific fund and commitment to the goals of MDGs. However, the IDB also retains the freedom to adapt any of the MDGs to suit particular countries' special needs and circumstances.

## THE IDB CHALLENGES

With its great financial capabilities, the IDB needs to act as a network builder for member countries, linking assets and knowledge from the sources of supply to the areas where it is most needed. IDB needs also to embrace global best practices in every aspect of its operations in order to become a world-class organization. Finally, the IDB need to revisit its strategy and focus more in providing substantial economic reforms for the strong and sustainable economic growth of its member states.

# Part III

—❖—

# The International Investment Banks

Sustaining the development of allies through long-term investments has led to many regional trade blocs (i.e., EU) to institute investment banks as a political tool to their overall agenda. The European Investment Bank and the Nordic Investment Bank are clear illustrations of that logic. They aim to sustain investment projects that embrace their stated goals and benefit the local businesses and the overall population. Through their sound expertise and preferential interest rates, they have become alternatives to international investment banks such as Goldman Sachs, Lazard Bank, and many others.

# CHAPTER 17

———❖———

# EUROPEAN INVESTMENT BANK

## GENERAL

The European Investment Bank (EIB), as the bank of the European Union created by the Treaty of Rome in 1958, has the core mission of supporting the balanced and steady development of the EU member states. The EIB is the only International Financial Institution (IFI) fully owned by the EU member states, and represents their interests.[1] The EIB is a powerful instrument to serve the EU external policies and related objectives, which have served the EU well so far.[2] The EIB Group consists of the European Investment Bank and the European Investment Fund (EIF). The EIB is different from MDBs, and its policies and procedures are mainly designed for its core business, which is within the EU.

Under Article 309 of the treaty of Rome, which created the EIB, the EIB operates on a nonprofit basis, as specified by the treaty on the functioning of the EU. The EIB applies sound banking practices in its operations and benefits from a first-class status as a borrower and lender.

In addition to its core activity within the EU, the EIB has been progressively and increasingly active in support of EU's external policies regarding most regions of the world since 1963.

The EIF focuses on innovative financing for SMEs. The EIB is the majority shareholder, with the remaining equity held by the European Union (represented by the European Commission) and other European private and public bodies. As both a bank and an institution of the EU, the EIB dedicates considerable resources to building partnerships aimed at improving the responsiveness of its operations.

## THE EIB'S CORE MISSIONS

The EIB provides finance and expertise for sound and sustainable investment projects that contribute to furthering EU policy objectives. More than 90 percent of the EIB's activity is focused on Europe, but it also implements, as an ancillary, the financial aspects of the EU's external and development policies. The European investment bank supports projects that make a significant contribution to growth, employment, regional cohesion, and environmental sustainability in Europe and beyond, within the six priorities defined in its operational plan. All the projects financed must not only be bankable, but also comply with strict economic, technical, environmental, and social standards.

The role of the EIB outside the EU is to support EU external policies (including enlargement, neighborhood, and development cooperation policies) through its financing operations in support of the economic, social, and environmental sustainability development of partner countries.[3]

## THE EIB'S ORGANIZATIONAL STRUCTURE

The organizational structure of the EIB is composed of (i) the board of governors, (ii) the board of directors, (iii) the president, and (iv) the Audit Committee.

### The Board of Governors

The board of governors comprises ministers designated by each of the 27 member states—usually finance ministers. It lays down credit policy guidelines, approves the annual accounts and balance sheet, and decides on the EIB's participation in financing operations outside the European Union as well as on capital increases. It also appoints the members of the board of directors, the Management Committee, and the Audit Committee.

### The Board of Directors

The board of directors consists of 28 directors, with one director nominated by each member state and one by the European Commission. There are 18 alternates, meaning that some of these positions will be shared by groupings of states. The board of directors has the sole power to take decisions in respect of loans, guarantees, and borrowings. As well as seeing that the EIB is properly run, it ensures that it is managed in keeping with the provisions of the treaty, the statute, and with the general directives laid down by the governors. Its members are appointed by the governors for a renewable period of five years following nomination by the member states, and are responsible solely to the EIB. Furthermore, in order to broaden the professional expertise of the board of directors in certain fields, the board is able to co-opt a maximum of six experts (three directors and three alternates), who participate in the board meetings in an advisory capacity, without voting rights.

Decisions are taken by a majority consisting of at least one-third of the members entitled to vote and representing at least 50% of the subscribed capital. The BoD organizes its activities through specific committees.

• The Board Committee on Remuneration

The Board Committee on Staff Remuneration discusses proposals concerning the EIB's staff budget and related issues, in preparation for the subsequent debates and decisions in the full board session.

• The Board Committee on Risk Policy

The Board Committee on Risk Policy reviews the EIB's policies with respect to credit, market, and liquidity risks, provides opinions to the board of directors as to whether these policies are appropriate, and follows their implementation by reviewing the EIB's risk profile.

• The Board Committee on Equity Participation Policy

The Board Committee on Equity Participation Policy examines the policy issues that arise from direct and indirect equity participations held or acquired by the EIB.

• The Management Committee

The Management Committee is the EIB's permanent collegiate executive body. It has nine members. Under the authority of the President and the supervision of the board of directors, it oversees the day-to-day running of the EIB, prepares decisions for directors, and ensures that these are implemented. The president chairs the meetings of the Management Committee. The members of the Management Committee are responsible solely to the EIB; and are appointed by the board of governors, based on proposals from the board of directors, for a renewable period of six years.

## The President

According to the EIB's statute, the president is also chairman of the board of directors. Since the beginning of the EIB's activities, the emoluments of the members of the Management Committee (president and vice presidents of the EIB) have been modelled on those of the president and vice presidents of the European Commission. As decided by the board of governors, social benefits for members of the Management Committee follow the same principles of analogy as applied to commissioners; as a result, certain benefits are the same as for the staff of the EIB, especially as regards medical insurance.

## The Audit Committee

The Audit Committee is an independent body answerable directly to the board of governors and responsible for verifying that the operations of the EIB have been conducted and that its books are kept in a proper manner. At the time of approval of the financial statements by the board of directors, the Audit Committee issues its statements thereon. The reports of the Audit Committee on the results of its work during the preceding year are sent to the board of governors together with the annual report of the board of directors. The Audit Committee is composed of six members, appointed by the board of governors for a nonrenewable term of office of six consecutive financial years. As the Audit Committee is nonresidential, members do not receive a remuneration from the EIB. For each meeting day of the committee (normally ten per year) in which they participate, members and observers of the Audit Committee receive an indemnity of €1050. In addition, the EIB pays a per diem of €200 as a lump-sum reimbursement for hotel and related expenses to be covered by individual committee members, and reimburses travel expenses.

## THE EIB's FINANCING

EIB's financing capacity is based on its significant ability to raise funds in international capital markets at attractive conditions and pass these benefits on to its counterparts. With the Community Guarantee, the EIB can maintain the gearing ratio of 250 percent without a negative impact on its AAA rating. The Community Guarantee has provided a very high financial leverage when compared to the budget resources allocated as provisions in the EU guarantee fund, which are equal to 9 percent of the net outstanding disbursed amounts. Given that the guarantee has been very rarely called upon and funds have always been recovered in full, the net actual cost for the EU budget has so far been negligible. The appropriateness of the provisioning rate of 9 percent has been studied in a parallel evaluation on the related EU guarantee fund, and has not been examined by the Steering Committee.

## THE EIB's ACTIVITIES

The cooperative ties that the EIB has forged with a number of different groups enable it to (i) ensure optimum interaction between its loans and EU budgetary aid through a number of joint initiatives such as JASPERS and the Risk-Sharing Finance Facility (RSFF), (ii) mobilize sound banking resources for projects by acting as a catalyst for other banks and finance institutions to become involved in EIB funded projects, and (iii) respond to the needs of civil society by ensuring transparency and providing information regarding the Bank's operations.

### Project Loans

The EIB lends to individual projects for which total investment cost exceeds €25 m. These loans can cover up to 50 percent of the total cost for both public and private sector promoters, but, on average, this share is about one-third. Besides individual project the loans, the EIB also finances multi-component, multi annual investment programs using a single "framework loan." This funds a range of projects, usually by a national or local public sector body, most frequently regarding infrastructure, energy efficiency/renewables, transport, and urban renovation.

To be eligible, projects must be in line with the EIB's lending objectives and be economically, financially, technically, and environmentally sound. Financing conditions depend on the investment type and the security offered by third parties (banks or banking syndicates, other financial institutions or the parent company). The EIB loans are assorted with interest payments, which can be fixed, revisable, or convertible (i.e., allowing for a change of interest rate formula during the lifetime of a loan at predetermined periods). In certain cases, the EIB charge fees for project-appraisals, legal services, commitments, non-utilization, and so on.

The functional currency of the EIB is the EURO. However, the EIB can also lend in GBP, US$, JPY, SEK, DKK, CHF, PLN, CZK, and HUF, as well as currencies of candidate countries and other EIB partner countries.

Repayment is normally on a semi-annual or annual basis. Grace periods for capital repayment may be granted for a project's construction phase.

## Intermediated Loans

The EIB makes loans to local banks and other intermediaries which subsequently "on-lend" to the final beneficiaries:

- Small-and-medium-sized businesses
- Mid-Cap businesses
- Large businesses
- Local authorities
- National administrations
- Public sector bodies.

All intermediated loans must meet at least one of the EIB's public policy goals, that is, they must enable:

(i) increase in growth and employment potential including SME and Mid-Cap support;
(ii) economic and social cohesion by addressing economic and social imbalances, promoting the knowledge economy/skills, and innovation and linking regional and national transport infrastructure;
(iii) environmental sustainability—including supporting competitive and secure energy supply; or
(iv) action for climate-resilient growth.

Intermediate loan conditions can be flexible in terms of the size, duration, structure, and so on. Lending decisions remain with the intermediary institutions, which also retain the financial risk of the on-lending. The intermediary must transfer a financial advantage reflecting the impact of the funding. The intermediary has to inform the end-client of this.

## Guarantees and Securitization

The EIB guarantees large and small projects to make them more attractive to other investors. They provide guarantees for senior and subordinated debt, either in a standard form or as a debt service guarantee similar to that offered by monoline insurers. Beneficiaries can be large private and public projects or partner intermediaries providing SME financing. Depending on the underlying funding structure of the operation, a guarantee may be more attractive than a loan. It may either provide greater value-added or require lower capital charges. Under capital adequacy rules, EIB guarantees provide a zero risk weightage to the guaranteed obligation. The Loan Guarantee Instrument for Trans-European Network Transport (LGTT) is designed to guarantee medium term revenue risks from public-private partnership transport schemes. Risk sharing instruments are also used in the SME funding schemes JEREMIE and CIP schemes, as well as complementing the Risk Sharing Finance Facility (RSFF), which boosts research, development and innovation.

## Venture Capital

The EIB finances venture capital funds and security packages for funds as well as offering conditional and subordinated loans. It bridges market gaps by working with the financial sector in each EU country. The venture capital activity is managed by the EIF, part of the EIB Group. The EIF sets up, manages, and advises venture capital fund-of-funds, most of which are entrusted by third parties such as the EIB, the European Commission, the Member States and regional authorities.

The EIB helps venture capital and private equity fund managers provide risk capital to growth SMEs. It also supports investment in funds that target early stage companies developing or using advanced technologies.

## NER300—Green-Tech Demonstration Support

The EIB supports the European Commission as an agent in the implementation of the NER300 initiative: the world's largest funding program for carbon capture and storage demonstration projects and innovative renewable energy technologies. A cooperation agreement details the respective roles of the two institutions in implementing the NER300 decision, notably, as far as it concerns the EIB.

Monetization of the 300 million EU allowances is set aside in the New Entrants Reserve of the EU emissions trading system for the initiative.

## Microfinance

The EIB Group has a longstanding record in microfinance. Since 2000, it has supported microfinancing institutions (MFIs), fund providers, and other industry stakeholders in addressing specific market failures and promoting financing solutions for micro, small, and medium Enterprises and low income self-employed. As of December 2011, the EIB group had €548m in active commitments to about 60 microfinance projects or intermediaries.

Operations are financed from the EIB's own resources or under the European Union's mandates, and uses a combination of financial and non-financial instruments. The EIB Group is to date active in microfinance in three regions: in sub-Saharan Africa, the Caribbean, and the Pacific countries (ACP region); the Mediterranean partner countries and in Europe.

Created in 2008, the Microfinance Centre of Expertise (MCE) acts as the knowledge-sharing platform for EIB professionals from a variety of backgrounds for exchanging and capitalizing on experiences, best practices, and industry developments. Through this joint resource, the EIB participates in various microfinancing sector initiatives

## Projects Financed

In 2012, the EIB lent €52 billion in support of the objectives of the European Union: €45 billion in the member states of the EU and €7 billion in the partner countries (figure 17.1).

Several other projects are within the pipelines of the EIB, including:

*ANDRITZ AG in Germany and Austria*[4]
The project comprises the promoter's European expenditures in research, development, and innovation (RDI) in the field of (i) electromechanical equipment for hydro-power plants (turbines and generators), pumps (e.g.,

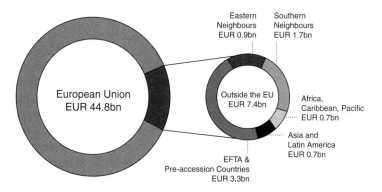

**Figure 17.1**   EIB—Projects Financed.
*Source*: http://www.eib.org/projects/loans/index.htm.

for water transport and irrigation), and turbo-generators for thermal power stations; (ii) systems and equipment for production of pulp; (iii) presses for metal-forming; and (iv) equipment for solid and liquid separation for various industries.

The main project deliverables include improvement of the energy efficiency for the final products, robust design, cost reduction, plant automation, as well as improvement of product-related environmental aspects such as the reduction of the risk of pollution during operation, the use of environmentally-friendly materials, reduced impact on wildlife, and the reduced use of resources and waste.

The R&D activities comprised in the proposed project do not fall under any annexes of the Directive 2011/92/EU; moreover, the project is expected to be carried out in existing facilities already authorized that will not change their scope due to the project and therefore the need for an EIA is unlikely. The EIB's services will however verify the environmental details during the due diligence.

## MEDITERRANEAN RAILWAY CORRIDOR[5]
*(Location: The Kingdom of Spain)*
*Sector: Transportation*
The project concerns the implementation of an interoperable dual gauge railway line along the Spanish Mediterranean coast from Castellbisbal (Barcelona) to Almussafes (Valencia), and the construction of a connection with the high-speed line Madrid-Barcelona-French border.

The project aims at ensuring railway interoperability for rail traffic between the French border and Algeciras in southern Spain along the Spanish Mediterranean coast.

Proposed EIB finance (Approximate amount): €750 million

Total cost (Approximate amount): €1500 million

The project is expected to decrease the negative impacts associated with road traffic and have positive impacts on the environment thanks to the modal transfer to rail.

## VASTERAS MUNICIPAL INVESTMENTS
*(Location: Sweden)*
*Sector(s): Education, Solid waste, Transport, Energy,*
*Services, Water, sewerage*
The project concerns the financing of investment schemes forming part of Municipality of Västerås' four-year investment program from 2014 to 2017.

The project is expected to comprise small to medium-sized schemes in the fields of municipal infrastructure, housing, schools, sports facilities, water and waste management, health infrastructure, and will benefit the Municipality of Västerås and its citizens.

The Proposed EIB finance (Approximate amount) is of SEK 1,800 million (€203 million), while the total cost (Approximate amount): SEK 6097 million (€688 million).

Sweden, as an EU member state, has transposed the Directives 2011/92/ EU and 2001/42/EC into the national environmental legislation. The EIB's appraisal will focus on the promoter's environmental management capacity to properly apply the EU SEA Directive 2001/42/EC, the EU EIA Directive 2011/92/EU, as well as the requirements of the habitats and birds directives, where appropriate. Compliance with the EU Directive on the Energy Performance of Buildings – recast (2010/31/EU) will be further examined during appraisal. All relevant key documents for the project will be published, in line with the EIB's disclosure policy.

### KBC—MID-CAP INITIATIVE
*(Location: Belgium)*
*Sector: Credit lines*
This Mid-Cap Initiative (MCI) operation will be set up as a risk-sharing instrument under the RSFF. The operation will be used to cover 50 percent of the credit risk associated with a portfolio of new loans originated by KBC Bank NV. The guaranteed portfolio will be composed of innovative mid-cap loans having eligible expenditures.

The proposed EIB finance (Approximate amount): €200 million, and the total cost (Approximate amount): Not applicable.

Final beneficiaries will be requested to comply with applicable national and EU legislation, as appropriate.

## THE EIB CHALLENGES

As an the EU's political arm, the EIB needs to reduce its bureaucracy in order to allocate funding more effectively and swiftly to small and medium Enterprises all over Europe. The EIB shall enhance transparency in its lending through financial intermediaries, increase further the transparency and accessibility of its activities, evaluations and outcomes through better access to information, both internally to EIB staff, by incorporating participation at relevant internal EIB meetings, and externally.[6]

# CHAPTER 18

⟦◆⟧

# NORDIC INVESTMENT BANK

## GENERAL

The Nordic Investment Bank (NIB) was established by a first-of-its-kind agreement entered into by the five Nordic countries in 1975. It is multilateral financial institution owned by the five Nordic countries—Denmark, Finland, Iceland, Norway, and Sweden—and operates in 44 countries all over the world.

The NIB is a common international financial institution having the same status as other legal persons conducting similar operations. That is, the capacity to enter into agreements, to acquire and dispose of immovable and movable property, and to be a party to legal proceedings before courts of law and/or other authorities.[1]

The NIB promotes the sustainable growth of its member countries by providing long-term complementary financing, based on sound banking principles, to projects that strengthen competitiveness and enhance the environment. NIB is owned by the five Nordic and the three Baltic countries: Denmark, Estonia, Finland, Iceland, Latvia, Lithuania, Norway, and Sweden. NIB member countries have subscribed authorized capital according to a distribution key based on the eight member countries' gross national income. NIB's authorized capital amounts to approximately € 6,142 million, which consists of paid-in capital and callable capital. The latest decision to increase the capital by € 2,000 million was taken by the board of governors in 2010. In addition to the paid-in and callable capital, the NIB has various reserves.

## NIB's CORE MISSIONS

The core mission of the NIB is to promote the growth of Nordic economies by means of long-term financing of projects in the private and public sectors. The NIB also finances emerging markets outside the Nordic countries.

The NIB is a financier of specific investment projects only, and all potential loans are assessed for their mandated contribution, with only those achieving a sufficiently high score in the internal mandate rating being accepted.

- Since 2001, under ordinary lending, the NIB has two special lending facilities that target the its priority areas: climate change, energy efficiency, and renewable energy facilities (CLEERE).
- NIB facilitates cooperation on and implementation of regional transport infrastructure and logistics projects.

Many projects relate to several sectors, particularly renewable energy, R&D, and transport projects, which often represent both the environment and the other mentioned sectors (energy; transport, logistics, and communications; and innovation).

## NIB's Corporate Governance

The NIB aims at following best practices of good governance. The NIB defines openness, transparency, predictability, accountability, objectivity, responsibility, and disclosure, with due regard to the safeguarding of clients' interests, as the general principles enhancing and further developing good governance.

- Openness

The NIB strives to make information concerning its strategies, policies, and activities available to the public in the absence of a compelling reason for confidentiality in line with the legal provisions of the NIB and the guiding principles of this policy.

- Transparency

The NIB is committed to being transparent in its activities. In so doing, the NIB supports stability on the international markets and in the member countries' economies.

- Accountability

The NIB is accountable to its public and aims to properly manage the funds and resources at its disposal

- Objectivity

The NIB is committed to provide accurate, timely information, And information provided by the NIB shall not be biased. In relation to information on financial activities, NIB applies principles of non-discrimination and simultaneous disclosure through appropriate regulatory channels.

## THE NIB's ORGANIZATIONAL STRUCTURE

The NIB organizational structure is composed of: (i) the board of governors, (ii) the board of directors, (iii) the president, (iv) the Control Committee and Auditors.

### The Board of Governors

The board of governors is the supreme decision-making body and is responsible for, inter alia, matters concerning NIB's agreement, statutes, and authorized capital. The board of governors is composed of eight governors, designated by each member country, respectively from among the ministers in its government. The board of governors appoints a chairman for one year according to a rotation scheme adopted by them.[2] The board of governors also approves the annual report of the board of directors and the audited financial statements of the NIB. Each member country appoints a member of its respective government to the board of governors. The chairmanship rotates among the member countries. The board of governors holds an annual meeting and such other meetings as deemed appropriate.

### The Board of Directors

According to Section 15 of the statutes, the non-resident board of directors consists of eight directors and alternates. One director and one alternate are appointed by each member country. A director and his or her alternate are appointed for a maximum term of four years at a time.

The board of directors makes policy decisions in matters that involve lending, borrowing, and administrative questions. The board of directors approves the financial transactions proposed by NIB's president. The board of directors is responsible for the financial statements, and may delegate its powers to the president to the extent considered appropriate. The board of directors appoints a chairman and a deputy chairman from among the directors. The chairmanship and the deputy chairmanship rotate among the member countries. The board of directors usually meets eight times a year. Except for the exclusive powers vested in the board of governors, all the powers are vested in the board of directors. The board of directors performs, inter alia, the following tasks:

- adopting policy decisions concerning the operations of the NIB;
- appointing the president and deciding on his/her remuneration;
- approving the loans and guarantees proposed by the president;
- authorizing the president under annual general authorizations to carry out borrowings and associated treasury activities;

- approving the principles for financial and cash management and setting limits for the NIB's risk management and risk control;
- deciding upon the annual financial plan and the financial statements;
- submitting proposals to the board of governors on matters that are within the exclusive powers of the board of governors;
- deciding upon other administrative matters outside the scope of the daily operations.

The board of directors can delegate its powers to the president to the extent it considers appropriate.

## The President

The president is appointed by the board of directors for a maximum term of five years at a time. The president shall not be a member of the board of directors, but may be present at the board meetings. He is considered the legal representative of the NIB and is responsible for the conduct of its current operations. The president is responsible for the management of the NIB and for the implementation and proposals for further development of its policies. The president is responsible for managing the risk profile of the NIB as a whole, within the framework set by the board of directors.

## Control Committee and Auditors

The Control Committee is the NIB's supervisory body. It ensures that the operations of the NIB are conducted in accordance with the statutes. The Control Committee is responsible for the audit of the NIB and submits its annual audit report to the board of governors. The Nordic Council and the parliaments of Estonia, Latvia, and Lithuania appointed members to the committee (with one member representing each member country). Furthermore, four members are appointed by the board of governors to serve as chairman and deputy chairman. The chairmanship and the deputy chairmanship rotate among the member countries. The Control Committee appoints two professional external auditors for the purpose of assisting the committee in carrying out its work and responsibilities. One of the professional auditors is appointed from the NIB's host country (Finland) and one from another member country.

Besides the institutions aforementioned, the NIB has established four separate bodies for its operations and administration: (i) the Management Committee, (ii) the Credit Committee; (iii) the Finance Committee; and (iv) the ICT Council, all to assist the president in his/her work.

- The Management Committee

The Management Committee consists of the president and six senior officers whose appointment to the Committee is confirmed by the board of directors. The Management Committee is the forum for addressing policy and management issues. It has the overall responsibility for risk management. The Management Committee meets once or twice a month and in addition as needed. The meetings are chaired by the president, who reaches decisions after consulting with the members of the Committee.

- The Credit Committee

The Credit Committee includes the president and six senior officers appointed to the committee by the board of directors. The Credit Committee is chaired by the president or, in the president's absence, by one of its members. The Credit Committee meets regularly—once a week. The Credit Committee is responsible for the preparation of and decision making on matters related to the lending operations of the NIB. The president exercises his delegated decision-making powers concerning lending operations through the Credit Committee.

- The Finance Committee

The Finance Committee is an advisory body to the president concerning treasury and risk management operations. The Committee monitors the market risk, borrowing activities, and treasury portfolio management of the NIB. The Committee is chaired by the president and consists four members appointed by the president. The Committee meets normally once a month.

- The ICT Council

The ICT Council advises the president in ICT matters. The president however, makes his decisions in ICT matters in the Management Committee. The ICT Council consists of the Head of ICT and of other staff members appointed by the president. The chairman of the ICT Council shall be a member of the Management Committee.

## THE NIB's FINANCING

By February 2011, the total authorized capital of the NIB amounts to approximately € 6,142 million. The authorized capital consists of a paid-in and a callable portion. The member countries have subscribed to the entire amount of the authorized capital in proportion to the their gross national income. The member countries shall pay in a portion corresponding to approximately 6.8 percent of the total authorized and subscribed capital of the NIB.[3] In addition to the paid-in and callable capital, the NIB has various reserves. The NIB's main source of income consists of net interest income, derived from its main business of lending, from the management of the Euro's fixed income portfolio, and from other liquid assets.

## NIB's ACTIVITIES

The NIB grants loans and issues guarantees up to a total amount equivalent to 250 percent of the sum of the authorized capital and accumulated reserves.[4]

In addition to the "ordinary lending" the NIB has two special loan facilities[5]: (i) Project Investment Loans (PIL) and (ii) Environmental Investment Loans (MIL).

### The Project Investment Loans

PILs provide long-term financing to creditworthy projects in emerging markets and the transition economies. The purpose of this loan facility is to promote the internationalization of business and industry, and the projects financed under the facility should be of mutual interest to the member countries and the country receiving such finance[6]. The authorization for the PIL facility is € 4,000 million. The NIB assumes 100 percent of any losses incurred on individual PIL loans, up to the amount available in the Special Credit Risk Fund for PIL (first loss principle). Only thereafter would the NIB be able to call on the member countries' guarantees that support the PIL facility.[7]

### The Environmental Investment Loans

MIL are granted for financing public and private sector environmental projects, of mutual interest, in the neighboring regions of the member countries.[8] The authorization for the MIL facility is € 300 million.[9] The MIL facility is 100 percent guaranteed by the member countries, based on an agreement between the NIB and each individual member country.

In 2011, new loans approved by NIB's board of directors amounted to € 2. Billion, whereas agreed loans increased substantially, reaching € 2.6 billion. Disbursements also increased and reached € 1.9 billion. The key driver for NIB's lending activities is fulfilment of its mandate: to support the competitiveness of its member countries and improve the environmental situation. Projects that comply with the NIB's mandate are above all found in the following sectors: environment; energy; transport, logistics, and communications; and innovation. The share of lending to these sectors accounted for 87 percent of loans agreed and $89 of loans disbursed in 2011. The NIB, however, also provides financing to other sectors of the economy. Loans were made for projects in manufacturing and the service sector as well as through lending programs with financial intermediaries. The amount of loans outstanding increased to €14,153 million by December 31, 2011. The amount of guarantees outstanding was €4 million.

## THE NIB's RISK MANAGEMENT POLICY

NIB assumes a conservative approach to risk taking. Credit risks, market risks, liquidity risks, and operational risks are managed carefully with risk management closely integrated into the business processes. As an international financial institution, NIB is not subject to any national or international banking regulations. The NIB's risk management systems and procedures are reviewed and refined on an ongoing basis in order to comply, in substance, with what the it identifies as the relevant market standards, recommendations, and best practices.

## THE NIB CHALLENGES

The future development of the Nordic-Baltic region is facing some significant challenges. As the Nordic countries are adjusting their welfare models to the changes in the structure in their population, the NIB's business model needs to be revisited or enhanced to keep track with its member countries. The NIB needs to re-shift its investment projects in infrastructure, education, and particularly high technology becomes imperative in the long run. The basis of the Nordic welfare model will change with the ageing of the population.

# CONCLUSION

The International Financial institutions studied in the book tend to perform their assignments on their own. There is almost no structural cooperation platform among the Bretton Woods institutions and the regional development and investment banks.

The Bretton Woods institutions (World Bank and IMF) work together in close cooperation, through regular and frequent interaction of economists and loan officers who work on the same country. Such a coordination is lacking on the global stage. A more coordinated effort among the Bretton Woods institutions, and other regional development and investment banks would be of greater value to their member countries. For instance, yearly joint-sessions among them would provide a better platform to align priorities in different regions whereby they intervene. Through a continuous flow of information exchange (commonly agreed matrix of evaluations and assessments) the Washington, DC institutions and their counterparts, development projects, could move more swiftly and the results assessed in a coordinated way.

# Appendix 1: IMF Code of Conduct for Staff May 6, 2011

Contents

## Introduction

The code of conduct applies to all International Monetary Fund staff. The code outlines in one document the guidelines for staff conduct, which are prescribed in various Fund rules and regulations. It also provides guidance on how to exercise good judgment in ethical matters, and it includes practical examples to illustrate how the rules can be applied.

The code clarifies and expands upon a number of rules. For example, it defines more clearly the obligations of staff as international civil servants with regard to conduct both at work and elsewhere. The section on use and disclosure of information provides clear and practical guidance to staff. The section on financial disclosure strengthens the safeguards needed to ensure that both the International Monetary Fund and its staff are seen as free of any conflict of interest and beyond reproach.

## Preamble

1. The goal of the International Monetary Fund (IMF) require that all who work for the institution observe the highest standards of professional ethics. We all have a responsibility to contribute to the good governance of the IMF and to help maintain its reputation for probity, integrity, and impartiality.

2. This code presents guidelines for staff conduct, which are intended to be consistent with the specific standards of conduct applicable to IMF staff members pursuant to the IMF's -Rules and Regulations.

3. The code outlines obligations of IMF staff. However, the IMF as employer also has the obligation to assist staff in these matters by providing information and advice and by being responsive to staff concerns about ethical issues.

Ethical conduct is not a passive process, but requires you to take conscious choices and decisions, and to exercise good judgment, consistent with the ethical values of the organization embodied in this code. A few basic guidelines to keep in mind:

- always act honestly and impartially when carrying out your duties;
- never make private use of, nor disclose without authorization, any confidential information you obtain through your work for the IEF;
- avoid outside activity that could reasonably be perceived as a conflict of interest; and always treat others in a courteous and professional manner.

4. You may sometimes find that the proper conduct in a given situation is not self-evident. This code can help you decide what to do in many, but not all, situations. When you are in doubt about the ethical implications of an action, seek advice before you act. Consult the documents posted on the IMF Web Service under the heading "Ethics and Staff Conduct." Address any questions to your supervisor or to the Staff Development Division of the Human Resources Department (HRD). And ask yourself these questions:

- Is it legal?
- Does it feel right?
- Will it reflect negatively or positively on me or the IMF?
- What would a reasonable person think about my action?
- Would I be embarrassed if others knew I took this action?
- Is there an alternative action that does not pose an ethical conflict?

5. Failure to observe the IMF's Rules and Regulations may be grounds for disciplinary action by the IMF, which may include termination of employment in the case of serious violations. Disciplinary action may be imposed for such misconduct depending on factors such as the nature and seriousness of the violation and the staff member's prior record of conduct. Before disciplinary action is imposed, staff will be given the opportunity to present his/her views on the alleged misconduct, and, in case of disagreement with the action, may appeal it.

## BASIC STANDARD OF CONDUCT

6. As a staff member, you are expected to observe the highest standards of ethical conduct, consistent with the values of integrity, impartiality and discretion. You should strive to avoid even the appearance of impropriety in your conduct. In the performance of your duties, you have a duty of exclusive loyalty to the IMF, and to its objectives, purposes, and principles.

### Integrity

7. You are expected to act with integrity in all your official activities, avoiding any behavior that would reflect adversely on you or on the IMF. Integrity

encompasses honesty, probity, and loyalty. You are expected to provide accurate and complete information needed by the IMF for the administration of personnel matters, and you must promptly report changes in your personal circumstances that affect your eligibility for benefits and allowances.

8. The IMF respects the privacy of staff members and does not wish to interfere with their personal lives and behavior outside the workplace. However, the status of an international civil servant carries certain obligations as regards conduct, both at work and elsewhere. The IMF attaches great importance to the observance of local laws by staff members, as well as the avoidance of actions that could be perceived as an abuse of the privileges and immunities conferred on the IMF and its staff, as the failure to do so would reflect adversely on the IMF. For example, staff members are expected to meet their private legal obligations to pay child support and alimony, and to comply with applicable laws concerning the treatment of G-5 domestic employees, as this program is available as a special privilege fob international organization personnel. The IMF would also be seriously concerned about notoriously disgraceful conduct by a staff member involving domestic violence or abuse of family members.

9. The IMF is not in a position to investigate allegations that a staff member has violated local law. However, if concerns about a staff member's behavior outside the workplace are brought to its attention by third parties, it is both appropriate and prudent that the staff member be involved about the matter. It is not the IMF's role to determine whether local laws have been violated by a staff member, as that as for the domestic courts to decide. However, if the IMF receives a lawful order from a court or other governmental authority instructing it to withhold an amount of salary to be paid to a staff member to satisfy an outstanding legal obligation, the IMF will not allow the staff member do take undue advantage of the fact that it is immune from such orders.

## Impartiality

10. You are expected to act with impartiality. You should take care that your expression of personal views and convictions does not compromise or appear to compromise the performance of your official duties or the interests of the IMF. Your official connect must at all times be characterized by objectivity and professionalism. You should not allow personal relationships or considerations, including bias or favoritism, to influence the performance of your official duties and you should avoid situations that create a conflict of interest.

## Discretion

11. You should exercise the utmost discretion in your actions and show pact and reserve in your pronouncements in a manner that is consistent with your status as an international civil servant. You should refrain from participating in any activity that is in conflict with the interests of the IMF or would

damage the IMF's reputation. You must respect and safeguard the confidentiality of information which is available or known to you by reason of your official functions.

## CONDUCT WITHIN THE IMF

12. The basic values of impartiality, integrity, and discretion should govern all aspects of your conduct in your work.

### Duty of Loyalty

13. By accepting appointment at the IMF, you have promised do discharge your functions under the sole authority of the Managing Director. You must respect the international character of your position and maintain your independence by not accepting any instructions relating to the performance of your official duties from any national government or from any other co5rces external to the IMF.

### Courtesy and Respect

14. You should treat your colleagues, whether supervisors, peers, or subordinates, with courtesy and respect, without harassment, or physical or verbal abuse. You should at all times avoid behavior at the workplace that, although not rising to the level of harassment or abuse, may nonetheless create an atmosphere of hostility or intimidation.

### Diversity

15. In view of the international character of the IMF and the value that the IMF attaches to diversity, you are expected to act with tolerance, sensitivity, respect, and impartiality toward other persons' cultures and backgrounds.

### Accountability

16. You must act within the scope of your authority at all times. You remain accountable for tasks you delegate to others and you are expected to exercise adequate control and supervision over matters for which you are responsible.

### Use of IMF Property, Facilities, and Supplies

17. You have a responsibility to ensure that IMF resources are used for the official business of the IMF and you are expected to devote your time during working hours to the official activities of the IMF.

18. A rule of reason applies to the personal use of IMF premises or equipment.

## Conflict Resolution

19. Managers have a responsibility to make themselves available to staff members who may wish to raise concerns in confidence and to deal with such situations in an impartial and sensitive manner. Managers should endeavor to create an atmosphere in which staff feels free to use, without fear of reprisal, the existing institutional channels for conflict resolution, and to express concerns about situations which are, or have the potential to be, conflictive.

# USE AND DISCLOSURE OF INFORMATION

## Use and Disclosure of Confidential Information

20. You have a responsibility to protect the security of any confidential information provided to, or generated by, the IMF. Accordingly, to avoid any unauthorized disclosure, you should be careful how you handle confidential information. The basic principle of the rules and guidelines on information security is that confidential information may be communicated among staff only in accordance with the rules/guidelines of document classification and must not be communicated to outsiders without authorization. Such authorization may take the form of either direct instructions from management to individuals or departments, or general policies established by management and the Executive Board. In addition, you must not use any such confidential information for your own advantage, for example, in your private business dealings (see Section V).

## Press Relations, Public Statements, and Publications

21. You should not, without authorization, provide to the news media, publish, or make public statements relating to the policies or activities of the IMF or to any national political question. You are free to publish and speak about other subjects, but you should avoid any public communication not in keeping with your position as an international civil servant, which calls for reserve and tact.

22. Special procedures have been established for handling news media contacts in the IMF. Normally, before responding to or initiating a press contact related to the policies or activities of the IMF or a national political question, you should consult your supervisor, who in turn may need to consult the head of your department and the External Relations Department before you proceed with the contact.

23. The IMF owns the copyright for all written material you produce as part of your official duties, and has the right to publish such work in a manner

it deems appropriate. If the IMF does not choose to publish your work, you may, with the approval of your department and the External Relations Department (EXR), publish your work elsewhere. The same joint approval is required for works (including public statements) prepared on your own time, or prior to joining the IMF staff, if the subject of the work relates to the IMF or its activities, or to any national political question. In contrast, no approval is required if the subject is unrelated to the IMF, its activities, or national political questions.

## CONFLICTS OF INTEREST, INCLUDING PERSONAL FINANCIAL AFFAIRS

### Conflicts of Interest

24. You should avoid any situation involving a conflict, or the appearance of a conflict, between your personal interests and performance of your official duties. In dealings with member country authorities, suppliers, and other parties, you should act in the best interest of the IMF to the exclusion of any personal advantage. To avoid potential conflicts of interest, the IMF will seek to avoid assigning nationals to work on policy issues relating specifically to IMF relations with their home country, unless needed for linguistic or other reasons. This would also apply to non-nationals who, given their individual circumstances, may have a particular conflict of interest vis-à-vis the country or its authorities. If a potential conflict exists, you should make prompt and full disclosure to your supervisor and seek his or her views as to whether you should recuse yourself from the situation that is creating the conflict or the appearance of conflict.

If you are engaged in IMF procurement activities and if you have, or are considering having, any direct or indirect outside interests, financial or otherwise, which might conflict or appear to conflict with the interests of the IMF, you should make this situation known to your supervisor and seek his/her view on whether you should withdraw from participating in the procurement activity.

If you are negotiating for, or have an arrangement concerning, prospective employment outside the IMF, you should maintain an arms-length relationship with the prospective employer in all matters relating to the work of the IMF. For example, you should recuse yourself from involvement in sensitive member country matters that could benefit, or could be perceived to benefit, the prospective employer. Similar conduct is expected of staff who are on temporary secondments to the IMF from their parent institution.

### Personal Financial Affairs

25. You are generally free to conduct your personal financial affairs as you see fit with two exceptions:

because of the IMF's role in exchange rate surveillance, all staff members are prohibited from engaging in short-term trading (i.e., a combination of buying and selling within six months) in gold, foreign currencies and closely related financial instruments, for speculative purposes. The term "combination" does not include one way transactions, such as the selling or buying of foreign exchange for household expenses, education or travel expenses;

staff members are prohibited from using, or providing to others, confidential information to which they have access for purposes of carrying out private financial transactions.

26. As many diverse situations may arise where the general principle mentioned in paragraph 25(b) above could be subject to various interpretations, further guidance is provided below. If you remain unsure on how to proceed in a given situation, you should seek the assistance of the officer designated to this effect by management.

> Confidential information includes market-sensitive information relating to pending IMF or government actions that, when disclosed, are likely to have a material impact on the market value of currency or other investment vehicles. Examples of such market-sensitive information may include information about pending exchange rate or interest rate changes, major fiscal or economic policy changes or initiatives, and, in some cases, pending changes in top government officials or developments in relations with the IMF (e.g., calendar of missions or Board meetings).

> The prohibitions above apply to financial transactions effected by yourselves and by your immediate family members, that is, spouse and dependents.

> The prohibitions above do not apply to pre-existing financial holdings. However, if you hold prior investments in financial assets of a country or group of countries to which you have been newly assigned and with respect to which you are likely to have access to confidential information, you should seek the views of the officer designated to this effect by management who would advise you whether you should divest these assets or refrain from effecting changes in asset positions during your assignment.

## Disclosures

27. You should disclose any financial or business interests that you or your immediate family members have that might be in actual or apparent conflict with your IMF duties. You should make this disclosure to your supervisor or to the officer designated by management for such matters. Supervisors and the officers designated by management should make a written record of the disclosure for the protection of the staff member.

28. All staff members shall certify, according to a periodicity and in a form to be prescribed by the Managing Director, that they have read the policy on conflicts of interest and that they are in compliance. If a staff member is unsure about the extent of his/her compliance, he/she should provide further explanations as provided for in the certification form. In addition,

the Managing Director may require certain categories of staff members to file a confidential statement of financial interests and activities, according to a periodicity and in a form prescribed by the Managing Director. These statements shall be filed with and examined by an officer designated by the Managing Director.

## EXTERNAL ACTIVITIES

29. You need permission from the IMF to engage in any outside employment, occupation, business activity, or profession. The IMF would not object to your engaging in such an activity, provided that (i) it does not interfere with your ability to perform your regular work for the IMF; (ii) it is compatible with the IMF's rules on staff conduct; (iii) it does not create a conflict of interest; and (iv) it does not violate applicable immigration rules. Your request should be cleared with your department and forwarded to HRD, with the endorsement of your department. In some cases, especially activities related to outside publications and speeches, your request will need to be cleared by EXR also.

30. You may participate in volunteer activities of a community or charitable nature without advance clearance. However, if you are in doubt as to whether an activity you are contemplating would run counter to the criteria in (i)-(iv) above, you should seek advice from the Staff Development Division, HRD.

### Political Activities

31. Staff members need permission to engage in political activities, except for activities such as voting, making legal political contributions, and participating at the local, grass roots, or community level. Staff members may not run for elected public office without obtaining permission. A staff member who accepts a political appointment must offer to resign from the IMF staff. The rules for public statements apply if, for example, you wish to make a public statement endorsing a national political candidate.

### Acceptance of Gifts, Decorations, and Honors

32. You should never solicit gifts or favours in connection with your IMF duties. Gifts that are offered should normally be declined. However, you may accept a small gift when it would create an embarrassment to refuse it. Under current rules, if its value is clearly less than $100, you may keep it and need not report it. If the value of the gift could exceed $100, you should report it, along with your estimate of its value. The gift may have to be turned in for an appraisal if there is a question about its value.

33. You are not allowed to accept any honours or decorations given to you in connection with your official duties with the IMF. If there is no advance notice of the honour or decoration, and it is impossible to refuse it, then you may accept it on behalf of the IMF and then report it to the IMF. However,

in cases where the honour or decoration is in recognition of services unrelated to the IMF, the IMF will permit acceptance of such recognition.

## Post-IMF Employment

34. Staff members who separate from the IMF, or are on leave status, including leave without pay, are expected to observe the respective IMF rules on use or disclosure of confidential information. In particular, staff members who separate from the IMF should not use or disclose confidential information known to them by reason of their service with the IMF and should not contact former colleagues to obtain confidential information. IMF employees are prohibited from providing confidential information to former colleagues, who should be treated like any other outside party.

## EXAMPLES

### Basic Standard of Conduct

1. A staff member fails to pay his or her spousal or child support obligations, notwithstanding a court order to do so. Does this violate the IMF's standards of conduct?

Yes. Staff members may not take improper advantage of the fact that the IMF is not subject to mandatory wage garnishments in order to avoid such obligations.

2. A staff member fails to comply with domestic violence laws or a court order regarding visitation rights. Does this violate the IMF's standards of conduct?

Yes. Staff members are required to comply with laws against domestic violence. This includes not only physical assault, but also violent acts and the threat of violent acts to those in the staff member's household. While the IMF will not become involved in purely domestic disputes, as an international organization, the IMF has an interest in ensuring that its staff members do not abuse any immunities, engage in acts of cruelty against household members, or violate court orders.

3. A staff member receives a traffic ticket in the operation of a motor vehicle. Does this violate the IMF's standards of conduct?

No. The type of unlawful conduct that would violate the IMF's standards on private conduct is conduct that is so serious, under the circumstances, that it would embarrass the IMF or call into question a staff member's ability to perform official duties. By contrast, fraud and theft would be serious unlawful acts in violation of the IMF's standards of conduct.

### Conduct within the IMF

4. I am taking orders for Girl Scout cookies on behalf of my daughter. May I ask colleagues whether they wish to place an order?

Yes, so long as there is no coercion or pressure placed on colleagues to make a purchase.

5. I am aware that my colleagues have made false claims on their travel claims following a mission. Should I report this?

You are not under any formal obligation to report unethical behaviour by colleagues. However, should you decide to report an ethical breach by another staff member, you should do so without fear of reprisal. You may also consider raising privately with the colleague your concern about the unethical behaviour. Under no circumstances should you actively participate in, or facilitate the commitment of, an ethical violation by another staff member. Staff should also be aware that malicious and unfounded whistle blowing is not acceptable behavior.

6. A staff member hangs a reproduction in his/her office of a famous painting of a nude. Another employee in an adjacent office reports that this picture makes him/her uncomfortable. Should the staff member be required to remove the painting?

Although not all norms of behavior constitute mandatory rules of conduct, it is nevertheless expected that staff members will avoid actions that could reasonably be deemed to create a hostile work environment or make others uncomfortable in the office. Assuming that this situation meets these criteria, the staff member should be respectful of his/her colleague's feelings and remove the painting.

7. My daughter is away at a university abroad. In order to cut down on the cost of telephone calls, I occasionally send her e-mails from the IMF. Is this a violation of the IMF's rules on conduct?

The primary purpose of the E-mail facilities is for official communications. The use of E-mail at headquarters for personal purposes is permitted as long as this does not encroach on work time, overburden the electronic network, or involve a significant extra expense for the IMF.

8. I am organizing a series of sermons to be delivered in my church by outside speakers. In this connection, I need to make and receive some phone calls. Can I do this from my office?

Yes, as long as the number and duration of such calls are limited and do not interfere with the performance of your duties. Generally, spending a small amount of time on personal calls is permitted within the constraints established by the supervisor. If significant time has to be spent on personal matters, you should make up the time by staying later in the office or you should make the calls during the lunch break. You are required to pay for any long distance calls.

## Use and Disclosure of Information

9. You receive a call from outside the IMF, requesting data on the balance of payments of Country X, as reported in the Recent Economic Developments (RED) for the last Article IV consultation. How do you respond?

You could refer the caller to EXR's public information number (623–7300) or you may provide the data if you know it is in the public domain.

10. You are the desk economist for Country Y, and receive a request from an international bank for information on the status of negotiations on a new IMF arrangement with Country Y. How do you answer?

You may disclose information about the negotiations only to the extent you have been authorized to do so. If you are uncertain as to how far such authorization extends or what is appropriate in the circumstances, you could pass the inquiry to either EXR or to the mission chief (or other senior officer in your area department), who can determine how much information should be disclosed.

11. You are working on Country Z, which has both an arrangement with the IMF and a Structural Adjustment Loan with the World Bank. Your Bank counterpart, seeking clarification of the monetary targets, specifically asks for a copy of the Board paper that incorporates the monetary projections, which he says have been published in a national newspaper in Country Z. How do you respond?

You may not give confidential IMF documents to outsiders, including the World Bank, without prior authorization. The fact that the paper has reportedly been leaked is irrelevant-it is a IMF document, and only the Executive Board can authorize its publication. Your best course of action is to seek guidance from the mission chief, or another senior officer of your department.

12. You are an expert on tax policy and would like to write a letter to the editor of a newspaper regarding a national sales tax. Does your letter need IMF clearance?

Whether your letter to the editor requires IMF clearance depends upon the issues covered and the context in which the letter is being written. This includes whether the author is identified as a IMF staff member, whether the letter could reasonably be expected to have an adverse effect on the policies or activities of the IMF, and whether a national sales tax is a significant issue in the IMF's relations with the country in question (the presumption is that it could be a significant issue).

13. You have expertise (acquired outside the IMF) on the problem of inadequate child care in your city and a local journalist would like to interview you. Do you need to clear this press contact in the IMF?

No, so long as you avoid commenting directly upon national policy issues such as controversies over national budget outlays for child care. If you do intend to touch on such controversies, you may need to seek IMF clearance for your comments in advance depending upon the issue.

14. I am invited to give a talk on the international agreement to ban land mines. Do I need to clear my outline within the IMF?

If this is currently a matter of national political controversy considering the context of the talk, and the content is such that it may reasonably be expected to embarrass the IMF or have an adverse effect on IMF policies and activities, you would need clearance from the IMF before accepting the invitation.

## Conflicts of Interest, Including Personal Financial Affairs

15. I work on emerging Country X, may I acquire mutual funds specialized in:

- this country?
- this region?

You may not if you make this acquisition on the basis of confidential information that you have obtained in the course of your work. For instance, you are prohibited from buying mutual funds if this decision is based on the information of a pending change in interest rates that you have learned about during confidential discussions with the authorities of the country to which you are assigned. In addition to this prohibition, you should not be perceived by a reasonable outsider to have acted on the basis of your access to confidential information in making an acquisition. This is why such acquisitions are generally discouraged. If in doubt, consult the officer designated to that effect by management before undertaking such investment.

16. I work on Country X desk. Do the rules above mean that I may not hold Country X mutual funds, equities, or Treasury bills?

No, they do not prohibit such holdings. They require that you refrain from conducting financial transactions which an outsider could reasonably consider to be influenced by your access to confidential information. As an example, selling Country X Treasury bills shortly after you have been discussing interest rate prospects with the authorities of Country X for your Article IV surveillance work could reasonably be perceived by an outsider to be influenced by confidential information obtained in the course of your work.

17. May I sell gold?

In general, you may, as long as you do not trade in gold. You may not, of course, make use of confidential information obtained in the course of your duties in the IMF as the basis for initiating a sale. Therefore, if you learned, for example, that the IMF was planning to sell gold, you would be prohibited from selling gold prior to the public announcement of a sale of gold by the IMF.

18. May I sell French Francs forward to protect the US dollar value of the proceeds that I am expecting to repatriate to Washington following the sale of my house in France?

Yes, you may. The prohibition stated in paragraph 25(a) (combination of buying and selling within six months) does not apply in this case.

19. I have recently been involved in the assessment of the financial sector of Country X where I came to learn about the financial situation of some commercial banks. Is it all right for me to take either a short or long position in their traded bonds or stocks?

No, it is not. You would be taking advantage of confidential information that you might have obtained in the course of your duties. Even if you had not been entrusted with any such information, others could reasonably perceive you as having been and, for that reason, you should abstain from such trading.

20. A staff member has been recruited by an investment bank. Before his departure, he is asked tm participate in a IMF mission to a country that is undergoing a financial crisis. In the course of this mission, he will no doubt come across confidential information that will be useful to his next employer. Should he go or should he recuse himself?

No, he should not go. This situation creates the appearance of impropriety in light of his imminent plans and it would be difficult or impossible for him to refrain from using information learned during the mission in his next job. He should bring this conflict of interest to the attention of his supervisor, who would be expected not to send him on the mission.

21. I learned through my brother-in-law, who works for a software firm of a new product that firm that may be useful for the IMF. May I arrange a meeting between the software firm and representatives of the IMF?

Yes, so long as you do nothing to influence the IMD's decision whether to acquire the software or otherwise use the products of this firm, as you would have a conflict of interest in dealing with such matters.

## External Activities

22. I have been invited by a university located in the US to teach a course on macroeconomics, for which I would be paid $5,000. Can I accept the invitation?

You can accept this invitation, provided that it is approved by your department, and the HR and that the work, including preparation, is dot done on office time. As prohibited by US law, you may not accept remuneration for the work you are not a US national or a Permanent Resident. (Currently, under US. law G-4, staff can accept "honoraria" of no more than $500 per occasion (no more than two occasions per year)).

23. I am a Resident Representative in Country H and I have been asked by a private investment fund to provide advice on a strategic plan for investment and to receive remuneration for this service. Can I accept this Offer?

· This would create at least the perception of a conflict of interest and perhaps also an actual conflict of interest because you have access to confidential Information.

24. I own an apartment that is currently rented to generate some income. Must I report it to the IMF to avoid violating the rules on outside activities?

No. You may rent your properties without advance clearance, as long as the rental has not become an organized business.

25. May I participate in a lawful public demonstration on an issue not closely related to the work of the IMF, for example, abortion policy or nuclear disarmament, without obtaining advance clearance?

Yes, provided that you participate in a manner that does not publicly identify your connection to the IMF. If, however, you intend to make a public statement on a "national political question," advance clearance is required (see paragraphs 21 through 23 above).

26. May I join and participate in the activities of a non-governmental environmental, animal rights, religious, or civic organization?

You may join both formal and Informal clubs and non-governmental organizations, if you can join and participate without identifying yourself in connection with the IMF, and without bringing embarrassment to the IMF or adversely affecting its interests.

27. May I sign a petition supporting a particular political candidate or endorse a candidate for elected office in my country?

You may sign a petition supporting a political candidate or endorse a candidate for elected office in the country in which you are qualified to vote, or join a political party, if you can do so without publicly identifying yourself in connection With the IMF and without bringing embarrassment to the IMF or adversely affecting its interests.

28. I am invited to accept an honorary degree in connection with my alumni activities and other services unrelated to the IMF. May I accept?

You should seek clearance from The IMF, which will grant permission to staff members to accept honorary degrees awarded in recognition of achievements and services unrelated to the IMF.

# Appendix 2: International Finance Corporation

## Articles of Agreement
### (as Amended through June 27, 2012)

Source: http://www.ifc.org/wps/wcm/connect/1c 95b500484cb68d9f3dbf5f4fc3f18b/IFC _ Articles _ of _ Agreement.pdf?MOD=AJPERES

### INTERNATIONAL FINANCE CORPORATION
## Articles Of Agreement (As amended through June 27, 2012)

The Governments on whose behalf this Agreement is signed agree as follows:

## Introductory Article

The International Finance Corporation (hereinafter called the Corporation) is established and shall operate in accordance with the following provisions:

## Article I
### Purpose

The purpose of the Corporation is to further economic development by encouraging the growth of productive private enterprise in member countries, particularly in the less developed areas, thus supplementing the activities of the International Bank for Reconstruction and Development (hereinafter called the Bank). In carrying out this purpose, the Corporation shall:

(i) in association with private investors, assist in financing the establishment, improvement and expansion of productive private enterprises which would contribute to the development of its member countries by making investments, without guarantee of repayment by the member government concerned, in cases where sufficient private capital is not available on reasonable terms;

(ii) seek to bring together investment opportunities, domestic and foreign private capital, and experienced management; and

(iii) seek to stimulate, and to help create conditions conducive to, the flow of private capital, domestic and foreign, into productive investment in member countries.

The Corporation shall be guided in all its decisions by the provisions of this Article.

## ARTICLE II

### Membership and Capital

*SECTION 1. Membership*

(a) The original members of the Corporation shall be those members of the Bank listed in Schedule A hereto which shall, on or before the date specified in Article IX, Section 2 (c), accept membership in the Corporation.

(b) Membership shall be open to other members of the Bank at such times and in accordance with such terms as may be prescribed by the Corporation.

*SECTION 2. Capital Stock*

(a) The authorized capital stock of the Corporation shall be $100,000,000, in terms of United States dollars.

(b) The authorized capital stock shall be divided into 100,000 shares having a par value of one thousand United States dollars each. Any such shares not initially subscribed by original members shall be available for subsequent subscription in accordance with Section 3 (d) of this Article.

(c) The amount of capital stock at any time authorized may be increased by the Board of Governors as follows:

(i) by a majority of the votes cast, in case such increase is necessary for the purpose of issuing shares of capital stock on initial subscription by members other than original members, provided that the aggregate of any increases authorized pursuant to this subparagraph shall not exceed 10,000 shares;

(ii) In any other case, by a four-fifths majority of the total voting power.

(d) In case of an increase authorized pursuant to paragraph (c)(ii) above, each member shall have a reasonable opportunity to subscribe, under such conditions as the Corporation shall decide, to a proportion of the increase of stock equivalent to the proportion which its stock theretofore subscribed bears to the total capital stock of the Corporation, but no member shall be obligated to subscribe to any part of the increased capital.

(e) Issuance of shares of stock, other than those subscribed either on initial subscription or pursuant to paragraph (d) above, shall require a three-fourths majority of the total voting power.

(f) Shares of stock of the Corporation shall be available for subscription only by, and shall be issued only to, members.

### SECTION 3. *Subscriptions*

(a) Each original member shall subscribe to the number of shares of stock set forth opposite its name in Schedule A. The number of shares of stock to be subscribed by other members shall be determined by the Corporation.

(b) Shares of stock initially subscribed by original members shall be issued at par.

(c) The initial subscription of each original member shall be payable in full within 30 days after either the date on which the Corporation shall begin operations pursuant to Article IX, Section 3 (b), or the date on which such original member becomes a member, whichever shall be later, or at such date thereafter as the Corporation shall determine. Payment shall be made in gold or United States dollars in response to a call by the Corporation which shall specify the place or places of payment.

(d) The price and other terms of subscription of shares of stock to be subscribed, otherwise than on initial subscription by original members, shall be determined by the Corporation.

### SECTION 4. *Limitation on Liability*
### SECTION 5. *Restriction on Transfers and Pledges of Shares*

Shares of stock shall not be pledged or encumbered in any manner whatever, and shall be transferable only to the Corporation.

## ARTICLE III

### Operations

### SECTION 1. *Financing Operations*

The Corporation may make investments of its funds in productive private enterprises in the territories of its members. The existence of a government or other public interest in such an enterprise shall not necessarily preclude the Corporation from making an investment therein.

### SECTION 2. *Forms of Financing*

The Corporation may make investments of its funds in such form or forms as it may deem appropriate in the circumstances.

### SECTION 3. *Operational Principles*

The operations of the Corporation shall be conducted in accordance with the following principles:

(i) the Corporation shall not undertake any financing for which in its opinion sufficient private capital could be obtained on reasonable terms;

(ii) the Corporation shall not finance an enterprise in the territories of any member if the member objects to such financing;

(iii) the Corporation shall impose no conditions that the proceeds of any financing by it shall be spent in the territories of any particular country;

(iv) the Corporation shall not assume responsibility for managing any enterprise in which it has invested and shall not exercise voting rights for such purpose or for any other purpose which, in its opinion, properly is within the scope of managerial control;

(v) the Corporation shall undertake its financing on terms and conditions which it considers appropriate, taking into account the requirements of the enterprise, the risks being undertaken by the Corporation and the terms and conditions normally obtained by private investors for similar financing;

(vi) the Corporation shall seek to revolve its funds by selling its investments to private investors whenever it can appropriately do so on satisfactory terms;

(vii) the Corporation shall seek to maintain a reasonable diversification in its investments.

*SECTION 4. Protection of Interests*

Nothing in this Agreement shall prevent the Corporation, in the event of actual or threatened default on any of its investments, actual or threatened insolvency of the enterprise in which such investment shall have been made, or other situations which, in the opinion of the Corporation, threaten to jeopardize such investment, from taking such action and exercising such rights as it may deem necessary for the protection of its interests.

*SECTION 5. Applicability of Certain Foreign*
*Exchange Restrictions*

Funds received by or payable to the Corporation in respect of an investment of the Corporation made in any member's territories pursuant to Section 1 of this Article shall not be free, solely by reason of any provision of this Agreement, from generally applicable foreign exchange restrictions, regulations and controls in force in the territories of that member.

*SECTION 6. Miscellaneous Operations*

In addition to the operations specified elsewhere in this Agreement, the Corporation shall have the power to:

(i) borrow funds, and in that connection to furnish such collateral or other security therefor as it shall determine; provided, however, that before making a public sale of its obligations in the markets of a member, the Corporation shall have obtained the approval of that member and of the member in whose currency the obligations are to be denominated; if and so long as the Corporation shall be indebted on loans from or guaranteed by the Bank, the total amount outstanding of borrowings incurred or guarantees given by the Corporation shall not be increased if, at the time or as a result thereof, the aggregate amount of debt (including the guarantee of any debt) incurred by the Corporation from any source and then outstanding shall exceed an amount equal to four times its unimpaired subscribed capital and surplus;

(ii)   invest funds not needed in its financing operations in such obligations as it may determine and invest funds held by it for pension or similar purposes in any marketable securities, all without being subject to the restrictions imposed by other sections of this Article;

(iii)  guarantee securities in which it has invested in order to facilitate their sale;

(iv)   buy and sell securities it has issued or guaranteed or in which it has invested;

(v)    exercise such other powers incidental to its business as shall be necessary or desirable in furtherance of its purposes.

### SECTION 7. *Valuation of Currencies*
Whenever it shall become necessary under this Agreement to value any currency in terms of the value of another currency, such valuation shall be as reasonably determined by the Corporation after consultation with the International Monetary Fund.

### SECTION 8. *Warning to be Placed on Securities*
Every security issued or guaranteed by the Corporation shall bear on its face a conspicuous statement to the effect that it is not an obligation of the Bank or, unless expressly stated on the security, of any government.

### SECTION 9. *Political Activity Prohibited*
The Corporation and its officers shall not interfere in the political affairs of any member; nor shall they be influenced in their decisions by the political character of the member or members concerned. Only economic considerations shall be relevant to their decisions, and these considerations shall be weighed impartially in order to achieve the purposes stated in this Agreement.

## ARTICLE IV

### Organization and Management

### SECTION 1. *Structure of the Corporation*
The Corporation shall have a Board of Governors, a Board of Directors, a Chairman of the Board of Directors, a President and such other officers and staff to perform such duties as the Corporation may determine.

*SECTION 2. Board of Governors*

(a) All the powers of the Corporation shall be vested in the Board of Governors.

(b) Each Governor and Alternate Governor of the Bank appointed by a member of the Bank which is also a member of the Corporation shall ex officio be a Governor or Alternate Governor, respectively, of the Corporation. No Alternate Governor may vote except in the absence of his principal. The Board of Governors shall select one of the Governors as Chairman of the Board of Governors. Any Governor or Alternate Governor shall cease to hold office if the member by which he was appointed shall cease to be a member of the Corporation.

(c) The Board of Governors may delegate to the Board of Directors authority to exercise any of its powers, except the power to:

   (i) admit new members and determine the conditions of their admission;

  (ii) increase or decrease the capital stock;

 (iii) suspend a member;

 (iv) decide appeals from interpretations of this Agreement given by the Board of Directors;

  (v) make arrangements to cooperate with other international organizations (other than informal arrangements of a temporary and administrative character);

 (vi) decide to suspend permanently the operations of the Corporation and to distribute its assets;

 (vii) declare dividends;

(viii) amend this Agreement.

(d) The Board of Governors shall hold an annual meeting and such other meetings as may be provided for by the Board of Governors or called by the Board of Directors.

(e) The annual meeting of the Board of Governors shall be held in conjunction with the annual meeting of the Board of Governors of the Bank.

(f) A quorum for any meeting of the Board of Governors shall be a majority of the Governors, exercising not less than two-thirds of the total voting power.

(g) The Corporation may by regulation establish a procedure whereby the Board of Directors may obtain a vote of the Governors on a specific question without calling a meeting of the Board of Governors.

(h) The Board of Governors, and the Board of Directors to the extent authorized, may adopt such rules and regulations as may be necessary or appropriate to conduct the business of the Corporation.

(i) Governors and Alternate Governors shall serve as such without compensation from the Corporation.

*SECTION 3. Voting*

(a) The voting power of each member shall be equal to the sum of its basic votes and share votes.

(i) The basic votes of each member shall be the number of votes that results from the equal distribution among all members of 5.55 percent of the aggregate sum of the voting power of all members, provided that there shall be no fractional basic votes.

(ii) The share votes of each member shall be the number of votes that results from the allocation of one vote for each share of stock held.

(b) Except as otherwise expressly provided, all matters before the Corporation shall be decided by a majority of the votes cast.

*SECTION 4. Board of Directors*

(a) The Board of Directors shall be responsible for the conduct of the general operations of the Corporation, and for this purpose shall exercise all the powers given to it by this Agreement or delegated to it by the Board of Governors.

(b) The Board of Directors of the Corporation shall be composed ex officio of each Executive Director of the Bank who shall have been either (i) appointed by a member of the Bank which is also a member of the Corporation, or (ii) elected in an election in which the votes of at least one member of the Bank which is also a member of the Corporation shall have counted toward his election. The Alternate to each such Executive Director of the Bank shall ex officio be an Alternate Director of the Corporation. Any Director shall cease to hold office if the member by which he was appointed, or if all the members whose votes counted toward his election, shall cease to be members of the Corporation.

(c) Each Director who is an appointed Executive Director of the Bank shall be entitled to cast the number of votes which the member by which he was so appointed is entitled to cast in the Corporation. Each Director who is an elected Executive Director of the Bank shall be entitled to cast the number of votes which the member or members of the Corporation whose votes counted toward his election in the Bank are entitled to cast in the Corporation. All the votes which a Director is entitled to cast shall be cast as a unit.

(d) An Alternate Director shall have full power to act in the absence of the Director who shall have appointed him. When a Director is present, his Alternate may participate in meetings but shall not vote.

(e) A quorum for any meeting of the Board of Directors shall be a majority of the Directors exercising not less than one-half of the total voting power.

(f) The Board of Directors shall meet as often as the business of the Corporation may require.

(g) The Board of Governors shall adopt regulations under which a member of the Corporation not entitled to appoint an Executive Director of the Bank may send a representative to attend any meeting of the Board of Directors of the Corporation when a request made by, or a matter particularly affecting, that member is under consideration.

*SECTION 5. Chairman, President and Staff*

(a) The President of the Bank shall be ex officio Chairman of the Board of Directors of the Corporation, but shall have no vote except a deciding vote in case of an equal division. He may participate in meetings of the Board of Governors but shall not vote at such meetings.

(b) The President of the Corporation shall be appointed by the Board of Directors on the recommendation of the Chairman. The President shall be chief of the operating staff of the Corporation. Under the direction of the Board of Directors and the general supervision of the Chairman, he shall conduct the ordinary business of the Corporation and under their general control shall be responsible for the organization, appointment and dismissal of the officers and staff. The President may participate in meetings of the Board of Directors but shall not vote at such meetings. The President shall cease to hold office by decision of the Board of Directors in which the Chairman concurs.

(c) The President, officers and staff of the Corporation, in the discharge of their offices, owe their duty entirely to the Corporation and to no other authority. Each member of the Corporation shall respect the international character of this duty and shall refrain from all attempts to influence any of them in the discharge of their duties.

(d) Subject to the paramount importance of securing the highest standards of efficiency and of technical competence, due regard shall be paid, in appointing the officers and staff of the Corporation, to the importance of recruiting personnel on as wide a geographical basis as possible.

*SECTION 6. Relationship to the Bank*

(a) The Corporation shall be an entity separate and distinct from the Bank and the funds of the Corporation shall be kept separate and apart from those of the Bank. The provisions of this Section shall not prevent the Corporation from making arrangements with the Bank regarding facilities, personnel and services and arrangements for reimbursement of administrative expenses paid in the first instance by either organization on behalf of the other.

(b) Nothing in this Agreement shall make the Corporation liable for the acts or obligations of the Bank, or the Bank liable for the acts or obligations of the Corporation.

*SECTION 7. Relations with other International Organizations*

The Corporation, acting through the Bank, shall enter into formal arrangements with the United Nations and may enter into such arrangements with other public international organizations having specialized responsibilities in related fields.

*SECTION 8. Location of Offices*

The principal office of the Corporation shall be in the same locality as the principal office of the Bank. The Corporation may establish other offices in the territories of any member.

*SECTION 9. Depositories*
Each member shall designate its central bank as a depository in which the Corporation may keep holdings of such member's currency or other assets of the Corporation or, if it has no central bank, it shall designate for such purpose such other institution as may be acceptable to the Corporation.

*SECTION 10. Channel of Communication*
Each member shall designate an appropriate authority with which the Corporation may communicate in connection with any matter arising under this Agreement.

*SECTION 11. Publication of Reports and Provision of Information*
(a) The Corporation shall publish an annual report containing an audited statement of its accounts and shall circulate to members at appropriate intervals a summary statement of its financial position and a profit and loss statement showing the results of its operations.
(b) The Corporation may publish such other reports as it deems desirable to carry out its purposes.
(c) Copies of all reports, statements and publications made under this Section shall be distributed to members.

*SECTION 12. Dividends*
(a) The Board of Governors may determine from time to time what part of the Corporation's net income and surplus, after making appropriate provision for reserves, shall be distributed as dividends.
(b) Dividends shall be distributed pro rata in proportion to capital stock held by members.
(c) Dividends shall be paid in such manner and in such currency or currencies as the Corporation shall determine.

# ARTICLE V

## Withdrawal; Suspension of Membership; Suspension of Operations

*SECTION 1. Withdrawal by Members*
Any member may withdraw from membership in the Corporation at any time by transmitting a notice in writing to the Corporation at its principal office. Withdrawal shall become effective upon the date such notice is received.

*SECTION 2. Suspension of Membership*
(a) If a member fails to fulfill any of its obligations to the Corporation, the Corporation may suspend its membership by decision of a majority of the Governors, exercising a majority of the total voting power. The member so suspended shall automatically cease to be a member one year from the date of its suspension unless a decision is taken by the same majority to restore the member to good standing.

(b) While under suspension, a member shall not be entitled to exercise any rights under this Agreement except the right of withdrawal, but shall remain subject to all obligations.

## SECTION 3. *Suspension or Cessation of Membership in the Bank*

Any member which is suspended from membership in, or ceases to be a member of, the Bank shall automatically be suspended from membership in, or cease to be a member of, the Corporation, as the case may be.

## SECTION 4. *Rights and Duties of Governments Ceasing to be Members*

(a) When a government ceases to be a member it shall remain liable for all amounts due from it to the Corporation. The Corporation shall arrange for the repurchase of such government's capital stock as a part of the settlement of accounts with it in accordance with the provisions of this Section, but the government shall have no other rights under this Agreement except as provided in this Section and in Article VIII(c).

(b) The Corporation and the government may agree on the repurchase of the capital stock of the government on such terms as may be appropriate under the circumstances, without regard to the provisions of paragraph (c) below. Such agreement may provide, among other things, for a final settlement of all obligations of the government to the Corporation.

(c) If such agreement shall not have been made within six months after the government ceases to be a member or such other time as the Corporation and such government may agree, the repurchase price of the government's capital stock shall be the value thereof shown by the books of the Corporation on the day when the government ceases to be a member. The repurchase of the capital stock shall be subject to the following conditions:

    (i) payments for shares of stock may be made from time to time, upon their surrender by the government, in such installments, at such times and in such available currency or currencies as the Corporation reasonably determines, taking into account the financial position of the Corporation;

    (ii) any amount due to the government for its capital stock shall be withheld so long as the government or any of its agencies remains liable to the Corporation for payment of any amount and such amount may, at the option of the Corporation, be set off as it becomes payable, against the amount due from the Corporation;

    (iii) if the Corporation sustains a net loss on the investments made pursuant to Article III, Section 1, and held by it on the date when the government ceases to be member, and the amount of such loss exceeds the amount of the reserves provided therefore on such date, such government shall repay on demand the amount by which the repurchase price of its shares of stock would have been reduced if such loss had been taken into account when the repurchase price was determined.

(d) In no event shall any amount due to a government for its capital stock under this Section be paid until six months after the date upon which the government ceases to be a member. If within six months of the date upon which any government ceases to be a member the Corporation suspends operations under Section 5 of this Article, all rights of such government shall be determined by the provisions of such Section 5 and such government shall be considered still a member of the Corporation for purposes of such Section 5, except that it shall have no voting rights.

*SECTION 5. Suspension of Operations and Settlement of Obligations*

(a) The Corporation may permanently suspend its operations by vote of a majority of the Governors exercising a majority of the total voting power. After such suspension of operations the Corporation shall forthwith cease all activities, except those incidents to the orderly realization, conservation and preservation of its assets and settlement of its obligations. Until final settlement of such obligations and distribution of such assets, the Corporation shall remain in existence and all mutual rights and obligations of the Corporation and its members under this Agreement shall continue unimpaired, except that no member shall be suspended or withdraw and that no distribution shall be made to members except as in this Section provided.

(b) No distribution shall be made to members on account of their subscriptions to the capital stock of the Corporation until all liabilities to creditors shall have been discharged or provided for and until the Board of Governors, by vote of a majority of the Governors exercising a majority of the total voting power, shall have decided to make such distribution.

(c) Subject to the foregoing, the Corporation shall distribute the assets of the Corporation to members pro rata in proportion to capital stock held by them, subject, in the case of any member, to prior settlement of all outstanding claims by the Corporation against such member. Such distribution shall be made at such times, in such currencies, and in cash or other assets as the Corporation shall deem fair and equitable. The shares distributed to the several members need not necessarily be uniform in respect of the type of assets distributed or of the currencies in which they are expressed.

(d) Any member receiving assets distributed by the Corporation pursuant to this Section shall enjoy the same rights with respect to such assets as the Corporation enjoyed prior to their distribution.

# ARTICLE VI

## Status, Immunities and Privileges

*SECTION 1. Purposes of Articles*

To enable the Corporation to fulfill the functions with which it is entrusted, the status, immunities and privileges set forth in this Article shall be accorded to the Corporation in the territories of each member.

## SECTION 2. *Status of the Corporation*

The Corporation shall possess full juridical personality and, in particular, the capacity:

  (i)  to contract;
 (ii)  to acquire and dispose of immovable and movable property:
(iii)  to institute legal proceedings.

## SECTION 3. *Position of the Corporation with Regard to Judicial Process*

Actions may be brought against the Corporation only in a court of competent jurisdiction in the territories of a member in which the Corporation has an office, has appointed an agent for the purpose of accepting service of process, or has issued or guaranteed securities. No actions shall, however, be brought by members or persons acting for or deriving claims from members. The property and assets of the Corporation shall, wheresoever located and by whomsoever held, be immune from all forms of seizure, attachment or execution before the delivery of final judgment against the Corporation.

## SECTION 4. *Immunity of Assets from Seizure*

Property and assets of the Corporation, wherever located and by whomsoever held, shall be immune from search, requisition, confiscation, expropriation or any other form of seizure by executive or legislative action.

## SECTION 5. *Immunity of Archives*

The archives of the Corporation shall be inviolable.

## SECTION 6. *Freedom of Assets from Restrictions*

To the extent necessary to carry out the operations provided for in this Agreement and subject to the provisions of Article III, Section 5, and the other provisions of this Agreement, all property and assets of the Corporation shall be free from restrictions, regulations, controls and moratoria of any nature.

## SECTION 7. *Privilege for Communications*

The official communications of the Corporation shall be accorded by each member the same treatment that it accords to the official communications of other members.

## SECTION 8. *Immunities and Privileges of Officers and Employees*

All Governors, Directors, Alternates, officers and employees of the Corporation:
  (i)  shall be immune from legal process with respect to acts performed by them in their official capacity;
 (ii)  not being local nationals, shall be accorded the same immunities from immigration restrictions, alien registration requirements and national service obligations and the same facilities as regards exchange restrictions as are accorded by members to the representatives, officials, and employees of comparable rank of other members;

(iii) shall be granted the same treatment in respect of travelling facilities as is accorded by members to representatives, officials and employees of comparable rank of other members.

*SECTION 9. Immunities from Taxation*

(a) The Corporation, its assets, property, income and its operations and transactions authorized by this Agreement, shall be immune from all taxation and from all customs duties. The Corporation shall also be immune from liability for the collection or payment of any tax or duty.

(b) No tax shall be levied on or in respect of salaries and emoluments paid by the Corporation to Directors, Alternates, officials or employees of the Corporation who are not local citizens, local subjects, or other local nationals.

(c) No taxation of any kind shall be levied on any obligation or security issued by the Corporation (including any dividend or interest thereon) by whomsoever held:

  (i) which discriminates against such obligation or security solely because it is issued by the Corporation; or

  (ii) if the sole jurisdictional basis for such taxation is the place or currency in which it is issued, made payable or paid, or the location of any office or place of business maintained by the Corporation.

(d) No taxation of any kind shall be levied on any obligation or security guaranteed by the Corporation (including any dividend or interest thereon) by whomsoever held:

  (i) which discriminates against such obligation or security solely because it is guaranteed by the Corporation; or

  (ii) if the sole jurisdictional basis for such taxation is the location of any office or place of business maintained by the Corporation.

*SECTION 10. Application of Article*

Each member shall take such action as is necessary in its own territories for the purpose of making effective in terms of its own law the principles set forth in this Article and shall inform the Corporation of the detailed action which it has taken.

*SECTION 11. Waiver*

The Corporation in its discretion may waive any of the privileges and immunities conferred under this Article to such extent and upon such conditions as it may determine.

# ARTICLE VII

## Amendments

(a) This Agreement may be amended by vote of three-fifths of the Governors exercising eighty-five percent of the total voting power.

(b) Notwithstanding paragraph (a) above, the affirmative vote of all Governors is required in the case of any amendment modifying:

   (i)   the right to withdraw from the Corporation provided in Article V, Section 1;
   (ii)  the pre-emptive right secured by Article II, Section 2 (d);
   (iii) the limitation on liability provided in Article II, Section 4.

(c) Any proposal to amend this Agreement, whether emanating from a member, a Governor or the Board of Directors, shall be communicated to the Chairman of the Board of Governors who shall bring the proposal before the Board of Governors. When an amendment has been duly adopted, the Corporation shall so certify by formal communication addressed to all members. Amendments shall enter into force for all members three months after the date of the formal communication unless the Board of Governors shall specify a shorter period.

## ARTICLE VIII

### Interpretation and Arbitration

(a) Any question of interpretation of the provisions of this Agreement arising between any member and the Corporation or between any members of the Corporation shall be submitted to the Board of Directors for its decision. If the question particularly affects any member of the Corporation not entitled to appoint an Executive Director of the Bank, it shall be entitled to representation in accordance with Article IV, Section 4 (g).

(b) In any case where the Board of Directors has given a decision under (a) above, any member may require that the question be referred to the Board of Governors, whose decision shall be final. Pending the result of the reference to the Board of Governors, the Corporation may, so far as it deems necessary, act on the basis of the decision of the Board of Directors.

(c) Whenever a disagreement arises between the Corporation and a country which has ceased to be a member, or between the Corporation and' any member during the permanent suspension of the Corporation, such disagreement shall be submitted to arbitration by a tribunal of three arbitrators, one appointed by the Corporation, another by the country involved and an umpire who, unless the parties otherwise agree, shall be appointed by the President of the International Court of Justice or such other authority as may have been prescribed by regulation adopted by the Corporation. The umpire shall have full power to settle all questions of procedure in any case where the parties are in disagreement with respect thereto.

## ARTICLE IX

### Final Provision

*SECTION 1. Entry into Force*
This Agreement shall enter into force when it has been signed on behalf of not less than 30 governments whose subscriptions comprise not less than

75 percent of the total subscriptions set forth in Schedule A and when the instruments referred to in Section 2 (a) of this Article have been deposited on their behalf, but in no event shall this Agreement enter into force before October 1, 1955.

*SECTION 2. Signature*
(a) Each government on whose behalf this Agreement is signed shall deposit with the Bank an instrument setting forth that it has accepted this Agreement without reservation in accordance with its law and has taken all steps necessary to enable it to carry out all of its obligations under this Agreement.
(b) Each government shall become a member of the Corporation as from the date of the deposit on its behalf of the instrument referred to in paragraph (a) above except that no government shall become a member before this Agreement enters into force under Section 1 of this Article.
(c) This Agreement shall remain open for signature until the close of business on December 31, 1956, at the principal office of the Bank on behalf of the governments of the countries whose names are set forth in Schedule A.
(d) After this Agreement shall have entered into force, it shall be open for signature on behalf of the government of any country whose membership has been approved pursuant to Article II, Section 1 (b).

*SECTION 3. Inauguration of the Corporation*
(a) As soon as this Agreement enters into force under Section 1 of this Article the Chairman of the Board of Directors shall call a meeting of the Board of Directors.
(b) The Corporation shall begin operations on the date when such meeting is held.
(c) Pending the first meeting of the Board of Governors, the Board of Directors may exercise all the powers of the Board of Governors except those reserved to the Board of Governors under this Agreement.

DONE at Washington, in a single copy which shall remain deposited in the archives of the International Bank for Reconstruction and Development, which has indicated by its signature below its agreement to act as depository of this Agreement and to notify all governments whose names are set forth in Schedule A of the date when this Agreement shall enter into force under Article IX, Section 1 hereof.

SCHEDULE A Subscriptions to Capital Stock of the International Finance Corporation (Table A.2.1).

**Table A.2.1**    IFC Subscription to Capital Stock

| Country | Number of Shares | Amount (in United States Dollars) |
| --- | --- | --- |
| Australia | 2,215 | 2,215,000 |
| Austria | 554 | 554,000 |
| Belgium | 2,492 | 2,492,000 |
| Bolivia | 78 | 78,000 |
| Brazil | 1,163 | 1,163,000 |
| Burma | 166 | 166,000 |
| Canada | 3,600 | 3,600,000 |
| Ceylon | 166 | 166,000 |
| Chile | 388 | 388,000 |
| China | 6,646 | 6,646,000 |
| Colombia | 388 | 388,000 |
| Costa Rica | 22 | 22,000 |
| Cuba | 388 | 388,000 |
| Denmark | 753 | 753,000 |
| Dominican Republic | 22 | 22,000 |
| Ecuador | 35 | 35,000 |
| Egypt | 590 | 590,000 |
| El Salvador | 11 | 11,000 |
| Ethiopia | 33 | 33,000 |
| Finland | 421 | 421,000 |
| France | 5,815 | 5,815,000 |
| Germany | 3,655 | 3,655,000 |
| Greece | 277 | 277,000 |
| Guatemala | 22 | 22,000 |
| Haiti | 22 | 22,000 |
| Honduras | 11 | 11,000 |
| Iceland | 11 | 11,000 |
| India | 4,431 | 4,431,000 |
| Indonesia | 1,218 | 1,218,000 |
| Iran | 372 | 372,000 |
| Iraq | 67 | 67,000 |
| Israel | 50 | 50,000 |
| Italy | 1,994 | 1,994,000 |
| Japan | 2,769 | 2,769,000 |
| Jordan | 33 | 33,000 |
| Lebanon | 50 | 50,000 |
| Luxembourg | 111 | 111,000 |
| Mexico | 720 | 720,000 |
| Netherlands | 3,046 | 3,046,000 |

continued

**Table A.2.1**   Continued

| Country | Number of Shares | Amount (in United States Dollars) |
|---|---|---|
| Nicaragua | 9 | 9,000 |
| Norway | 554 | 554,000 |
| Pakistan | 1,108 | 1,108,000 |
| Panama | 2 | 2,000 |
| Paraguay | 16 | 16,000 |
| Peru | 194 | 194,000 |
| Philippines | 166 | 166,000 |
| Sweden | 1,108 | 1,108,000 |
| Syria | 72 | 72,000 |
| Thailand | 139 | 139,000 |
| Turkey | 476 | 476,000 |
| South Africa | 1,108 | 1,108,000 |
| United Kingdom | 14,400 | 14,400,000 |
| United States | 35,168 | 35,168,000 |
| Uruguay | 116 | 116,000 |
| Venezuela | 116 | 116,000 |
| Yugoslavia | 443 | 443,000 |
| Total | 1000,000 | 100,000,000 |

*Source*: IFC, http://www.ifc.org/wps/wcm/connect/1c95b500484cb68d9f3dbf5f4fc3f18b/IFC_
Articles_of_Agreement.pdf?MOD=AJPERES.

# Appendix 3: Statutes of the Bank for International Settlements

## (of January 20, 1930; text as amended on March 10, 2003)
### Source: www.bis.org/about/statut.pdf

## Chapter I
### Name, Seat and Objects

*Article 1*

*There is constituted under the name of the Bank for International Settlements (hereinafter referred to as the Bank) a Company limited by shares.*

*Article 2*

The registered office of the Bank shall be situated at Basle, Switzerland.

*Article 3*

The objects of the Bank are: to promote the co-operation of central banks and to provide additional facilities for international financial operations; and to act as trustee or agent in regard to international financial settlements entrusted to it under agreements with the parties concerned.

## Chapter II
### Capital

*Article 4*

(1) The authorized capital of the Bank shall be three thousand million Special Drawing Rights(SDR), as defined from time to time by the International Monetary Fund.

(2) It shall be divided into 600,000 shares of equal nominal value, consisting of three tranches of 200,000 shares each.

(3) The nominal value of each share and the amount remaining to be paid up shall be stated on the face of the share certificates which may be issued by the Bank pursuant to Article 16.

*Article 5*
The two first tranches of 200,000 shares each have already been issued.

*Article 6*
The Board, upon a decision taken by a two-thirds majority, may, when it considers it advisable, issue on one or more occasions a third tranche of 200,000 shares and distribute them in accordance with the provisions of Article 8.

*Article 7*
(1) Twenty-five per cent only of the value of each share shall be paid up at the time of subscription. The balance may be called up at a later date or dates at the discretion of the Board. Three months' notice shall be given of any such calls.
(2) If a shareholder fails to pay any call on a share on the day appointed for payment thereof the Board may, after giving reasonable notice to such shareholder, forfeit the share in respect of which the call remains unpaid. A forfeited share may be sold on such terms and in such manner as the Board may think fit, and the Board may execute a transfer in favor of the person or corporation to whom the share is sold. The proceeds of sale may be received by the Bank, which will pay to the defaulting shareholder any part of the net proceeds over and above the amount of the call due and unpaid.

*Article 8*
(1) The capital of the Bank may be increased or reduced on the proposal of the Board acting by a two-thirds majority and adopted by a two-thirds majority of the General Meeting.
(2) In the event of an increase in the authorized capital of the Bank and of a further issue of shares, the distribution among countries shall be decided by a two-thirds majority of the Board. The central banks of Belgium, England, France, Germany, Italy and the United States of America, or some other financial institution of the last-named country acceptable to the foregoing central banks, shall be entitled to subscribe or arrange for the subscription in equal proportions of at least fifty-five per cent of such additional shares.
(3) In extending invitations to subscribe for the amount of the increase in capital not taken up by the banks referred to in clause (2), consideration shall be given by the Board to the desirability of associating with the Bank the largest possible number of central banks that make a substantial contribution to international monetary co-operation and to the Bank's activities.

*Article 9*
Shares subscribed in pursuance of Article 8 by the banks referred to in clause (2) of that Article may be placed at the Bank's disposal at any time for the

purposes of cancellation and the issue of an equivalent number of shares. The necessary measures shall be taken by the Board by a two-thirds majority.

*Article 10*
No shares shall be issued below par.

*Article 11*
The liability of shareholders is limited to the nominal value of their shares.

*Article 12*
(1) The shares shall be registered and transferable in the books of the Bank.
(2) No share may be transferred without the prior consent of the Bank and of the central bank, or the institution acting in lieu of a central bank, by or through whom the shares in question were issued.

*Article 13*
The shares shall carry equal rights to participate in the profits of the Bank and in any distribution of assets under Articles 51, 52 and 53 of the Statutes.

*Article 14*
The ownership of shares of the Bank carries no right of voting or representation at the General Meeting. The right of representation and of voting, in proportion to the number of shares subscribed in each country, may be exercised by the central bank of that country or by its nominee. Should the central bank of any country not desire to exercise these rights, they may be exercised by a financial institution of widely recognized standing and of the same nationality, appointed by the Board, and not objected to by the central bank of the country in question. In cases where there is no central bank, these rights may be exercised, if the Board thinks fit, by an appropriate financial institution of the country in question appointed by the Board.

*Article 15*
Shares may be subscribed or acquired only by central banks, or by financial institutions appointed by the Board in accordance with the terms and conditions laid down in Article 14.

*Article 16*
The Bank may at its discretion issue share certificates to its shareholders.

*Article 17*
Ownership of shares of the Bank implies acceptance of the Statutes of the Bank.

*Article 18*
The registration of the name of a shareholder in the books of the Bank establishes the title to ownership of the shares so registered.

*Article 18(A)*
*(Transitional provisions)*
In accordance with the resolutions of the Extraordinary General Meeting held on 8 January 2001 and in order to implement Article 15 of the Statutes as amended, the Bank will, on a compulsory basis, repurchase each share which, as of that date, is registered in the name of a shareholder other than a central bank (a "private shareholder"), against payment of compensation of CHF 16,000 for each share, as follows:

(1)  On 8 January 2001, the registration of each private shareholder will be cancelled in the books of the Bank. As from this cancellation, every private shareholder will lose all rights appertaining to shares which are repurchased (including all rights to the payment of any future dividend), subject to the provisions of Article 54; every private shareholder will receive, in exchange for every share which is ipso jure transferred to the Bank, a statutory right to the payment of the amount of compensation referred to above.

(2)  With a view to the payment of the compensation, the Bank will promptly send each private shareholder a notice inviting that private shareholder: (a) to provide written confirmation that he or she has not transferred or otherwise disposed of any share registered on 8 January 2001 in his or her name; (b) to provide written instructions for payment of the compensation by the Bank; and (c) to return the corresponding share certificates to the Bank.

(3)  Upon receiving a complete response to the notice sent out pursuant to Article 18(A)(2), and after it has carried out all appropriate verifications, the Bank will pay each private shareholder the amount of compensation due to that shareholder. If a private shareholder has transferred or otherwise disposed of any share for which he or she is the registered shareholder prior to 8 January 2001, and the Bank is aware of that transfer, the Bank will pay the amount of compensation due from it to the successor in title of the registered shareholder after it has carried out all appropriate verifications. If there is any doubt as to any entitlement to compensation in respect of any share, or if there is no response or only an incomplete response to the notice sent by the Bank pursuant to Article 18(A)(2), the Bank may, on such terms as it may deem appropriate, place in escrow the amount of compensation until such time as the interested parties appropriately establish their rights. Any transfer of a share which has not been notified to the Bank before the date on which the compensation is paid will have no effect with regard to the Bank.

(4)  The Board will redistribute, in the manner in which it considers appropriate, the shares repurchased from private shareholders either (a) by offering them for sale to central bank shareholders against payment of an amount equal to that of the compensation paid to the private shareholders, or (b) by offering them for subscription as bonus shares by central bank shareholders in proportion to the number of shares held (including, if applicable, any share purchased pursuant to (a) above), it being

understood that this redistribution may be achieved by a combination of (a) and (b).

(5) The Board is authorized to take all decisions it deems necessary in connection with the implementation of these transitional provisions, including delegating to the General Manager as appropriate responsibility for practical execution.

## CHAPTER III

### Powers of the Bank

*Article 19*

The operations of the Bank shall be in conformity with the monetary policy of the central banks of the countries concerned.

Before any financial operation is carried out by or on behalf of the Bank on a given market or in a given currency, the Board shall afford to the central bank or central banks directly concerned an opportunity to dissent. In the event of disapproval being expressed within such reasonable time as the Board shall specify, the proposed operation shall not take place. A central bank may make its concurrence subject to conditions and may limit its assent to a specific operation, or enter into a general arrangement permitting the Bank to carry on its operations within such limits as to time, character and amount as may be specified. This Article shall not be read as requiring the assent of any central bank to the withdrawal from its market of funds to the introduction of which no objection had been raised by it, in the absence of stipulations to the contrary by the central bank concerned at the time the original operation was carried out.

Any Governor of a central bank, or his alternate or any other Director specially authorized by the central bank of the country of which he is a national to act on its behalf in this matter, shall, if he is present at the meeting of the Board and does not vote against any such proposed operation, be deemed to have given the valid assent of the central bank in question.

If the representative of the central bank in question is absent or if a central bank is not directly represented on the Board, steps shall be taken to afford the central bank or banks concerned an opportunity to express dissent.

*Article 20*

The operations of the Bank for its own account shall only be carried out in currencies deemed suitable by the Board.

*Article 21*

The Board shall determine the nature of the operations to be undertaken by the Bank.

The Bank may in particular:

(a) buy and sell gold coin or bullion for its own account or for the account of central banks;
(b) hold gold for its own account under earmark in central banks;

(c) accept the custody of gold for the account of central banks;

(d) make advances to or borrow from central banks against gold, bills of exchange and other short-term obligations of prime liquidity or other approved securities;

(e) discount, rediscount, purchase or sell with or without its endorsement bills of exchange, cheques and other short-term obligations of prime liquidity, including Treasury bills and other such government short-term securities as are currently marketable;

(f) buy and sell exchange for its own account or for the account of central banks;

(g) buy and sell negotiable securities other than shares for its own account or for the account of central banks;

(h) discount for central banks bills taken from their portfolio and rediscount with central banks bills taken from its own portfolio;

(i) open and maintain current or deposit accounts with central banks;

(j) accept:

   (i) deposits from central banks on current or deposit account;

   (ii) deposits in connection with trustee agreements that may be made between the Bank and Governments in connection with international settlements;

   (iii) such other deposits as in the opinion of the Board come within the scope of the Bank's functions.

The Bank may also:

(k) act as agent or correspondent of any central bank;

(l) arrange with any central bank for the latter to act as its agent or correspondent. If a central bank is unable or unwilling to act in this capacity, the Bank may make other arrangements, provided that the central bank concerned does not object. If in such circumstances it should be deemed advisable that the Bank should establish its own agency, the sanction of a two-thirds majority of the Board will be required;

(m) enter into agreements to act as trustee or agent in connection with international settlements, provided that such agreements shall not encroach on the obligations of the Bank towards third parties; and carry out the various operations laid down therein.

## Article 22
Any of the operations which the Bank is authorized to carry out with central banks under the preceding Article may be carried out with banks, bankers, corporations or individuals of any country provided that the central bank of that country does not object.

## Article 23
The Bank may enter into special agreements with central banks to facilitate the settlement of international transactions between them.

For this purpose it may arrange with central banks to have gold earmarked for their account and transferable on their order, to open accounts through which central banks can transfer their assets from one currency to another and to take such other measures as the Board may think advisable within the limits of the powers granted by these Statutes. The principles and rules governing such accounts shall be fixed by the Board.

*Article 24*
The Bank may not:

(a)  issue notes payable at sight to bearer;
(b)  "accept" bills of exchange;
(c)  make advances to Governments;
(d)  open current accounts in the name of Governments;
(e)  acquire a predominant interest in any business concern;
(f)  except so far as is necessary for the conduct of its own business, remain the owner of real property for any longer period than is required in order to realize to proper advantage such real property as may come into the possession of the Bank in satisfaction of claims due to it.

*Article 25*
The Bank shall be administered with particular regard to maintaining its liquidity, and for this purpose shall retain assets appropriate to the maturity and character of its liabilities. Its short-term liquid assets may include bank-notes, cheques payable on sight drawn on first-class banks, claims in course of collection, deposits at sight or at short notice in first-class banks, and prime bills of exchange of not more than ninety days' usance, of a kind usually accepted for rediscount by central banks.

The proportion of the Bank's assets held in any given currency shall be determined by the Board with due regard to the liabilities of the Bank.

# CHAPTER IV

## Management

*Article 26*
The administration of the Bank shall be vested in the Board.

*Article 27*
The Board shall be composed as follows:

(1) The Governors for the time being of the central banks of Belgium, France, Germany, Great Britain, Italy and the United States of America (hereinafter referred to as ex-officio Directors).

Any ex-officio Director may appoint one person as his alternate who shall be entitled to attend and exercise the powers of a Director at meetings of the Board if the Governor himself is unable to be present.

(2) Six persons representative of finance, industry or commerce, appointed one each by the Governors of the central banks mentioned in clause (1), and being of the same nationality as the Governor who appoints him.

If for any reason the Governor of any of the six institutions above mentioned is unable or unwilling to serve as Director, or to make an appointment under the preceding paragraph, the Governors of the other institutions referred to or a majority of them may invite to become members of the Board two nationals of the country of the Governor in question, not objected to by the central bank of that country.

Directors appointed as aforesaid, other than ex-officio Directors, shall hold office for three years but shall be eligible for reappointment.

(3) Not more than nine persons to be elected by the Board by a two-thirds majority from among the Governors of the central banks of countries in which shares have been subscribed but of which the central bank does not delegate ex-officio Directors to the Board.

The Directors so elected shall remain in office for three years but may be re-elected.

*Article 28*
In the event of a vacancy occurring on the Board for any reason other than the termination of a period of office in accordance with the preceding Article, the vacancy shall be filled in accordance with the procedure by which the member to be replaced was selected. In the case of Directors other than ex-officio Directors, the new Director shall hold office for the unexpired period only of his predecessor's term of office. He shall, however, be eligible for re-election at the expiration of that term.

*Article 29*
Directors must be ordinarily resident in Europe or in a position to attend regularly at meetings of the Board.

*Article 30*
No person shall be appointed or hold office as a Director who is a member or an official of a Government unless he is the Governor of a central bank and no person shall be so appointed or hold office who is a member of a legislative body unless he is the Governor or a former Governor of a central bank.

*Article 31*

(1) Meetings of the Board shall be held not less than six times a year. At least four of these shall be held at the registered office of the Bank.
(2) In addition, decisions of the Board may be taken by means of teleconferencing or by correspondence, unless at least five Directors request that the decisions be referred to a meeting of the Board.

*Article 32*

A member of the Board who is not present in person at a meeting of Directors may give a proxy to any other member authorizing him to vote at that meeting on his behalf.

*Article 33*

Unless otherwise provided by the Statutes, decisions of the Board shall be taken by a simple majority of those present or represented by proxy. In the case of an equality of votes, the Chairman shall have a second or casting vote.

The Board shall not be competent to act unless a quorum of Directors is present. This quorum shall be laid down in a regulation adopted by a two-thirds majority of the Board.

*Article 34*

The members of the Board may receive, in addition to out-of-pocket expenses, a fee for attendance at meeting and/or a remuneration, the amounts of which will be fixed by the Board, subject to the approval of the General Meeting.

*Article 35*

The proceedings of the Board shall be summarized in minutes which shall be signed by the Chairman. Copies of or extracts from these minutes for the purpose of production in a court of justice must be certified by the General Manager of the Bank.

A record of decisions taken at each meeting shall be sent within eight days of the meeting to every member.

*Article 36*

The Board shall represent the Bank in its dealings with third parties and shall have the exclusive right of entering into engagements on behalf of the Bank. It may, however, delegate this right to the Chairman of the Board, to another member or other members of the Board, to the President of the Bank or to a member or members of the permanent staff of the Bank, provided that it defines the powers of each person to whom it delegates this right.

*Article 37*

The Bank shall be legally committed vis-à-vis third parties either by the signature of the President of the Bank, or by the signatures of two members of the Board or of two members of the staff of the Bank who have been duly authorized by the Board to sign on its behalf.

*Article 38*

The Board shall elect from among its members a Chairman and one or more Vice-Chairmen, one of whom shall preside at meetings of the Board in the absence of the Chairman.

The Board shall elect a President of the Bank. If the President of the Bank is not Chairman of the Board nor a member thereof, he shall nevertheless be entitled to attend all meetings of the Board, to speak, to make proposals to the Board and, if he so desires, to have his opinions specially recorded in the minutes.

The appointments referred to in this Article shall be made for a maximum of three years and may be renewed.

The President of the Bank will carry out the policy decided upon by the Board and will control the administration of the Bank. He shall not hold any other office which, in the judgment of the Board, might interfere with his duties as President.

### Article 39
At the meeting at which the Board elects its Chairman, the Chair shall be taken by the oldest member of the Board present.

### Article 40
A General Manager and a Deputy General Manager shall be appointed by the Board on the proposal of the Chairman of the Board. The General Manager will be responsible to the President of the Bank for the operations of the Bank and will be the chief of its operating staff.

The Heads of Departments and any other officers of similar rank shall be appointed by the Board on recommendations made by the President of the Bank after consultation with the General Manager.

The remainder of the staff shall be appointed by the General Manager with the approval of the President of the Bank.

### Article 41
The departmental organization of the Bank shall be determined by the Board.

### Article 42
The Board may, if it thinks fit, appoint from among its members an Executive Committee to assist the President of the Bank in the administration of the Bank.

The President of the Bank shall be a member of this Committee.

### Article 43
The Board may appoint Advisory Committees chosen wholly or partly from persons not concerned in the Bank's management.

## CHAPTER V
### General Meeting

### Article 44
General Meetings of the Bank may be attended by nominees of the central banks or other financial institutions referred to in Article 14.

Voting rights shall be in proportion to the number of shares subscribed in the country of each institution represented at the meeting.

The Chair shall be taken at General Meetings by the Chairman of the Board or in his absence by a Vice-Chairman.

At least three weeks' notice of General Meetings shall be given to those entitled to be represented. Subject to the provisions of these Statutes, the General Meeting shall decide upon its own procedure.

*Article 45*
Within four months of the end of each financial year of the Bank, an Annual General Meeting shall be held upon such date as the Board may decide. The meeting shall take place at the registered office of the Bank. Voting by proxy will be permitted in such manner as the Board may have provided in advance by regulation.

*Article 46*
The Annual General Meeting shall be invited:

(a)  to approve the Annual Report, the Balance Sheet upon the Report of the Auditors, and the Profit and Loss Account, and any proposed changes in the remuneration, fees or allowances of the members of the Board;
(b)  to make appropriations to reserve and to special funds, and to consider the declaration of a dividend and its amount;
(c)  to elect the Auditors for the ensuing year and to fix their remuneration; and
(d)  to discharge the Board from all personal responsibility in respect of the past financial year.

*Article 47*
Extraordinary General Meetings shall be summoned to decide upon any proposals of the Board:

(a)  to amend the Statutes;
(b)  to increase or decrease the capital of the Bank;
(c)  to liquidate the Bank.

# CHAPTER VI

## Accounts and Profits

*Article 48*
The financial year of the Bank will begin on 1st April and end on 31st March. The first financial period will end on 31st March, 1931.

*Article 49*
The Bank shall publish an Annual Report, and at least once a month a Statement of Account in such form as the Board may prescribe. The Board

shall cause to be prepared a Profit and Loss Account and Balance Sheet of the Bank for each financial year in time for submission to the Annual General Meeting.

*Article 50*
The Accounts and Balance Sheet shall be audited by independent auditors. The Auditors shall have full power to examine all books and accounts of the Bank and to require full information as to all its transactions. The Auditors shall report to the Board and to the General Meeting and shall state in their Report:

(a) whether they have obtained all the information and explanations they have required; and
(b) whether, in their opinion, the Balance Sheet and the Profit and Loss Account dealt with in the Report are properly drawn up so as to exhibit a true and fair view of the state of the Bank's affairs according to the best of their information and the explanations given to them, and as shown by the books of the Bank.

*Article 51*
The yearly net profits of the Bank shall be applied as follows:

(1) Five per cent. of such net profits, or such proportion of five per cent as may be required for the purpose, shall be paid to a reserve fund called the Legal Reserve Fund until that Fund reaches an amount equal in value to ten per cent. of the amount of the paid-up capital of the Bank for the time being.
(2) Thereafter the net profits shall be applied in or towards payment of the dividend which is declared by the General Meeting on the proposal of the Board. The portion of the net profits so applied shall take into account the amount (if any) which the Board decides to draw from the Special Dividend Reserve Fund of the Bank pursuant to Article 52.
(3) After making provision for the foregoing, one-half of the yearly net profits then remaining shall be paid into the General Reserve Fund of the Bank until it equals the paid-up capital. Thereafter forty per cent shall be so applied until the General Reserve Fund equals twice the paid-up capital; thirty per cent until it equals three times the paid-up capital; twenty per cent until it equals four times the paid-up capital; ten per cent until it equals five times the paid-up capital; and from that point onward, five per cent.
In case the General Reserve Fund, by reason of losses or by reason of an increase in the paid-up capital, falls below the amounts provided for above after having once attained them, the appropriate proportion of the yearly net profits shall again be applied until the position is restored.

(4) The disposal of the remainder of the net profits shall be determined by the General Meeting on the proposal of the Board, provided that a portion of such remainder may be allotted to the shareholders by way of a transfer to the Special Dividend Reserve Fund.

*Article 52*
Reserve Funds
The General Reserve Fund shall be available for meeting any losses incurred by the Bank. In case it is not adequate for this purpose, recourse may be had to the Legal Reserve Fund provided for in clause (1) of Article 51.

The Special Dividend Reserve Fund shall be available, in case of need, for paying the whole or any part of the dividend declared pursuant to clause (2) of Article 51.

These reserve funds, in the event of liquidation, and after the discharge of the liabilities of the Bank and the costs of liquidation, shall be divided among the shareholders.

## Chapter VII

### General Provisions

*Article 53*
(1) The Bank may not be liquidated except by a three-fourths majority of the General Meeting.
(2) In the event of the liquidation of the Bank, the obligations assumed by the Bank under the Staff Pension Scheme and any related special funds, in particular the corresponding liability as published in the latest Balance Sheet or Statement of Account, shall enjoy priority over the discharge of any other liabilities of the Bank, irrespective of whether or not the pension fund of the Bank, which covers the relevant obligations, has separate legal personality at the time of liquidation.

*Article 54*
(1) If any dispute shall arise between the Bank, on the one side, and any central bank, financial institution, or other bank referred to in the present Statutes, on the other side, or between the Bank and its shareholders, with regard to the interpretation or application of the Statutes of the Bank, the same shall be referred for final decision to the Tribunal provided for by the Hague Agreement of January, 1930.
(2) In the absence of agreement as to the terms of submission either party to a dispute under this Article may refer the same to the Tribunal, which shall have power to decide all questions (including the question of its own jurisdiction) even in default of appearance by the other party.
(3) Before giving a final decision and without prejudice to the questions at issue, the President of the Tribunal, or, if he is unable to act in any case,

a member of the Tribunal to be designated by him forthwith, may, on the request of the first party applying therefor, order any appropriate provisional measures in order to safeguard the respective rights of the parties.

(4) The provisions of this Article shall not prejudice the right of the parties to a dispute to refer the same by common consent to the President or a member of the Tribunal as sole arbitrator.

*Article 55*

(1) The Bank shall enjoy immunity from jurisdiction, save:

(a) to the extent that such immunity is formally waived in individual cases by the President, the General Manager of the Bank, or their duly authorized representatives; or

(b) in civil or commercial suits, arising from banking or financial trans-actions, initiated by contractual counterparties of the Bank, except in those cases in which provision for arbitration has been or shall have been made.

(2) Property and assets of the Bank shall, wherever located and by whomsoever held, be immune from any measure of execution (including seizure, attachment, freeze or any other measure of execution, enforcement or sequestration), except if that measure of execution is sought pursuant to a final judgment rendered against the Bank by any court of competent jurisdiction pursuant to subparagraph 1(a) or (b) above.

(3) All deposits entrusted to the Bank, all claims against the Bank and the shares issued by the Bank shall, without the express prior agreement of the Bank, wherever located and by whomsoever held, be immune from any measure of execution (including seizure, attachment, freeze or any other measure of execution, enforcement or sequestration).

*Article 56*

For the purposes of these Statutes:

(a) central bank means the bank or banking system in any country to which has been entrusted the duty of regulating the volume of currency and credit in that country; or, in a cross-border central banking system, the national central banks and the common central banking institution which are entrusted with such duty;

(b) the Governor of a central bank means the person who, subject to the control of his Board or other competent authority, has the direction of the policy and administration of the bank;

(c) a two-thirds majority of the Board means not less than two-thirds of the votes (whether given in person or by proxy) of the whole directorate;

(d) country means a sovereign state, a monetary zone within a sovereign state or a monetary zone extending over more than one sovereign state.

*Article 57*
Amendments of any Articles of these Statutes other than those enumerated in Article 58 may be proposed by a two-thirds majority of the Board to the General Meeting and if adopted by a majority of the General Meeting shall come into force, provided that such amendments are not inconsistent with the provisions of the Articles enumerated in Article 58.

*Article 58*
Articles 2, 3, 8, 14, 19, 24, 27, 44, 51, 54, 57 and 58 cannot be amended except subject to the following conditions: the amendment must be adopted by a two-thirds majority of the Board, approved by a majority of the General Meeting and sanctioned by a law supplementing the Charter of the Bank.

# Appendix 4: ICSID Convention, Regulations, and Rules

As of April 2006. Source: https://icsid.worldbank. org/ICSID/StaticFiles/basicdoc/CRR _ English- final.pdf

## Convention On The Settlement Of Investment Disputes Between States and Nationals of Other States

### Preamble

**The Contracting States**

Considering the need for international cooperation for economic development, and the role of private international investment therein;

Bearing in mind the possibility that from time to time disputes may arise in connection with such investment between Contracting States and nationals of other Contracting States;

Recognizing that while such disputes would usually be subject to national legal processes, international methods of settlement may be appropriate in certain cases;

Attaching particular importance to the availability of facilities for international conciliation or arbitration to which Contracting States and nationals of other Contracting States may submit such disputes if they so desire;

Desiring to establish such facilities under the auspices of the International Bank for Reconstruction and Development;

Recognizing that mutual consent by the parties to submit such disputes to conciliation or to arbitration through such facilities constitutes a binding agreement which requires in particular that due consideration be given to any recommendation of conciliators, and that any arbitral award be complied with; and

Declaring that no Contracting State shall by the mere fact of its ratification, acceptance or approval of this Convention and without its consent be deemed to be under any obligation to submit any particular dispute to conciliation or arbitration.

Have agreed as follows:

# CHAPTER I

## International Centre for Settlement of Investment Disputes

*Section 1*
*Establishment and Organization*
Article 1
(1) There is hereby established the International Centre for Settlement of Investment Disputes (hereinafter called the Centre).
(2) The purpose of the Centre shall be to provide facilities for conciliation and arbitration of investment disputes between Contracting States and nationals of other Contracting States in accordance with the provisions of this Convention.

Article 2
The seat of the Centre shall be at the principal office of the International Bank for Reconstruction and Development (hereinafter called the Bank). The seat may be moved to another place by decision of the Administrative Council adopted by a majority of two-thirds of its members.

Article 3
The Centre shall have an Administrative Council and a Secretariat and shall maintain a Panel of Conciliators and a Panel of Arbitrators.

*Section 2*
*The Administrative Council*
Article 4
(1) The Administrative Council shall be composed of one representative of each Contracting State. An alternate may act as representative in case of his principal's absence from a meeting or inability to act.
(2) In the absence of a contrary designation, each governor and alternate governor of the Bank appointed by a Contracting State shall be ex officio its representative and its alternate respectively.

Article 5
The President of the Bank shall be ex officio Chairman of the Administrative Council (hereinafter called the Chairman) but shall have no vote. During his absence or inability to act and during any vacancy in the office of President of the Bank, the person for the time being acting as President shall act as Chairman of the Administrative Council.

Article 6
(1) Without prejudice to the powers and functions vested in it by other provisions of this Convention, the Administrative Council shall:
   (a) adopt the administrative and financial regulations of the Centre;
   (b) adopt the rules of procedure for the institution of conciliation and arbitration proceedings;

(c) adopt the rules of procedure for conciliation and arbitration proceedings (hereinafter called the Conciliation Rules and the Arbitration Rules);

(d) approve arrangements with the Bank for the use of the Bank's administrative facilities and services;

(e) determine the conditions of service of the Secretary-General and of any Deputy Secretary-General;

(f) adopt the annual budget of revenues and expenditures of the Centre;

(g) approve the annual report on the operation of the Centre.

The decisions referred to in sub-paragraphs (a), (b), (c) and (f) above shall be adopted by a majority of two-thirds of the members of the Administrative Council.

(2) The Administrative Council may appoint such committees as it considers necessary.

(3) The Administrative Council shall also exercise such other powers and perform such other functions as it shall determine to be necessary for the implementation of the provisions of this Convention.

Article 7

(1) The Administrative Council shall hold an annual meeting and such other meetings as may be determined by the Council, or convened by the Chairman, or convened by the Secretary-General at the request of not less than five members of the Council.

(2) Each member of the Administrative Council shall have one vote and, except as otherwise herein provided, all matters before the Council shall be decided by a majority of the votes cast.

(3) A quorum for any meeting of the Administrative Council shall be a majority of its members.

(4) The Administrative Council may establish, by a majority of two-thirds of its members, a procedure whereby the Chairman may seek a vote of the Council without convening a meeting of the Council. The vote shall be considered valid only if the majority of the members of the Council cast their votes within the time limit fixed by the said procedure.

Article 8

Members of the Administrative Council and the Chairman shall serve without remuneration from the Centre.

*Section 3*
*The Secretariat*
Article 9

The Secretariat shall consist of a Secretary-General, one or more Deputy Secretaries-General and staff.

Article 10

(1) The Secretary-General and any Deputy Secretary-General shall be elected by the Administrative Council by a majority of two-thirds of its members upon the nomination of the Chairman for a term of service not exceeding six years and shall be eligible for re-election. After consulting the members of the Administrative Council, the Chairman shall propose one or more candidates for each such office.

(2) The offices of Secretary-General and Deputy Secretary-General shall be incompatible with the exercise of any political function. Neither the Secretary-General nor any Deputy Secretary-General may hold any other employment or engage in any other occupation except with the approval of the Administrative Council.

(3) During the Secretary-General's absence or inability to act, and during any vacancy of the office of Secretary-General, the Deputy Secretary-General shall act as Secretary-General. If there shall be more than one Deputy Secretary-General, the Administrative Council shall determine in advance the order in which they shall act as Secretary-General.

Article 11

The Secretary-General shall be the legal representative and the principal officer of the Centre and shall be responsible for its administration, including the appointment of staff, in accordance with the provisions of this Convention and the rules adopted by the Administrative Council. He shall perform the function of registrar and shall have the power to authenticate arbitral awards rendered pursuant to this Convention, and to certify copies thereof.

*Section 4*
*The Panels*

Article 12

The Panel of Conciliators and the Panel of Arbitrators shall each consist of qualified persons, designated as hereinafter provided, who are willing to serve thereon.

Article 13

(1) Each Contracting State may designate to each Panel four persons who may but need not be its nationals.

(2) The Chairman may designate ten persons to each Panel. The persons so designated to a Panel shall each have a different nationality.

Article 14

(1) Persons designated to serve on the Panels shall be persons of high moral character and recognized competence in the fields of law, commerce, industry or finance, who may be relied upon to exercise independent judgment. Competence in the field of law shall be of particular importance in the case of persons on the Panel of Arbitrators.

(2) The Chairman, in designating persons to serve on the Panels, shall in addition pay due regard to the importance of assuring representation on the Panels of the principal legal systems of the world and of the main forms of economic activity.

Article 15
(1) Panel members shall serve for renewable periods of six years.
(2) In case of death or resignation of a member of a Panel, the authority which designated the member shall have the right to designate another person to serve for the remainder of that member's term.
(3) Panel members shall continue in office until their successors have been designated.

Article 16
(1) A person may serve on both Panels.
(2) If a person shall have been designated to serve on the same Panel by more than one Contracting State, or by one or more Contracting States and the Chairman, he shall be deemed to have been designated by the authority which first designated him or, if one such authority is the State of which he is a national, by that State.
(3) All designations shall be notified to the Secretary-General and shall take effect from the date on which the notification is received.

*Section 5*
*Financing the Centre*
Article 17
If the expenditure of the Centre cannot be met out of charges for the use of its facilities, or out of other receipts, the excess shall be borne by Contracting States which are members of the Bank in proportion to their respective subscriptions to the capital stock of the Bank, and by Contracting States which are not members of the Bank in accordance with rules adopted by the Administrative Council.

*Section 6*
*Status, Immunities and Privileges*
Article 18
The Centre shall have full international legal personality. The legal capacity of the Centre shall include the capacity:

(a) to contract;
(b) to acquire and dispose of movable and immovable property;
(c) to institute legal proceedings.

Article 19
To enable the Centre to fulfil its functions, it shall enjoy in the territories of each Contracting State the immunities and privileges set forth in this Section.

Article 20
The Centre, its property and assets shall enjoy immunity from all legal process, except when the Centre waives this immunity.

Article 21
The Chairman, the members of the Administrative Council, persons acting as conciliators or arbitrators or members of a Committee appointed pursuant to paragraph (3) of Article 52, and the officers and employees of the Secretariat

(a)  shall enjoy immunity from legal process with respect to acts performed by them in the exercise of their functions, except when the Centre waives this immunity;
(b)  not being local nationals, shall enjoy the same immunities from immigration restrictions, alien registration requirements and national service obligations, the same facilities as regards exchange restrictions and the same treatment in respect of travelling facilities as are accorded by Contracting States to the representatives, officials and employees of comparable rank of other Contracting States.

Article 22
The provisions of Article 21 shall apply to persons appearing in proceedings under this Convention as parties, agents, counsel, advocates, witnesses or experts; provided, however, that sub-paragraph (b) thereof shall apply only in connection with their travel to and from, and their stay at, the place where the proceedings are held.

Article 23
(1)  The archives of the Centre shall be inviolable, wherever they may be.
(2)  With regard to its official communications, the Centre shall be accorded by each Contracting State treatment not less favourable than that accorded to other international organizations.

Article 24
(1)  The Centre, its assets, property and income, and its operations and transactions authorized by this Convention shall be exempt from all taxation and customs duties. The Centre shall also be exempt from liability for the collection or payment of any taxes or customs duties.
(2)  Except in the case of local nationals, no tax shall be levied on or in respect of expense allowances paid by the Centre to the Chairman or members of the Administrative Council, or on or in respect of salaries, expense allowances or other emoluments paid by the Centre to officials or employees of the Secretariat.
(3)  No tax shall be levied on or in respect of fees or expense allowances received by persons acting as conciliators, or arbitrators, or members of

a Committee appointed pursuant to paragraph (3) of Article 52, in proceedings under this Convention, if the sole jurisdictional basis for such tax is the location of the Centre or the place where such proceedings are conducted or the place where such fees or allowances are paid.

## CHAPTER II

### Jurisdiction of the Centre

Article 25

(1) The jurisdiction of the Centre shall extend to any legal dispute arising directly out of an investment, between a Contracting State (or any constituent subdivision or agency of a Contracting State designated to the Centre by that State) and a national of another Contracting State, which the parties to the dispute consent in writing to submit to the Centre. When the parties have given their consent, no party may withdraw its consent unilaterally.

(2) "National of another Contracting State" means:

   (a) any natural person who had the nationality of a Contracting State other than the State party to the dispute on the date on which the parties consented to submit such dispute to conciliation or arbitration as well as on the date on which the request was registered pursuant to paragraph (3) of Article 28 or paragraph (3) of Article 36, but does not include any person who on either date also had the nationality of the Contracting State party to the dispute; and

   (b) any juridical person which had the nationality of a Contracting State other than the State party to the dispute on the date on which the parties consented to submit such dispute to conciliation or arbitration and any juridical person which had the nationality of the Contracting State party to the dispute on that date and which, because of foreign control, the parties have agreed should be treated as a national of another Contracting State for the purposes of this Convention.

(3) Consent by a constituent subdivision or agency of a Contracting State shall require the approval of that State unless that State notifies the Centre that no such approval is required.

(4) Any Contracting State may, at the time of ratification, acceptance or approval of this Convention or at any time thereafter, notify the Centre of the class or classes of disputes which it would or would not consider submitting to the jurisdiction of the Centre. The Secretary-General shall forthwith transmit such notification to all Contracting States. Such notification shall not constitute the consent required by paragraph (1).

Article 26
Consent of the parties to arbitration under this Convention shall, unless otherwise stated, be deemed consent to such arbitration to the exclusion of

any other remedy. A Contracting State may require the exhaustion of local administrative or judicial remedies as a condition of its consent to arbitration under this Convention.

Article 27

(1) No Contracting State shall give diplomatic protection, or bring an international claim, in respect of a dispute which one of its nationals and another Contracting State shall have consented to submit or shall have submitted to arbitration under this Convention, unless such other Contracting State shall have failed to abide by and comply with the award rendered in such dispute.

(2) Diplomatic protection, for the purposes of paragraph (1), shall not include informal diplomatic exchanges for the sole purpose of facilitating a settlement of the dispute.

# CHAPTER III

## Conciliation

*Section 1*
*Request for Conciliation*
Article 28

(1) Any Contracting State or any national of a Contracting State wishing to institute conciliation proceedings shall address a request to that effect in writing to the Secretary-General who shall send a copy of the request to the other party.

(2) The request shall contain information concerning the issues in dispute, the identity of the parties and their consent to conciliation in accordance with the rules of procedure for the institution of conciliation and arbitration proceedings.

(3) The Secretary-General shall register the request unless he finds, on the basis of the information contained in the request, that the dispute is manifestly outside the jurisdiction of the Centre. He shall forthwith notify the parties of registration or refusal to register.

*Section 2*
*Constitution of the Conciliation Commission*
Article 29

The Conciliation Commission (hereinafter called the Commission) shall be constituted as soon as possible after registration of a request pursuant to Article 28.

(1) (a) The Commission shall consist of a sole conciliator or any uneven number of conciliators appointed as the parties shall agree.

(b) Where the parties do not agree upon the number of conciliators and the method of their appointment, the Commission shall consist of three conciliators, one conciliator appointed by each party and the third, who shall be the president of the Commission, appointed by agreement of the parties.

## Article 30

If the Commission shall not have been constituted within 90 days after notice of registration of the request has been dispatched by the Secretary-General in accordance with paragraph (3) of Article 28, or such other period as the parties may agree, the Chairman shall, at the request of either party and after consulting both parties as far as possible, appoint the conciliator or conciliators not yet appointed.

## Article 31

(1) Conciliators may be appointed from outside the Panel of Conciliators, except in the case of appointments by the Chairman pursuant to Article 30.

(2) Conciliators appointed from outside the Panel of Conciliators shall possess the qualities stated in paragraph (1) of Article 14.

*Section 3*
*Conciliation Proceedings*
## Article 32

(1) The Commission shall be the judge of its own competence.

(2) Any objection by a party to the dispute that that dispute is not within the jurisdiction of the Centre, or for other reasons is not within the competence of the Commission, shall be considered by the Commission which shall determine whether to deal with it as a preliminary question or to join it to the merits of the dispute.

## Article 33

Any conciliation proceeding shall be conducted in accordance with the provisions of this Section and, except as the parties otherwise agree, in accordance with the Conciliation Rules in effect on the date on which the parties consented to conciliation. If any question of procedure arises which is not covered by this Section or the Conciliation Rules or any rules agreed by the parties, the Commission shall decide the question.

## Article 34

(1) It shall be the duty of the Commission to clarify the issues in dispute between the parties and to endeavour to bring about agreement between them upon mutually acceptable terms. To that end, the Commission may at any stage of the proceedings and from time to time recommend terms of settlement to the parties. The parties shall cooperate in good faith with the Commission in order to enable the Commission to carry out its functions, and shall give their most serious consideration to its recommendations.

(2) If the parties reach agreement, the Commission shall draw up a report noting the issues in dispute and recording that the parties have reached agreement. If, at any stage of the proceedings, it appears to the Commission that there is no likelihood of agreement between the parties, it shall close the proceedings and shall draw up a report noting the submission of the dispute and recording the failure of the parties to reach agreement. If one party fails to appear or participate in the proceedings, the Commission shall close the proceedings and shall draw up a report noting that party's failure to appear or participate.

Article 35

Except as the parties to the dispute shall otherwise agree, neither party to a conciliation proceeding shall be entitled in any other proceeding, whether before arbitrators or in a court of law or otherwise, to invoke or rely on any views expressed or statements or admissions or offers of settlement made by the other party in the conciliation proceedings, or the report or any recommendations made by the Commission.

# CHAPTER IV

## Arbitration

*Section 1*
*Request for Arbitration*
Article 36

(1) Any Contracting State or any national of a Contracting State wishing to institute arbitration proceedings shall address a request to that effect in writing to the Secretary-General who shall send a copy of the request to the other party.

(2) The request shall contain information concerning the issues in dispute, the identity of the parties and their consent to arbitration in accordance with the rules of procedure for the institution of conciliation and arbitration proceedings.

(3) The Secretary-General shall register the request unless he finds, on the basis of the information contained in the request, that the dispute is manifestly outside the jurisdiction of the Centre. He shall forthwith notify the parties of registration or refusal to register.

*Section 2*
*Constitution of the Tribunal*
Article 37

(1) The Arbitral Tribunal (hereinafter called the Tribunal) shall be constituted as soon as possible after registration of a request pursuant to Article 36.

(2) (a) The Tribunal shall consist of a sole arbitrator or any uneven number of arbitrators appointed as the parties shall agree.

(b) 'Where the parties do not agree upon the number of arbitrators and the method of their appointment, the Tribunal shall consist of three arbitrators, one arbitrator appointed by each party and the third, who shall be the president of the Tribunal, appointed by agreement of the parties.

## Article 38

If the Tribunal shall not have been constituted within 90 days after notice of registration of the request has been dispatched by the Secretary-General in accordance with paragraph (3) of Article 36, or such other period as the parties may agree, the Chairman shall, at the request of either party and after consulting both parties as far as possible, appoint the arbitrator or arbitrators not yet appointed. Arbitrators appointed by the Chairman pursuant to this Article shall not be nationals of the Contracting State party to the dispute or of the Contracting State whose national is a party to the dispute.

## Article 39

The majority of the arbitrators shall be nationals of States other than the Contracting State party to the dispute and the Contracting State whose national is a party to the dispute; provided, however, that the foregoing provisions of this Article shall not apply if the sole arbitrator or each individual member of the Tribunal has been appointed by agreement of the parties.

## Article 40

(1) Arbitrators may be appointed from outside the Panel of Arbitrators, except in the case of appointments by the Chairman pursuant to Article 38.

(2) Arbitrators appointed from outside the Panel of Arbitrators shall possess the qualities stated in paragraph (1) of Article 14.

## Section 3
### Powers and Functions of the Tribunal
## Article 41

(1) The Tribunal shall be the judge of its own competence.

(2) Any objection by a party to the dispute that that dispute is not within the jurisdiction of the Centre, or for other reasons is not within the competence of the Tribunal, shall be considered by the Tribunal which shall determine whether to deal with it as a preliminary question or to join it to the merits of the dispute.

## Article 42

(1) The Tribunal shall decide a dispute in accordance with such rules of law as may be agreed by the parties. In the absence of such agreement, the Tribunal shall apply the law of the Contracting State party to the dispute (including its rules on the conflict of laws) and such rules of international law as may be applicable.

(2) The Tribunal may not bring in a finding of non liquet on the ground of silence or obscurity of the law.

(3) The provisions of paragraphs (1) and (2) shall not prejudice the power of the Tribunal to decide a dispute ex aequo et bono if the parties so agree.

## Article 43

Except as the parties otherwise agree, the Tribunal may, if it deems it necessary at any stage of the proceedings,

(a) call upon the parties to produce documents or other evidence, and
(b) visit the scene connected with the dispute, and conduct such inquiries there as it may deem appropriate.

## Article 44

Any arbitration proceeding shall be conducted in accordance with the provisions of this Section and, except as the parties otherwise agree, in accordance with the Arbitration Rules in effect on the date on which the parties consented to arbitration. If any question of procedure arises which is not covered by this Section or the Arbitration Rules or any rules agreed by the parties, the Tribunal shall decide the question.

## Article 45

(1) Failure of a party to appear or to present his case shall not be deemed an admission of the other party's assertions.
(2) If a party fails to appear or to present his case at any stage of the proceedings the other party may request the Tribunal to deal with the questions submitted to it and to render an award. Before rendering an award, the Tribunal shall notify, and grant a period of grace to, the party failing to appear or to present its case, unless it is satisfied that that party does not intend to do so.

## Article 46

Except as the parties otherwise agree, the Tribunal shall, if requested by a party, determine any incidental or additional claims or counterclaims arising directly out of the subject-matter of the dispute provided that they are within the scope of the consent of the parties and are otherwise within the jurisdiction of the Centre.

## Article 47

Except as the parties otherwise agree, the Tribunal may, if it considers that the circumstances so require, recommend any provisional measures which should be taken to preserve the respective rights of either party.

*Section 4*
*The Award*
## Article 48

(1) The Tribunal shall decide questions by a majority of the votes of all its members.

(2) The award of the Tribunal shall be in writing and shall be signed by the members of the Tribunal who voted for it.

(3) The award shall deal with every question submitted to the Tribunal, and shall state the reasons upon which it is based.

(4) Any member of the Tribunal may attach his individual opinion to the award, whether he dissents from the majority or not, or a statement of his dissent.

(5) The Centre shall not publish the award without the consent of the parties.

Article 49

(1) The Secretary-General shall promptly dispatch certified copies of the award to the parties. The award shall be deemed to have been rendered on the date on which the certified copies were dispatched.

(2) The Tribunal upon the request of a party made within 45 days after the date on which the award was rendered may after notice to the other party decide any question which it had omitted to decide in the award, and shall rectify any clerical, arithmetical or similar error in the award. Its decision shall become part of the award and shall be notified to the parties in the same manner as the award. The periods of time provided for under paragraph (2) of Article 51 and paragraph (2) of Article 52 shall run from the date on which the decision was rendered.

*Section 5*
*Interpretation, Revision and Annulment of the Award*
Article 50

(1) If any dispute shall arise between the parties as to the meaning or scope of an award, either party may request interpretation of the award by an application in writing addressed to the Secretary-General.

(2) The request shall, if possible, be submitted to the Tribunal which rendered the award. If this shall not be possible, a new Tribunal shall be constituted in accordance with Section 2 of this Chapter. The Tribunal may, if it considers that the circumstances so require, stay enforcement of the award pending its decision.

Article 51

(1) Either party may request revision of the award by an application in writing addressed to the Secretary-General on the ground of discovery of some fact of such a nature as decisively to affect the award, provided that when the award was rendered that fact was unknown to the Tribunal and to the applicant and that the applicant's ignorance of that fact was not due to negligence.

(2) The application shall be made within 90 days after the discovery of such fact and in any event within three years after the date on which the award was rendered.

(3) The request shall, if possible, be submitted to the Tribunal which rendered the award. If this shall not be possible, a new Tribunal shall be constituted in accordance with Section 2 of this Chapter.

(4) The Tribunal may, if it considers that the circumstances so require, stay enforcement of the award pending its decision. If the applicant requests a stay of enforcement of the award in his application, enforcement shall be stayed provisionally until the Tribunal rules on such request.

Article 52

(1) Either party may request annulment of the award by an application in writing addressed to the Secretary-General on one or more of the following grounds:

   (a) that the Tribunal was not properly constituted;

   (b) that the Tribunal has manifestly exceeded its powers;

   (c) that there was corruption on the part of a member of the Tribunal;

   (d) that there has been a serious departure from a fundamental rule of procedure; or

   (e) that the award has failed to state the reasons on which it is based.

(2) The application shall be made within 120 days after the date on which the award was rendered except that when annulment is requested on the ground of corruption such application shall be made within 120 days after discovery of the corruption and in any event within three years after the date on which the award was rendered.

(3) On receipt of the request the Chairman shall forthwith appoint from the Panel of Arbitrators an ad hoc Committee of three persons. None of the members of the Committee shall have been a member of the Tribunal which rendered the award, shall be of the same nationality as any such member, shall be a national of the State party to the dispute or of the State whose national is a party to the dispute, shall have been designated to the Panel of Arbitrators by either of those States, or shall have acted as a conciliator in the same dispute. The Committee shall have the authority to annul the award or any part thereof on any of the grounds set forth in paragraph (1).

(4) The provisions of Articles 41–45, 48, 49, 53 and 54, and of Chapters VI and VII shall apply mutatis mutandis to proceedings before the Committee.

(5) The Committee may, if it considers that the circumstances so require, stay enforcement of the award pending its decision. If the applicant requests a stay of enforcement of the award in his application, enforcement shall be stayed provisionally until the Committee rules on such request.

(6) If the award is annulled the dispute shall, at the request of either party, be submitted to a new Tribunal constituted in accordance with Section 2 of this chapter.

*Section 6*
*Recognition and Enforcement of the Award*
Article 53
(1) The award shall be binding on the parties and shall not be subject to any appeal or to any other remedy except those provided for in this Convention. Each party shall abide by and comply with the terms of the award except to the extent that enforcement shall have been stayed pursuant to the relevant provisions of this Convention.
(2) For the purposes of this Section, "award" shall include any decision interpreting, revising or annulling such award pursuant to Articles 50, 51 or 52.

Article 54
(1) Each Contracting State shall recognize an award rendered pursuant to this Convention as binding and enforce the pecuniary obligations imposed by that award within its territories as if it were a final judgment of a court in that State. A Contracting State with a federal constitution may enforce such an award in or through its federal courts and may provide that such courts shall treat the award as if it were a final judgment of the courts of a constituent state. A party seeking recognition or enforcement in the territories of a Contracting State shall furnish to a competent court or other authority which such State shall have designated for this purpose a copy of the award certified by the Secretary-General. Each Contracting State shall notify the Secretary-General of the designation of the competent court or other authority for this purpose and of any subsequent change in such designation.
(2) Execution of the award shall be governed by the laws concerning the execution of judgments in force in the State in whose territories such execution is sought.

Article 55
Nothing in Article 54 shall be construed as derogating from the law in force in any Contracting State relating to immunity of that State or of any foreign State from execution.

# CHAPTER V

## Replacement and Disqualification of Conciliators and Arbitrators

Article 56
(1) After a Commission or a Tribunal has been constituted and proceedings have begun, its composition shall remain unchanged; provided, however, that if a conciliator or an arbitrator should die, become incapacitated, or resign, the resulting vacancy shall be filled in accordance with the provisions of Section 2 of Chapter III or Section 2 of Chapter IV.

(2) A member of a Commission or Tribunal shall continue to serve in that capacity notwithstanding that he shall have ceased to be a member of the Panel.

(3) If a conciliator or arbitrator appointed by a party shall have resigned without the consent of the Commission or Tribunal of which he was a member, the Chairman shall appoint a person from the appropriate Panel to fill the resulting vacancy.

## Article 57

A party may propose to a Commission or Tribunal the disqualification of any of its members on account of any fact indicating a manifest lack of the qualities required by paragraph (1) of Article 14. A party to arbitration proceedings may, in addition, propose the disqualification of an arbitrator on the ground that he was ineligible for appointment to the Tribunal under Section 2 of Chapter IV.

## Article 58

The decision on any proposal to disqualify a conciliator or arbitrator shall be taken by the other members of the Commission or Tribunal as the case may be, provided that where those members are equally divided, or in the case of a proposal to disqualify a sole conciliator or arbitrator, or a majority of the conciliators or arbitrators, the Chairman shall take that decision. If it is decided that the proposal is well-founded the conciliator or arbitrator to whom the decision relates shall be replaced in accordance with the provisions of Section 2 of Chapter III or Section 2 of Chapter IV.

# CHAPTER VI

## Cost of Proceedings

## Article 59

The charges payable by the parties for the use of the facilities of the Centre shall be determined by the Secretary-General in accordance with the regulations adopted by the Administrative Council.

## Article 60

(1) Each Commission and each Tribunal shall determine the fees and expenses of its members within limits established from time to time by the Administrative Council and after consultation with the Secretary-General.

(2) Nothing in paragraph (1) of this Article shall preclude the parties from agreeing in advance with the Commission or Tribunal concerned upon the fees and expenses of its members.

## Article 61

(1) In the case of conciliation proceedings the fees and expenses of members of the Commission as well as the charges for the use of the facilities of

the Centre, shall be borne equally by the parties. Each party shall bear any other expenses it incurs in connection with the proceedings.

(2) In the case of arbitration proceedings the Tribunal shall, except as the parties otherwise agree, assess the expenses incurred by the parties in connection with the proceedings, and shall decide how and by whom those expenses, the fees and expenses of the members of the Tribunal and the charges for the use of the facilities of the Centre shall be paid. Such decision shall form part of the award.

## CHAPTER VII

### Place of Proceedings

Article 62
Conciliation and arbitration proceedings shall be held at the seat of the Centre except as hereinafter provided.

Article 63
Conciliation and arbitration proceedings may be held, if the parties so agree,
(a) at the seat of the Permanent Court of Arbitration or of any other appropriate institution, whether private or public, with which the Centre may make arrangements for that purpose; or
(b) at any other place approved by the Commission or Tribunal after consultation with the Secretary-General.

## CHAPTER VIII

### Disputes Between Contracting States

Article 64
Any dispute arising between Contracting States concerning the interpretation or application of this Convention which is not settled by negotiation shall be referred to the International Court of Justice by the application of any party to such dispute, unless the States concerned agree to another method of settlement.

## CHAPTER IX

### Amendment

Article 65
Any Contracting State may propose amendment of this Convention. The text of a proposed amendment shall be communicated to the Secretary-General not less than 90 days prior to the meeting of the Administrative Council at which such amendment is to be considered and shall forthwith be transmitted by him to all the members of the Administrative Council.

Article 66

(1) If the Administrative Council shall so decide by a majority of two-thirds of its members, the proposed amendment shall be circulated to all Contracting States for ratification, acceptance or approval. Each amendment shall enter into force 30 days after dispatch by the depositary of this Convention of a notification to Contracting States that all Contracting States have ratified, accepted or approved the amendment.

(2) No amendment shall affect the rights and obligations under this Convention of any Contracting State or of any of its constituent subdivisions or agencies, or of any national of such State arising out of consent to the jurisdiction of the Centre given before the date of entry into force of the amendment.

## CHAPTER X

### Final Provisions

Article 67

This Convention shall be open for signature on behalf of States members of the Bank. It shall also be open for signature on behalf of any other State which is a party to the Statute of the International Court of Justice and which the Administrative Council, by a vote of two-thirds of its members, shall have invited to sign the Convention.

Article 68

(1) This Convention shall be subject to ratification, acceptance or approval by the signatory States in accordance with their respective constitutional procedures.

(2) This Convention shall enter into force 30 days after the date of deposit of the twentieth instrument of ratification, acceptance or approval. It shall enter into force for each State which subsequently deposits its instrument of ratification, acceptance or approval 30 days after the date of such deposit.

Article 69

Each Contracting State shall take such legislative or other measures as may be necessary for making the provisions of this Convention effective in its territories

Article 70

This Convention shall apply to all territories for whose international relations a Contracting State is responsible, except those which are excluded by such State by written notice to the depositary of this Convention either at the time of ratification, acceptance or approval or subsequently.

Article 71

Any Contracting State may denounce this Convention by written notice to the depositary of this Convention. The denunciation shall take effect six months after receipt of such notice.

Article 72
Notice by a Contracting State pursuant to Articles 70 or 71 shall not affect the rights or obligations under this Convention of that State or of any of its constituent subdivisions or agencies or of any national of that State arising out of consent to the jurisdiction of the Centre given by one of them before such notice was received by the depositary.

Article 73
Instruments of ratification, acceptance or approval of this Convention and of amendments thereto shall be deposited with the Bank which shall act as the depositary of this Convention. The depositary shall transmit certified copies of this Convention to States members of the Bank and to any other State invited to sign the Convention.

Article 74
The depositary shall register this Convention with the Secretariat of the United Nations in accordance with Article 102 of the Charter of the United Nations and the Regulations thereunder adopted by the General Assembly.

Article 75
The depositary shall notify all signatory States of the following:

(a)  signatures in accordance with Article 67;
(b)  deposits of instruments of ratification, acceptance and approval in accordance with Article 73;
(c)  the date on which this Convention enters into force in accordance with Article 68;
(d)  exclusions from territorial application pursuant to Article 70;
(e)  the date on which any amendment of this Convention enters into force in accordance with Article 66; and
(f)  denunciations in accordance with Article 71.

DONE at Washington, in the English, French and Spanish languages, all three texts being equally authentic, in a single copy which shall remain deposited in the archives of the International Bank for Reconstruction and Development, which has indicated by its signature below its agreement to fulfil the functions with which it is charged under this Convention.

# NOTES

## 1 INTERNATIONAL FINANCIAL INSTITUTIONS: ARCHITECTURE, FLAWS, AND LEGITIMACY

1. Andrés Solimano (1999) *Can Reforming Global Institutions Help Developing Countries Share in the Benefits from Globalization?* (Washington, DC: The World Bank Paper).
2. Report of the High-Level Commission on Modernization of World Bank Group Governance, p. 8.
3. Jose Antonio Ocampo (2005) "The Democratic Deficit of International Arrangements," in *Protecting the Poor: Global Financial Institutions and the Vulnerability of Low-Income Countries*, pp. 117–118.
4. The World Bank and the IMF are two distinct institutions: the bank is primarily a development institution, while the IMF is a cooperative institution that seeks to maintain an orderly system of payments and receipts between nations.

   The IMF is small (about 2,300 staff members) and, unlike the World Bank, has no affiliates or subsidiaries. Most of its staff members work at the headquarters in Washington, DC, although three small offices are maintained in Paris, Geneva, and at the United Nations in New York. Its professional staff members are, for the most part, economists and financial experts. With over 7,000 staff members, the World Bank Group is about three times as large as the IMF, and maintains about 40 offices across the world, although 95 percent of its staff works at its Washington, DC, headquarters.
5. Benjamin J. Cohen (2008) "Bretton Woods System," in *Routledge Encyclopedia of International Political Economy*.
6. Niall Fergusson (2008) *The Ascent of Money: A Financial History of the World* (New York: Penguin), p. 305.
7. Kenneth A. Reinert (2012) *An Introduction to International Economics: New Perspectives on the World Economy* (New York: Cambridge University Press), Chapter 17.
8. Cheol S. Eun and Bruce G. Resnick (2007) *International Financial Management*, 4th ed. (Boston: McGraw-Hill), p. 30.
9. West Germany, France, the United States, Japan, and the United Kingdom.
10. Carlos Cottarelli (2005) "Efficiency and Legitimacy: Trade-Offs in IMF Governance." IMF working papers WP/05/107.

## 2 THE INTERNATIONAL MONETARY FUND

1. Martin Weiss (2012) "International Monetary Fund: Background and Issues for Congress," p. 3 Martin Weiss (2012) "International Monetary Fund: Background and Issues for Congress," p. 3 -Congressional Research Service 7–5700 at www.crs.gov.

2. Felix Lessambo (2013) *The International Banking System: Capital Adequacy, Core Business, and Risk Mangement* (Hampshire: Palgrave Macmillan), p. 79.
3. The NAB is a credit arrangement between the IMF and a group of countries. The funds remain at the hand of the agreed-upon countries until the IMF request their return.
4. Jose Antonio Ocampo (2005) "The Democratic Deficit of International Arrangements," in *Protecting the Poor: Global Financial Institutions and the Vulnerability of Low-Income Countries*, p. 120 Jose Antonio Ocampo (2005) "The Democratic Deficit of International Arrangements," in Protecting the Poor: Global Financial Institutions and the Vulnerability of Low-Income Countries, Chapter 7 (The Democratic Deficit of International Arrangements), p. 120, Fondad, The Hague, November 2005. www.fondad org.
5. Weiss, "International Monetary Fund," p. 14.
6. The structural adjustment programs started on February 5, 1980, by the former president of the World Bank, Robert McNamara.
7. William Easterly (2005) "What Did Structural Adjustment Adjust? The Association of Policies and Growth with Repeated IMF and World Bank Adjustment Loans," *Journal of Development Economics* 76, p. 10 (Elsevier).
8. Joseph Stiglitz (2003) *Globalization and Its Discontents* (New York: W.W. Norton), Chapter 5.
9. John Odling-Smee (2004) "The IMF and Russia in the 1990s," IMF Working Paper, International Monetary Fund, p. 7. https://www.imf.org/external/pubs/ft/wp/2004/wp04155.pdf.
10. Odling-Smee, "The IMF and Russia in the 1990s," p. 22.
11. Odling-Smee, "The IMF and Russia in the 1990s," p. 29.
12. Odling-Smee, "The IMF and Russia in the 1990s," p. 30.
13. Odling-Smee, "The IMF and Russia in the 1990s," p. 32.
14. Odling-Smee, "The IMF and Russia in the 1990s," p. 35.
15. Odling-Smee, "The IMF and Russia in the 1990s," p. 36.
16. Odling-Smee, "The IMF and Russia in the 1990s," p. 37.
17. Odling-Smee, "The IMF and Russia in the 1990s," p. 39.
18. Jeffrey Sachs (2012) "What I Did in Russia," at http://Jeffsachs.org.
19. Sachs, "What I Did in Russia."
20. Sachs, "What I Did in Russia."
21. Sachs, "What I Did in Russia."
22. Sachs, "What I Did in Russia."
23. Odling-Smee, "The IMF and Russia in the 1990s," p. 11 or footnote 16.
24. Odling-Smee, "The IMF and Russia in the 1990s," p. 11.
25. Sachs, "What I Did in Russia."
26. Richard J. Self (2011) "Policy Development and Implementation in the Bretton Woods Institutions: A Consideration of the Legality, Human Rights Impact and Effectiveness of their Programmes," *International Journal of Arts & Sciences*, 4: 172.
27. Idem.
28. Self, "Policy Development and Implementation in the Bretton Woods Institutions," p. 201.
29. J. E. Stiglitz (1999) Whither Reform?: Ten Years of the Transition, World Bank: Annual Bank Conference on Development Economics, Keynote Address, p. 3.

30. International Monetary Fund (IMF) Managing Director Christine Lagarde speech during the China Development Forum in Beijing March 23, 2014.
31. The annual World Bank/IMF 2014 Spring meetings, in Washington, DC.
32. The New Development Bank is the newly created development bank for the Brazil, Russia, India, China, and South Africa (BRICS).

## 3 THE WORLD BANK

1. The World Bank, the IFA, the IDA, the MIGA, and the International Center for the Settlement of Investment Disputes (ICSID).
2. Jeffrey Sachs (2006) *The End of Poverty: Economic Possibilities for Our Time* (New York: Penguin).
3. William Easterly (2007) *The White Man's Burdens: Why the West's Efforts to Aid the Rest Have Done So Much Ill and So Little Good* (New York: Penguin).
4. Moyo Dambisa (2010) D*ead Aid: Why Aid Is Not Working and How There Is a Better Way for Africa* (New York: Farrar, Straus and Giroux).
5. Abhijit V. Barnejee and Esther Duflo (2011) *Poor Economics: A Radical Rethinking of the Way to Fight Global poverty* (New York: PublicAffairs).
6. Idem, p. 271.
7. Idem, p. 272.
8. World Bank Annual Report (2008): Development Impact Report, p. 48.
9. CPIA is discussed in depth in chapter 5, which analyzes the International Development Agency.
10. Felix Lessambo (2014) *The International Corporate Governance System: Audit Roles & Board Oversight* (Basingstoke: Palgrave Macmillan), Chapter 18, p. 225.
11. *Repowering the World Bank for the 21st Century: The Report of the High-Level Commission on Modernization of World Bank Group Governance*, p. X.
12. World Bank Annual Report (2008): Development Impact Report, p. 13.
13. *Repowering the World Bank for the 21st Century: Report of the High-Level Commission on Modernization of World Bank Group Governance*, p. 23.

## 4 THE INTERNATIONAL FINANCE CORPORATION

1. Steven Hess &and Annette Swahla: Moody's Investors Service (2013) The International Financial Corporation: Credit Analysis p. 2, New York, at www.moodys.com.
2. Hess and Swahla, The International Financial Corporation, p. 6.
3. Hess and Swahla, The International Financial Corporation, p. 6.
4. Australian Multilateral Assessment (AMA) (2011) Submission by the International Finance Corporation, p. 4 at http://www.ag.gov.au/cca.
5. Australian Multilateral Assessment, Submission by the International Finance Corporation, p. 5.
6. Australian Multilateral Assessment, Submission by the International Finance Corporation, p. 6.
7. CAO Audit Report (2013) CAO Audit of IFC Advisory Services Project with the Korporata Energjetike e Kosoves, Kosovo, p. 10.
8. Australian Multilateral Assessment, Submission by the International Finance Corporation, p. 33.
9. http://ieg.worldbankgroup.org.

## 5 The International Development Association

1. IDA (2002) "IDA, Grants and the Structure of Official Development Assistance." http://siteresources.worldbank.org/IDA/Resources/Seminar%20PDFs/grantsANDstructure.pdf.
2. IDA, Article of Agreement, Article VIII, Section 4.
3. IDA, Article of Agreement, Article VIII, Section 5.
4. IDA Articles of Agreement, Article VI, Section 2(c).
5. IDA Articles of Agreement. Article VI, Section 4.
6. IDA Articles of Agreement, Article VI, Section 5.
7. The Report of the High-Level Commission on Modernization of World Bank Group Governance, p. Xii.
8. IDA, "IDA, Grants and the Structure of Official Development Assistance," p. 5.
9. Martin Weiss (2008). The World Bank International Development Association, CRS Report to Congress, p. 7.
10. IEG (2010) *The World Bank's Country Policy and Institutional Assessment: An Evaluation* (Washington, DC: The World Bank), p. 29.
11. IEG, *The World Bank's Country Policy and Institutional Assessment*, p. 8.
12. IEG, *The World Bank's Country Policy and Institutional Assessment*, p. 41.
13. IEG, *The World Bank's Country Policy and Institutional Assessment*, p. 26.
14. A. Economic Management
     1. Macroeconomic Management
     2. Fiscal Policy
     3. Debt Policy
   B. Structural Policies
     4. Trade
     5. Financial Sector
     6. Business Regulatory Environment
   C. Policies for Social Inclusion
     7. Gender Equality
     8. Equity of Public Resource Use
     9. Building Human Resources
     10. Social Protection and Labour
     11. Policies and Institutions for Environmental Sustainability
   D. Public Sector Management and Institutions
     12. Property Rights and Rule-based Governance
     13. Quality of Budgetary and Financial Management
     14. Efficiency of Revenue Mobilization
     15. Quality of Public Administration
     16. Transparency, Accountability, and Corruption in the Public Sector.
15. Julia Cage (2013) "Measuring Policy Performance: Can We Do Better Than the World Bank?," p. 2. https://jica-ri.jica.go.jp/publication/assets/Measuring%20Policy%20Performance,%20Cage%20-%20JICA%20IPD%20Working%20Papers.pdf.
16. Cage, "Measuring Policy Performance," p. 8.
17. Elisa Van Waeyenberge (2009) "Selectivity at Work: Country Policy and Institutional Assessments at the World Bank," *European Journal of Development Research* 21, No. 5, p. 792.
18. IDA Article of Agreement, Article V, Section 2.
19. IDA Article of Agreement, Article V, Section 5.

## 6 THE INTERNATIONAL CENTER FOR SETTLEMENT OF INVESTMENT DISPUTES

1. ICSID Convention, Article 1.
2. ICSID Convention, Article 3.
3. ICSID Convention, Article 4.
4. ICSID Convention, Article 5.
5. ICSID Convention, Article 7.
6. ICSID Convention, Article 8.
7. ICSID Convention, Article 6.
8. ICSID Convention, Article 9.
9. ICSID Convention, Article 11.
10. ICSID Convention, Article 10(1).
11. ICSID Convention, Article 10(2).
12. http://icsid.worldbank.org/.
13. ICSID Convention, Article 13(1).
14. ICSID Convention, Article 13(2).
15. ICSID Convention, Article 15.
16. ICSID Convention, Article 25(1).
17. ICSID Convention, Article 25(3).
18. ICSID Convention, Article 26.
19. ICSID, Article 36.
20. ICSID Convention, Article 37(2)(a).
21. Holiday Inns S. A. v. Morocco, ICSID Case No. ARB/72/1 (1972); see also ICSID (1972) Annual Report.
22. Sergio Puig (2013) "Emergence & Dynamism in International Organizations: ICSID, Investor-State Arbitration & International Investment Law," *Georgetown Journal of International Law* 44, p. 536.

## 7 THE MUTUAL INVESTMENT GUARANTEE AGENCY

1. Report of the High-Level Commission on Modernization of World Bank Group Governance, p. 26.
2. MIGA Annual Report, at: http://www.miga.org/resources/index.cfm?stid=1854.
3. MIGA Website at: www.miga.org.
4. MIGA Website at: www.miga.org.
5. MIGA Website at: www.miga.org.
6. MIGA (2013) World Investment and Political Risk—World Investment Trends and Corporate Perspectives- The Political Risk Insurance Industry (Breach of Contract), p. 41.
7. MIGA Investment Guarantees at: http://www.miga.org/investmentguarantees/index.cfm?stid=-1548.
8. MIGA Website- Terms and Conditions, at: http://www.miga.org/investmentguarantees/index.cfm?stid=1799.
9. Ibid.
10. MIGA "Who Are We," at: http:// www.miga.org/whoweare/index.cfm?stid=1792m.
11. MIGA (2012) *Investors and Experts Debate: Is the Glass Half Full or Half Empty?* http://www.miga.org/news/index.cfm?aid=3415.
12. MIGA(2009) *Working Today for Tomorrow* http://www.miga.org/news/index.cfm?aid=2354.

## 8   The Bank for International Settlement

1. The ten founders included the central banks of Belgium, France, Germany, Italy, Japan, and the United Kingdom along with three leading commercial banks from the United States (J. P. Morgan Chase & Co., First National Bank of New York, and First National Bank of Chicago).
2. Adam LeBor (2013) *Tower of Basel: The Shadow History of the Secret Bank That Runs the World* (New York : Public Affairs), p. Xiv.
3. Bank for International Settlements, Archive guide, 2007, p. 2 http://www. bis.org/about/arch_guide.pdf>.
4. Murray N. Rothbard (2005) *A History of Money and Banking in the United States: The Colonial Era to World War II* (Auburn: Ludwig Von Mises Institute), p. 276.
5. LeBor, *Tower of Basel*, p. XX.
6. Felix Lessambo (2013) *The International Banking System: Capital Adequacy, Core Business and Risk Management* (New York: Palgrave Macmillan), p. 79.
7. The Irving Fisher Committee is in charge of central banks' statistics.
8. LeBor, *Tower of Basel*, p. xv.
9. LeBor, *Tower of Basel*, p. 259.
10. LeBor, *Tower of Basel*, p. 272.
11. James C. Baker (2002) *The Bank for International Settlements* (Wesport, CO: Quorum Books), p. 141.
12. Baker, *The Bank for International Settlements*, p. 143.
13. Baker, *The Bank for International Settlements*, p. 167.
14. Baker, *The Bank for International Settlements*, p. 5.

## 10   The European Bank for Reconstruction and Development

1. Agreement Establishing the European Bank for Reconstruction and Development, Chapter 6, Article 25.
2. Agreement Establishing the European Bank for Reconstruction and Development, Chapter 6, Article 27.
3. Agreement Establishing the European Bank for Reconstruction and Development, Chapter 6, Article 26.
4. Agreement Establishing the European Bank for Reconstruction and Development, Chapter 6, Article 29(1).
5. Agreement Establishing the European Bank for Reconstruction and Development, Chapter 6, Article 30(4).
6. Agreement Establishing the European Bank for Reconstruction and Development, Chapter 6, Article 30(5).
7. Agreement Establishing the European Bank for Reconstruction and Development, Chapter 6, Article 30(1).
8. Agreement Establishing the European Bank for Reconstruction and Development, Chapter 6, Article 30(2).
9. Idem.
10. Agreement Establishing the European Bank for Reconstruction and Development, Chapter 6, Article 31(1).
11. Agreement Establishing the European Bank for Reconstruction and Development, Chapter 6, Article 31(2).

12. Cap and Collar refers to an agreement in which a financial organization puts an upper (= the cap) and a lower (= the collar) limit on an interest rate for a loan, a share price, etc.

## 11 THE COUNCIL OF EUROPE DEVELOPMENT BANK

1. Members are: Albania, Belgium, Bosnia and Herzegovina, Bulgaria, Croatia Cyprus, Czech Republic, Denmark, Estonia, Finland, France, Georgia, Germany, Greece, Holy See, Hungary, Iceland, Ireland, Italy, Kosovo, Latvia, Liechtenstein, Lithuania, Luxembourg, Malta, Republic of Moldova Montenegro, The Netherlands, Norway, Poland, Portugal, Romania, San Marino, Serbia, Slovak Republic, Spain, Slovenia, Sweden, Switzerland "the former Yugoslav Republic of Macedonia," and Turkey.
2. Council of Europe-Parliamentary Assembly (2014) "Challenges for the Council of Europe Development Bank," p. 5. http://assembly.coe.int/ASP/Doc/XrefViewPDF.asp?FileID=20915&Language=EN.
3. Theodore Ivanov (2005) The Council of Europe Development Bank (CEB) as a funding source for social housing projects.
4. Albania, Belgium, Bosnia and Herzegovina, Bulgaria, Croatia, Cyprus, Czech Republic, Denmark, Estonia, France, Finland, Georgia, Germany, Greece, Holy See, Hungary, Iceland, Ireland, Italy, Latvia, Liechtenstein, Lithuania, Luxembourg, Malta, Republic of Moldova, Montenegro, Netherlands, Norway, Poland, Portugal, Romania, San Marino, Serbia, Slovak Republic, Slovenia, Spain, Sweden, Switzerland, and Turkey.
5. CEB at: http://coe.org.
6. CEB at: http://coe.org.
7. CEB at: http://coe.org.
8. Council of Europe-Parliamentary Assembly, "Challenges for the Council of Europe Development Bank," p. 10.

## 12 THE ASIAN DEVELOPMENT BANK

1. ADB (2012) ADB Financial Profile in 2012 http://www.adb.org/documents/adb-financial-profile-2012.
2. ADB (2009) "Aid for Trade in Asia and Pacific."
3. ADB, "Aid Trade in Asian and Pacific."
4. ADB (2014) "Midterm Review of Strategy 2020: Meeting the Challenges of a Transforming Asia and Pacific," p. 40.

## 13 THE AFRICAN DEVELOPMENT BANK

1. Nigeria is the largest shareholder with 8.586 percent of the voting power, followed by Egypt as the second largest regional member with 5.455 percent.
2. The three big non-regional members are: the USA (over 6%), Japan (5.5%), and Germany (4%).
3. Agreement Establishing the African Development Bank (2011), Article 29.
4. Agreement Establishing the African Development Bank (2011), Article 29(2).
5. Agreement Establishing the African Development Bank (2011), Article 30.
6. Agreement Establishing the African Development Bank (2011), Article 31.

7. The Board of Directors for the African Development Fund does not appear in the organizational structure of the AfDB.
8. Agreement Establishing the African Development Bank (2011), Article 33.
9. Agreement Establishing the African Development Bank (2011), Article 33(3).
10. Agreement Establishing the African Development Bank (2011), Article 36 (1).
11. Agreement Establishing the African Development Bank (2011), Article 1.
12. Agreement Establishing the African Development Bank (2011), Article 2.
13. African Development Bank Group, "Auditor General's Office," http://www.afdb.org/en/aboutus/ structure/auditor-generals-office.
14. African Development Bank Group, "Operations Evaluation," http://www.afdb.org/en/aboutus/ structure/operations-evaluation.
15. African Development Bank Group, "Independent Review Mechanism (IRM)," http://www.afdb.org/en/about-us/structure/independent-review -mechanism-irm/ and "About the IRM," http://www.afdb.org/en/about-us/structure/independent-review-mechanism-irm/aboutthe-Irm.
16. http://siteresources.worldbank.org/INTDOII/Resources/FinalIFITaskForceFramework&Gdlines.pdf.

## 14   THE LATIN AMERICA DEVELOPMENT BANK

1. Argentina, Bolivia, Brazil, Chile, Colombia, Costa Rica, Ecuador, Spain, Jamaica, Mexico, Panama, Paraguay, Peru, Portugal, Dominican Republic, Trinidad& Tobago, Uruguay, and Venezuela.

## 15   THE CARIBBEAN DEVELOPMENT BANK

1. Antigua and Barbuda/St Kitts and Nevis, The Bahamas, Barbados, Belize and British Dependencies (Anguilla, British Virgin Islands, Cayman Islands, Montserrat and Turks, and Caicos Islands), Dominica and St Lucia, Grenada and St Vincent and the Grenadines, Guyana, Haiti, Jamaica, and Trinidad and Tobago. Other regional members include Colombia, Mexico, and Venezuela.
2. Canada, China, Germany, Italy, and the United Kingdom.
3. Lending Policies; Direct Lending Policy (upcoming); Disaster Management Strategy and Operational Guidelines, 2009; Environment Policy; Urban Revitalization Strategy and Operational Guidelines; Private Sector Development Strategy; Gender Equality Policy Information Disclosure Policy.

## 16   THE ISLAMIC DEVELOPMENT BANK

1. Comoros, Syria, Albania, Bangladesh, Somalia, Burkina Faso, Chad, Cameroon, Kazakhstan, Egypt, Togo, Turkey, Uganda, Yemen, Tajikistan, Djibouti, Tunisia, Uzbekistan, Afghanistan, Gabon, Indonesia, Gambia, Jordan, Guinea, Iran Iraq, Kyrgyz, Lebanon, Maldives, Mali, Mauritania, Morocco, Pakistan, Mozambique, Niger, Palestine, Qatar, Kuwait, Sierra Leone, Cote D'Ivoire, Brunei, Guinea Bissau, Lybia, Malaysia, Nigeria, Oman, Bahrain, Algeria, Azerbaijan, Benin, Turkmenistan, United Arab Emirates, Saudi Arabia, Sudan, Suriname, and Senegal.

2. ID is the unit of account of the IDB, which is equivalent to one Special Drawing Right (SDR) of the International Monetary Fund (IMF).
3. The Islamic Development Bank (Articles of Agreement), Article 29.
4. The Islamic Development Bank (Articles of Agreement), Article 31.
5. The Islamic Development Bank (Articles of Agreement), Article 35.
6. The Islamic Development Bank (Articles of Agreement), Article 36.

## 17 EUROPEAN INVESTMENT BANK

1. EIB's external mandate 2007–2013, Mid-Term Review (2010) "Report and Recommendations of the Steering Committee of Wise Persons," p. 8 http://www.eib.org/attachments/documents/eib_external_mandate_2007-2013_mid-term_review.pdf.
2. EIB's external mandate 2007–2013, Mid-Term Review, "Report and Recommendations of the Steering Committee of Wise Persons," p. 2.
3. EIB (2013) "Report and Recommendations of the Steering Committee of 'Wise Persons,'" p. 8.
4. EIB at: www.eib.org.
5. EIB at www.eib.org.
6. European Parliament Resolution of March 11, 2014 on the European Investment Bank (EIB)—Annual Report 2012 [2013/2131(INI)].

## 18 NORDIC INVESTMENT BANK

1. Article 1 of the 1957 Agreement.
2. NIB (2009) "Financial Policy," p. 6. https://www.nib.int/filebank/a/133 7759087/8cb170a10b7fc5d84b3016d6c24051e0/1076-Financial_Policies. pdf. Also, NIB Status, section 14.
3. NIB Statutes, Section 4.
4. NIB Statutes, Section 7.
5. NIB Statutes, Section 7.
6. NIB, "Financial policy," p. 11.
7. NIB, "Financial policy," p. 12.
8. The neighboring regions of the member countries are defined to include Poland, the Kaliningrad enclave, and Northwest Russia consisting of the St. Petersburg, Leningrad, Novgorod, Pskov, and Vologda regions as well as the Barents region and the Republic of Karelia. The neighboring regions also include Belarus and Ukraine to the extent covered by the drainage area of the Baltic Sea or by projects that cause emissions having a direct impact on the member countries.
9. NIB Statutes, Section 9.

# Glossary of the Terms

**Balance of Payment (BoP):** Is a statistical statement that summarizes, for a specific period (a year or a quarter), the economic transactions of an economy with the rest of the world.

**Callable Capital:** Is the commitment by each shareholder to make additional capital available to the institution in case of financial distress.

**Comprehensive Development Framework (CDF):** Framework developed by the World Bank to coordinate all actors in the development process towards implementing a coherent framework of macroeconomic, structural and social reforms for poverty reduction.

**Concessional Loan:** Loan provided to poorest countries with lower interest rates and longer repayment periods than typical or standard market or multilateral loans, that is, less than market interest rates and extended grace period.

**Conditionalities:** Economic policies or structural reforms that a borrowing member state country agrees to follow as a condition for the use of the IMF/WB resources (loans) often called performance criteria or benchmarks.

**Contingency Credit Line (CCL):** IMF credit line established after the financial crisis in 1997–1999. Countries are required to satisfy certain conditions in order to join the CCL to provide emergency assistance. This facility was expired in November 2003.

**Corporate Governance:** Refers to the mechanism that frames duties and powers of corporations to deliver benefits to investors and those directly impacted by the corporation's activities.

**Corporate Social Responsibility:** Refers to legal compliance, business ethics, sustainable development, and corporate citizenship.

**Country Policy and Institutional Assessment (CPIA):** Initiated by the Bank in the late 1970s, CPIAs consist of a set of criteria representing the different policy and institutional dimensions of an effective poverty reduction and growth strategy (e.g., quality of budgetary and financial management, debt policy, gender equality...), and are intended to guide the allocation of IDA lending resources. For each criterion, countries are rated on a scale of one (very weak performance) to six (very strong performance), and a total rating for each country is calculated.

**Disclosure:** Refers to the act of revealing a fact or condition stated on the balance sheet or in footnotes. It is made of a whole array of different forms of information produced by companies, such as the annual reports.

**Enhanced Structural Adjustment Facility (ESAF):** Facility established in 1987 to provide assistance on concessional terms to low-income member countries facing protracted balance of payments problems. It has been replaced in 2000 by the Poverty Reduction and Growth Facility (PRGF).

**Extended Credit Facility (ECF):** The ECF follows the PRGF as the main concessional financing tool for low-income countries (LICs), and aims to help countries with protracted balance of payments problems. Compared to other IMF concessional loans, the ECF has higher levels of access and more concessionary terms.

**Extended Fund Facility (EFF):** The EFF is a longer-term IMF loan facility that focuses on the structural problems behind balance of payments issues and contains broader conditions.

**Fairness:** Means treaty people with equality. It entails avoiding of bias towards one or more entities as compared to the others.

**Financial Statements:** Consist of reports about an organization's financial condition: balance sheet, statement of income and statement of cash flows.

**Flexible Credit Line (FCL):** The FCL is available to IMF member states that already have stable records of policy implementation and have fulfilled a set of prior conditions. Once a state has qualified, they have condition-free access to the funds.

**Global Public Goods:** Are defined as goods whose benefits extend to all countries, people, and generations.

**Governance:** Refers to a new cooperative relationship between and among government, the private sector and the civil societies.

**Heavily-Indebted Poor Countries Initiative (HiPCI):** Arrangement for reducing multilateral, bilateral and private sector debt for the poorest, most indebted countries.

**Interim Poverty Reduction Strategy Paper (IPRSP):** Document which outlines actions the government intends to take to develop a full a full Poverty Reduction Strategy Paper (PRSP). It also contains details of intended macroeconomic policy reforms and may also include information on the country's poverty situation.

**International Financial Institutions (IFIs):** Generic name given to all financial institutions operating on an international level, ranging from development banks, such as the World Bank and Asian Development Bank (ADB), and monetary authorities, such as the IMF.

**Middle Income Countries (MICs):** MICs are defined by the World Bank as having: "1. Similar incomes (by definition between $3,036 and 9,385 per capita); 2. Better Policies (but not consistently so); 3. Better institutions (but not all); 4. Better access to external finance (but only 22 out of 69 were investment grade and another 20 had volatile access); 5. Alternatives to the Bank for funds and advice; a test of the Bank's value added." From WB Conference on Effectiveness of Policies and Reforms: 4/10/2004.

**Multilateral Debt Relief Initiative (MDRI):** The MDRI was agreed at the G8 in Gleneagles in 2005 and allowed for the cancellation of debts of certain qualified countries to the IMF, International Development Association and African Development Fund.

**Performance Criteria:** Refer to conditions that are formally specified in a member country's financing arrangement with the IMF.

**Policy Implementation:** Refers to the translation of strategic goals into actionable tasks, as well as their execution.

**Poverty Reduction and Growth Facility (PRGF):** The IMF's concessional lending facility, which provides finance for Poverty Reduction Strategy Papers (PRSPs). Previously, this facility was called the Enhanced Structural Adjustment Facility (ESAF).

**Precautionary and Liquidity Line (PLL):** The PLL aims at consolidating market confidence by improving policies prior to loan qualification. Similar to the Flexible Credit Line (FCL) it can be used for actual or potential balance of payments needs.

**Precautionary Credit Line (PCL):** The IMF's PCL was designed for those countries in need of precautionary finance from the IMF in the face of external shocks but do not qualify for the Flexible Credit Line (FCL).

**Private Equity:** A pool of investors and funds that make investments directly into private companies or conduct buyouts of public companies that result in de-listing of public equity.

**Process Tracing:** A standard analytical tool in history and political science, which consists of splitting up the policy-making process into small steps and looking for observable evidence at each step.

**Quantitative Performance Criteria:** Are specific and measurable conditions that have to be met to complete a review. They relate to macroeconomic variables under the control of the authorities, such as monetary and credit aggregates, international reserves, fiscal balances, and external borrowing.

**Rapid Credit Facility (RCF):** The RCF focuses on rapid concessional financing for low-income countries (LICs) in urgent need due to balance of payments problems. The RCF has more flexibility in terms of use, less conditionality and emphasizes poverty reduction and growth.

**Rapid Financing Instrument (RFI):** The RFI is not a full-fledged IMF loan facility but provides fast and low-access financing to help recipients with balance of payments needs.

**Structural Adjustments:** Reforms that required to developing country when seeking a loan from the IMF/WB. Structural adjustments often include a commitment to a free market where goods and services are bought and sold according to supply and demand, privatization.

**Structural Adjustment Participatory Review Initiative (SAPRI):** Joint World Bank, government and civil society initiative to review the impact of adjustment lending in seven borrowing countries.

**Structural Benchmarks:** Reform measures that are critical to achieve the program goals and are intended as markers to assess program implementation during a review.

**Supplemental Reserve Facility (SRF):** A facility to provide financial assistance for countries experiencing exceptional capital account problems resulting from a sudden and disruptive loss of market confidence.

**Technical Cooperation:** Includes both (1) Grants to nationals of aid recipient countries receiving education or training at home or abroad and (2) Payments to consultants, advisors and similar personnel in recipient countries.

**Triangulation:** An evaluation technique based on the principle that questions are approached through different and independent perspectives.

# BIBLIOGRAPHY

African Development Bank Group. 2011. "Agreement Establishing the African Development Bank." http://www.afdb.org/fileadmin/uploads/afdb/Documents /Legal-Documents/Agreement%20Establishing%20the%20ADB%20final%20 2011.pdf.

———. 2014a. "About the IRM." http://www.afdb.org/en/about-us/structure/ independent-review-mechanism-irm/about-the-irm/.

———. 2014b. "Auditor General's Office." http://www.afdb.org/en/about-us/ structure/auditor-generals-office/.

———. 2014c. "Independent Review Mechanism (IRM)." http://www.afdb.org/ en/about-us/structure/independent-review-mechanism-irm/.

———. 2014d. "Operations Evaluation." http://www.afdb.org/en/about-us/ structure/operations-evaluation/.

Asian Development Bank. 2009. "Aid for Trade in Asia and the Pacific. Asian Development Bank." http://www.wto.org/english/tratop_e/devel_e/a4t_e/ asian_devel_bank_report_e.pdf.

———. 2012. "ADB Financial Profile 2012." http://www.adb.org/sites/default/ files/institutional-document/33497/files/adb-financial-profile-2012.pdf.

———. 2014. "Midterm Review of Strategy 2020: Meeting the Challenges of a Transforming Asia and Pacific." http://www.adb.org/sites/default/files/publi-cation/39388/midterm-review-strategy2020-brochure.pdf.

Baker, James C. 2002. *"Bank for International Settlements.* Westport, CO: Quorum Books.

Bank for International Settlements. 2007. *BIS Archive Guide.* Basel: Bank for International Settlements. http://www.bis.org/about/arch_guide.pdf.

Barnejee, Abhijit V. and Esther Duflo. 2011. *Poor Economics: A Radical Rethinking of the Way to Fight Global Poverty.* New York: Public Affairs.

Cage, Julia. 2013. "Measuring Policy Performance: Can We Do Better than the World Bank?." Working paper prepared for JICA/IPD Africa Task Force meet-ing. https://jica-ri.jica.go.jp/publication/assets/Measuring%20Policy%20 Performance,%20Cage%20%20-%20JICA%20IPD%20Working%20Papers.pdf.

Cohen, Benjamin J. 2008. "Bretton Woods System." In *Routledge Encyclopedia of International Political Economy*, edited by R. J. Barry Jones. New York: Routledge.

Cottarelli, Carlo. 2005. "Efficiency and Legitimacy: Trade-Offs in IMF Governance." http://papers.ssrn.com/sol3/papers.cfm?abstract_id=887976##.

Council of Europe-Parliamentary Assembly. 2014. "Challenges for the Council of Europe Development Bank." Doc. 13513. http://assembly.coe.int/ASP/Doc/ XrefViewPDF.asp?FileID=20915&Language=EN.

Dambisa, Moyo. 2010. *Dead Aid: Why Aid Is Not Working and How There Is a Better Way for Africa.* New York: Farrar, Straus and Giroux.

Easterly, William. 2005. "What Did Structural Adjustment Adjust? The Association of Policies and Growth with Repeated IMF and World Bank Adjustment Loans." *Journal of Development Economics* 76 (1): 1–22.

———. 2007. *The White Man's Burdens: Why the West's Efforts to Aid the Rest Have Done So Much Ill and So Little Good*. New York: Penguin.

European Commission Council. 1990. "Agreement Establishing the European Bank for Reconstruction and Development." In *Official Journal of the EC*, Office for Official Publications of the European Communities, 1999, pp. 4–26. Luxembourg: EC.

Eun, Cheol S. and Bruce G. Resnick. 2007. *International Financial Management*, 4th ed. Boston: McGraw-Hill/Irwin.

European Investment Bank. 2010. "Mid-Term Review of EIB External Mandate: Report of the Steering Committee of 'Wise Persons.'" http://www.eib.org/attachments/documents/eib_external_mandate_2007-2013_mid-term_review.pdf.

Fergusson, Niall. 2008. *The Ascent of Money: A Financial History of the World*. New York: Penguin.

Holiday Inns S. A. v. Morocco ICSID Case No. ARB/72/1.

International Centre for Settlement of Investment Disputes. 2003. *ICSID Convention, Regulations and Rules*. Washington, DC: International Centre for Settlement of Investment Disputes.

International Development Association. 1962. *Articles of Agreement of the International Development Association, Effective September 24, 1960*. Washington, DC: IDA.

———. 2002. "IDA, Grants, and the Structure of Official Development Assistance." http://siteresources.worldbank.org/IDA/Resources/Seminar%20PDFs/grantsANDstructure.pdf.

International Finance Corporation. 2011. "Australian Multilateral Assessment." http://aid.dfat.gov.au/partner/Documents/ama-ifc.pdf.

International Financial Institutions Anti-Corruption Task Force. 2006. *"Uniform Framework for Preventing and Combating Fraud and Corruption."* http://siteresources.worldbank.org/INTDOII/Resources/FinalIFITaskForceFramework&Gdlines.pdf.

Islamic Development Bank. 1974. *"Articles of Agreement. Jeddah, Saudi Arabia: Islamic Development Bank."* http://www.isdb.org/irj/go/km/docs/documents/IDBDevelopments/Internet/English/IDB/CM/About%20IDB/Articles%20of%20Agreement/IDB_Articles-of-Agreement.pdf.

LeBor, Adam. 2013. *Tower of Basel: The Shadowy History of the Secret Bank That Runs the World*. New York: Public Affairs.

Lessambo, Felix. 2013. *The International Banking System: Capital Adequacy, Core Businesses, and Risk Management*. Houndmills, Basingstoke, Hampshire, and New York: Palgrave Macmillan.

———. 2014. *The International Corporate Governance System: Audit Roles and Board Oversight*. Basingstoke, Hampshire: Palgrave Macmillan.

MIGA. 2013. "MIGA Annual Report 2013." http://www.miga.org/documents/Annual_Report13.pdf.

Moody's Investors Service. 2013. "Credit Analysis: The International Financial Corporation." http://www.ifc.org/wps/wcm/connect/e5aaba0042929868a63aae0dc33b630b/Moody%27s+IFC+credit+analysis+Nov2013.pdf?MOD=AJPERES.

Multilateral Investment Guarantee Agency. 2009. "Working Today for Tomorrow." *News: Feature Stories*, June 8. http://www.miga.org/news/index.cfm?aid=2354.

———. 2012. "Investors and Experts Debate: Is the Glass Half Full or Half Empty?" *News: Feature Stories*, December 12. http://www.miga.org/news/index.cfm?aid=3415.

———. 2013a. "MIGA Annual Report 2013." http://www.miga.org/documents/Annual_Report13.pdf.

———. 2013b. *World Investment and Political Risk: World Investment Trends and Corporate Perspectives, the Political Risk Insurance Industry, Breach of Contract.* Washington, DC: World Bank. http://www.miga.org/documents/WIPR13.pdf.

———. 2014a. "Investment Guarantees." Accessed December 19, 2014. http://www.miga.org/investmentguarantees/index.cfm.

———. Investment Guarantees: Terms and Conditions. http://www.miga.org/investmentguarantees/index.cfm?stid=1799.

———. MIGA Website: Terms and Conditions. http://www.miga.org/investment-guarantees/index.cfm?stid=1799.

———. "Who We Are." http://www.miga.org/whoweare/index.cfm.

Nordic Investment Bank. 2005. "Statutes of the Nordic Investment Bank." In *Agreement, Statutes*, pp. 5–8. Helsinki: Nordic Investment Bank. http://www.nib.int/filebank/45-Agreement_and_Statutes.pdf.

———. 2009. *Financial Policy, Part I.* https://www.nib.int/filebank/a/1337759087/8cb170a10b7fc5d84b3016d6c24051e0/1076-Financial_Policies.pdf.

Ocampo, Jose Antonio. 2005. "The Democratic Deficit of International Arrangements." In *Protecting the Poor: Global Financial Institutions and the Vulnerability of Low-Income Countries,* Fondad, The Hague, November 2005. www.fondad.org.

Odling-Smee, John. 2004. "The IMF and Russia in the 1990s." IMF Working Paper. International Monetary Fund. https://www.imf.org/external/pubs/ft/wp/2004/wp04155.pdf.

Office of the Compliance Advisor Ombudsman (CAO). 2013. CAO Audit of IFC Advisory Services Project with the Korporata Energjetike E Kosovës, Kosovo. Audit Report C-I-R4-Y12-F158. International Finance Corporation (IFC). http://www.cao-ombudsman.org/documents/Audit_Report_C-I-R4-Y12-F158_KOSOVO.pdf.

Parlimentary Assembly of the Council of Europe. 2014. Challenges for the Council of Europe Development Bank. Doc. 13513. http://assembly.coe.int/ASP/Doc/XrefViewPDF.asp?FileID=20915&Language=EN.

Prada, Fernando. 2012. *World Bank, Inter-American Development Bank, and Subregional Development Banks in Latin America: Dynamics of a System of Multilateral Development Banks. No. 380.* ADBI Working Paper Series. Tokyo, Japan: Asian Development Bank Institute. http://www.adbi.org/files/2012.09.05.wp380.dynamics.system.multilateral.dev.banks.pdf.

Puig, Sergio. 2013. "Emergence and Dynamism in International Organizations: ICSID, Investor-State Arbitration, and International Investment." *Georgetown Journal of International Law* 44 (531). https://www.law.georgetown.edu/academics/law-journals/gjil/recent/upload/zsx00213000531.PDF.

Reinert, Kenneth A. 2012. *An Introduction to International Economics: New Perspectives on the World Economy.* New York: Cambridge University Press.

Rothbard, Murray N. 2005. *A History of Money and Banking in the United States: The Colonial Era to World War II.* Auburn, AL: Ludwig von Mises Institute.

Sachs, Jeffrey. 2006. *The End of Poverty: Economic Possibilities for Our Time.* New York: Penguin.

———. 2012. "What I Did in Russia." March 14. http://jeffsachs.org/2012/03/what-i-did-in-russia/.

Self, Richard. 2011. "Policy Development and Implementation in the Bretton Woods Institutions: A Consideration of the Legality, Human Rights Impact and Effectiveness of Their Programmes." *International Journal of Arts & Sciences* 4 (23): 171–210.

Solimano, Andres. 2001. *Can Reforming Global Institutions Help Developing Countries Share More in the Benefits from Globalization?.* Washington, DC: World Bank. http://elibrary.worldbank.org/doi/pdf/10.1596/1813-9450-2518.

Stiglitz, Joseph. 2002. *Globalization and Its Discontents.* New York: W.W. Norton.

Waeyenberge, Elisa V. 2009. "Selectivity at Work: Country Policy and Institutional Assessments at the World Bank." *European Journal of Development Research* 21 (5): 792–810.

Weiss, Martin A. 2008. The World Bank's International Development Association (IDA). CRS Report to Congres. https://www.hsdl.org/?view&did=717441.

———. 2011. *International Monetary Fund: Background and Issues for Congress.* Congressional Research Service. December, 19, 2014. http://fpc.state.gov/documents/organization/174242.pdf.

World Bank. Independent Evaluation Group. 2010. *The World Bank's Country Policy and Institutional Assessment: An IEG Evaluation.* Washington, DC: World Bank. https://ieg.worldbankgroup.org/Data/reports/cpia_eval.pdf.

Zoellick, Robert B. 2009. *Repowering the World Bank for the 21st Century: The Report of the High: Level Commission on Modernization of World Bank Group Governance.* Washington, DC: World Bank. http://siteresources.worldbank.org/NEWS/Resources/WBGovernanceCOMMISSIONREPORT.pdf.

# About the Author

**Dr. Felix Lessambo** is an Adjunct Associate Professor at St. John's University (The Peter J. Tobin College of Business), where he teaches International taxation, Corporate tax, Business tax, Individual Tax Planning, International Transfer Pricing, and Financial Reporting: Evaluation and Analysis. Prior to his St. John's appointment, Dr. Lessambo taught International Finance Management, International Markets and Institutions, Mergers and Acquisitions. He specializes in the Taxation of International Business Transactions, EU laws, International Finance, and Alternative Investment Vehicles. He is the author of "*Taxation of International Business Transactions*," "*Fundamentals of European Union Direct Tax*," "*Fundamentals of Hedge Funds: Alternative Investment Vehicles*," "*International Banking: Capital Adequacy, Core Businesses, and Risk Management*," and "*International Corporate Governance*." Dr. Lessambo has co-authored two best-selling BNA- Special Reports on Hedge Funds and Real Estate Investment Trust (REIT). He has published over fifty leading articles in international tax law reviews.

Dr. Lessambo practiced in International Tax and Alternative Investment Management Groups where he structured, and advised on Hedge Funds and Private Equity cross-border transactions. Dr. Lessambo is the first scholar to argue against the incompatibility of the French Controlled Foreign Corporation (CFC), the French transfer pricing provision (Article 57); the French thin-capitalization rules (Article 212), the French tax regime of artists (Article 155A), and the Luxembourg securitization law, with respect to both the EU laws and the OECD treaty. Ten years earlier in 1999, ahead of his time, Dr. Lessambo came out, for the first time, according to professor Bernard Castagnede, with the opinion that the sole way to crack-down on the use of "preferred tax regimes" is to broaden the scope of the exchange of information among tax and financial authorities. The G-20 summit in London has adopted the opinion in the midst of the world financial crisis (2009). He lectured with the European American Tax Institute (EATI), ISDE, and other business organizations. He lives in New York and serves on the boards of various Christian organizations.

# INDEX